IN MY BLOOD

I WAS BORN TO FOLLOW
LIVERPOOL FC

GERRY BLAYNEY

EMPIRE
PUBLICATIONS

First published in 2014

EMPIRE PUBLICATIONS
1 Newton Street, Manchester M1 1HW
© Gerry Blayney 2014

ISBN: 9781909360327

Printed in Great Britain.

Cover design by Elliot Blayney.

CONTENTS

INTRODUCTION v

FOREWORD ix

ACKNOWLEDGEMENTS xi

MY DEBUT SEASON 1956-57 1

THE SHANKS.. 9

ARISE SIR BOB 65

A SEASON ON THE BENCH 87

JOE FAGAN TAKES OVER 106

KING KENNY 121

SOUNESS - WHAT A MISTAKE!............................ 140

ROY EVANS - CLOSE BUT NO CIGAR 145

HOULLIER AND THE TREBLE 160

RAFA AND ISTANBUL 182

THE MANAGERIAL MERRY-GO-ROUND.......... 210

INTRODUCTION

THROUGH-OUT THE 1970s, once the football season ended, hordes of lads from all over the north-west set out looking for work in hotels, holiday camps and caravan parks in southern seaside resorts. I was in Minehead in 1974 when one day I got talking to a group of Kirkby pickpockets who had been following Ken Dodd's tour opening supermarkets and pushing pennies over in the swanky hotels. We soon clicked and they mentioned they were going down to Newton Abbot racecourse picking pockets and would I fancy doing the job of blocking the targets or marks and receiving their wallets? "Does the pope wear a funny hat? Stick me in lads!" For the rest of that summer on my days off we'd meet in Exeter and then get to work. In the late 60's I use to sell newspapers at football matches, soon I was using the papers to block the old men's pockets, whilst my free hand dipped in feeling for cigs. Now and then I'd come out with a couple of shillings or a ten bob note which was a major result. Now I could fulfil my wish to learn the noble art of dipping with a team.

The next summer we switched to the west coast of Bognor Regis. The Scouse Zap Squad had just got back from Paris where Leeds had played Bayern Munich in the European Cup final. Soon the lads were telling me about the craic over the water where most dips brought bigger wedges than in England. We soon hit the disco on the pier where I met Gerry Blayney. The first thing I noticed was how all the Kirkby Bandits looked up to him, even though he was from Huyton. Gerry was 24 and being only 19 it made sense to take on-board any advice I got from him about learning the sneaking game. What really impressed me was his passion for the beautiful game, stories about Liverpool in the Second Division, the rise of the Shankly era and funny stories about the fans who stood on the Kop. The only Evertonion amongst this crew was Steven

McLean (Maca) from Thornton. He got constant stick and was made up to link up with me - being a Manc never came into it or made any difference.

Together we spent the next couple of months bang at it, the local papers reported a tidal wave of crime hitting the coast all the way down to Brighton. One hot day on the beach Gerry pulled me and Maca aside and said "Listen lads, youse best get offside whilst the goings good, the bizzies are ready to kick in doors." After chewing the fat about our next move I suggested a trip overseas, my blood was pumping just thinking about the five finger discounts on the continent and getting a chance to pull a chic French lady so two days later we landed in Calais sporting sore heads from duty free bottles of Pernod. We never made it to any farms checking for work grape-picking, instead we banged a jack (till) in a book shop, copped for four ton (a fortune back then) and we were doing cart-wheels all the way to the train station and jumped the first rattler back up to the north coast and got work picking apples for ten long days earning decent wages before heading back on the ferry from Dieppe to Newhaven.

Like a true dickhead instead of travelling back up north with Maca I called into Bognor. Butlin's was closing up that same week for the season, all the grafters had done one bar Gerry who had moved into a seaside flat and said to me "There's nothing to hang around for, lad!" Call it over confidence but I wanted to show off my top quality French clobber, plus I had a wedge to spread and like any young buck I wanted my last fling or blow out of the summer. No surprise, the very next morning whilst snoring my bollocks with a Red Coat, her Chalet door was booted in and I got my collar felt. If I'd have headed home the witnesses would have forgotten all about me and I would have slipped the net. Instead a few weeks later I was sentenced to 6 months to 2 years in Borstal. Just my luck that between May and September 1976 the UK experienced the best heat wave of all time and being banged up in them sweaty cells was mundane to say the least. The only bright spots came via post cards from the lads in mid-August that if I kept my nose clean, home leave was on the menu. I was wired to the moon when Maca wrote saying he'd moved into a flatlet and had a spare room for me, and I'd have my choice of women to chill with.

A week later I landed in Bognor, jibbed over Butlin's fence and bumped into all the lads sporting sad faces, Maca had passed away after snorting speed – a freak death! Never in my life up to that day had I ever felt so low. I was sad, lost even. You have to remember I'd spent the full summer day dreaming that I would be lucky enough to catch a weekend by the sea with the lads with Roxy Music on the airwaves and perhaps a beach party that night with lots of young darling cockney babes on tap. Reality sank in at that point. Fuck going back to Borstal! I thought I'd get over to France as getting a bent passport back then was simple (a 12 month passie could be anyone's with some snide ID at a Post Office). At this point Gerry pulled me to one side and pointed out that doing one was probably not the best move. It'd be better to get back to Borstal and serve my time. I was gobsmacked – surely he'd know how much I was in need of a serious blowout! However the next morning I was on the first train out and back inside.

Christmas and New Year 1976-77 saw me back at Butlin's cooking 3,000 fried eggs every morning for the campers. At night I went into town and saw Gerry cruising in his new jag. I said thanks for the sound advice – see once I'd got back to Borstal the remaining six weeks were more like a convalescence so my head was straight once I came out.

By the mid 80's I worked selling merchandice at rock and pop concerts with Jerry's cousin Colin O'Brien (Snap). On Boxing Day 1986 I had to meet Snap at 8.30am in the pub outside The Kop to load my boot up with football swag. I was then ready to park up safe over near the away supporters' section, get inside with a pie and a hot Bovril ready for the 11.30 kick-off.

Let's say Colin had a way with words... "Now zen Blaney, let's get in the Ale house lad, landlord's sweet as, we'll sink a few Don Revie's, you'll need them to take the edge off all that Crimbo boozing."

He did have a valid point and somehow even blagged me into

The Kop where I just keep schtum and never said a word till half time. I was more than pleased to see Gerry grinning there. His first words hit me "Remember the last time you were in here Col?" referring to August 1971 when United had to play Arsenal at Anfield as punishment for rowdy behaviour in the Stretford End the season before. That night you had around 4,000 United fans stood on The Kop right up until ten minutes before kick-off when all of a sudden thousands of Kopites attacked United from every angle forcing us all onto the pitch and over to the safety of the Annie Road End. After the game it got even worse as we tried to make it back in one piece to Lime Street. The Red Army received its biggest ever hiding in Liverpool and I'm sure Jerry and Snap would have been in the thick of it. This wasn't really what I wanted to think about as the second half loomed, so I was glad of a few slaps on the back as a bottle of Brandy got passed around.

I realised at this point what a proper old school Grafter and gentleman Mr Blayney is. I can honestly say it's been a real privilege to contribute these pages, I know how much it means for Gerry and his family to have his story out there. I'm looking forward to working on a few projects with Gerry in the near future.

Colin Blaney
Author of Grafters, Jibbers and The Undesirables.

FOREWORD

L IVERPOOL FOOTBALL CLUB have some truly amazing supporters worldwide but there are a select few who are granted the term "super fan". There's no doubt Gerry Blayney falls into that category. From his first game in 1957 until the present day his life has revolved around Liverpool Football Club, taking in all the highs and lows, witnessing all 7 European cup finals, seeing his red men lift the the trophy with the big ears on 5 occasions, never mind all the other trophies; league titles, UEFA, FA and League cups, but also being present in two of the darkest days for his beloved reds, Heysel and Hillsborough. Amongst the 96 who lost their lives one was felt more deeply in the Blayney household as Gerry's son Peter was sadly lost on that fateful day.

When I started in the team there are faces you see home & away that you begin to recognise; Bobby Wilcox, Tony Hall, Sully and the lads from the Holt and Gerry was part of that band of supporters who never missed a game. I got to know him more as we live locally to one another and I was never surprised by his enthusiasm and passion for the Liverbird.

He then demanded I salute him before every home game! Which I duly did. I am still asked today who I used to wave at in the Upper Centenary Stand. It wasn't only home games as I used to warm up in away grounds or far flung lands I would hear a shout from behind the goal and a thumbs up exchanged with Gerry.

Every new manager and every player who plays ten years or more for the club is presented with a silver salver from Gerry and mine stands proudly at home. Gerry will continue to give his life to

Liverpool FC. Like many others their support has been a massive help to the players of different eras and is greatly appreciated.

Jamie Carragher

ACKNOWLEDGEMENTS

I WOULD LIKE TO DEDICATE this book to my late, great father Harry. Without a doubt, this book would not have been possible without him. Also, I would like to thank the other bird (apart from the liver bird) in my life, my beautiful wife Annmarie. How she has put up with me for the last thirty years I'll never know, especially when we get beat. I've got to be honest, I'm not very good company after a defeat. It usually takes me three days to get over it. I'd also like to say a huge thank you to all the fabulous Liverpool supporters I've met on my amazing journey, from the second division to become not only champions of England, but also the champions of Europe (five times baby). Also I'd like to pay a big thank you to Nicky Holt and Frank Bentley (Banna). I'd just like to thank those two for going on at me to write a book, they would say "for fuck's sake lad, write a book. You're a legend!" I'd say to them "more like a leg-end". Anyway here we go…

MY DEBUT SEASON 1956-57

FIRST I SHOULD TELL YOU ABOUT my dad, Harry. He was born in Belfast, Ireland in 1923. His mother and father had big problems. His father, a Mr Gillespie, was not only a drunk and a wife beater, but he was also a policeman! I could hear all my mates laughin, "Blayney's grandad was a bizzie!" My dad was eventually taken into care, where a Mr & Mrs Blayney adopted him as a 7 year old in 1930. They decided to make a new life for themselves and move across the water to live in Liverpool. My step grandad got a job in Camel Laird's, the biggest shipbuilders in England. He also liked watching football when he was living in Ireland. He used to go and watch Glentoran Football Club. For the first couple of years living in Liverpool he would go to watch both Liverpool and Everton, one week to Anfield, and one week to Goodison. Me Dad tells me he was 9 years old when his new dad asked him if he wanted to go and watch a football match. Me dad says "Yes please". Then he said "I only wanna watch one of the teams". He said "The atmosphere at both grounds was amazing!" So the Saturday comes and he says to me dad "I'm taking you to Goodison this week, then next week I'll take you to Anfield. I'll let you choose which team you follow". So it was off to Goodison Park. "It was brilliant, I think I'll pick Everton now!" me dad said, but his stepdad said "don't jump the gun lad, I'll take you to Anfield next week and you can make your own mind up". He also said "I don't mind which team you pick, I just want us to watch one team". So Saturday finally comes, and me dad and his dad are off to Anfield together for the very first time. Then me dad says to me grandad after only 10 or 15 minutes of play that he'd made his mind up. He said "There is only one team for me, and that's the reds!" Thank fuck he never picked the blue shite! It makes me sick that I was so close to becoming an Everton fan.

I love listening to his stories about going to Anfield and later on, all over England to watch our beloved redmen. I just knew I was born to follow my great father. I miss him so much. And like anyone's father who fought in the war, he had a story or two to tell. He loved telling them and I just loved listening to them. Me dad was a cook in the merchant navy. He tells me one day the ship was in the middle of the ocean when this Jerry bomber bastard (not you Gerry lad!) was trying to blast him out of the ocean. Me dad said "everyone was duckin' an' divin' to dodge the bullets" One of the gunners took one in the arm and fell. Me dad says he'd never fired a gun in his life, never mind one of these monsters! "I just grabbed a bottle of rum, took the biggest swig I've ever had in my life (about a third of a bottle), then I rushed over and took over the gun, firing all over the place. My ass was gone! I was just screamin' and shoutin' 'Come on you German bastards!', then I got the hang of it. Then this jerry bomber came right into my sight. I just started blasting away. The next thing I've got him! His plane was burning up. Fuck me I've got him!" He was so proud, but his pants were in a terrible mess as you could imagine! Anyway, after the war me dad decided he would stay in the merchant navy for another 6 years, to 1951 as work was very hard to find, no jobs around anywhere! That's when he found out I was in my mother's belly. So he says to Elsie, me maa "I'll just do the one more trip to New Zealand. I'll be well home before the baby's due" Me dad tells me he just fell in love with New Zealand, and he very nearly bought a small sheep farm. He'd been saving all his wages for a few good years so that he could give me and me mam a good start in life. Anyway, he actually done the deal with farmer on one condition, that being he would send me maa a telegram (no phones in them days lads!) to see whether me maa fancied it. Me maa sent him one back, which took about three weeks, which read something like "Get your ass back here to Liverpool. Our baby will be here soon". And that was the end of that. Phew! Thanks maa. I didn't fancy being a sheep farmer because I might've been tempted! Me dad told me he was absolutely gutted but "what could I do lad, I love your maa". He told me he really wanted a son so he could take me to see the other bird in his life, the liver bird. He got his wish, but I wasn't so little. 9lbs 2oz!

So now it was time for him to find a job. He eventually got one after 12 years travelling all over the world, Liverpool was just like most cities in England (got bombed a little bit more though), everywhere people trying to rebuild their lives. Money was so tight, to put it mildly. Eventually me dad found a job in Lucas-Engineering factory in Broad Green, as a capstan setter (machinist) making parts for aeroplanes. He told me he was really missing the sea but what could he do. He stayed at Lucas's for 33 years, yes 33 years, gold watch and all, and you could count the days on one hand that he was off sick. The pay was shite for the first five or six years so he decided to buy an old Bedford van, with a wooden floor and column gear change. In other words the gearstick was at the back of the steering wheel. He started his own little earner. At the weekend he would travel all over Liverpool buying scrap metal. Boy was there loads of it! Then off to the scrap yard to sell it. He started to take me with him when I was five, mainly to give me mam a break, I was a handful. I loved it, driving all over Liverpool to builders' yards, plumbers and so on. Not many people had a car, van, or any other kind of vehicle in 1956. I think there was only two other cars in our whole road. Nowadays everyone's got a car.

Anyway I've just turned 6 on the fourth of June. The football season not far away, August 18th, the opening game of the season. I'd never been to a game up to now. The Saturday morning comes, it's about 7 o'clock in the morning. Me dad shouts up to the bedroom "Come on lad, it's time to earn your match money". I shouts back "Wa". He says "It's about time you made your debut". I says "Wa" yet again. Me dad says "Your first game. I'm taking you to Anfield today". Me maa, Elsie was made up as it gave her a well-earned rest from me as I was shall we say 'a hard faced little bastard'. Apart from me, there were two other young boys to look after, ar Billy, just over a year younger than me, then the baby, Bimbo. His proper name was Frank. He got the nickname because he was a little fucker! Always sneaking off on his own. At the time there was a record in the charts called 'Bimbo Bimbo Where you gonna Go e o". It just stuck to this very day.

Anyway me maa was well happy. She was just the same as me dad, work wise that is. She used to sell toffee apples from our back yard on Ivy St, on the back of Faulkner St, Liverpool 8, for a penny each. Loads of kids every school day, loads of pennies. Don't forget, fish & chips out of the chippy was one shilling and 3d (six pence in today's money). So all those pennies add up. Credit crunch it's called today. Credit crunch my ass! People today are 100 times better off than they were in the 50's. In our school, St Saviours on Canning St, Liverpool 8, just at the back of Parliament St, some of the kids would come to the school with their ass hangin' out of their pants, worn out, or even a pair of wellies in the summer coz their shoes were worn out. Don't fuckin laugh, its true! That was the proper credit crunch. It was very hard times but thanks to my mum and dad working all the hours god sent, things were never that bad for me and my two brothers.

Believe me, only about one in twenty families, maybe more, had a television set. Wow, I'd never seen one before. None of my mates had one. So as you could imagine, when me dad got us a television, black and white of course, everyone wanted to be my mate. Me mam would let me bring three mates in to watch the telly after school. We lived in a very small two bedroom terraced house. It was fuckin funny looking back. Me maa would leave the curtains open so all me other mates could get a look. It was hilarious! About eight or ten lads climbing over each other, trying to get a good look. I'll never forget those times, it was magical. Boy you young lads don't know how lucky you are! Everything on a plate for you.

Well that's a brief account of my family so it's time to get back to my amazing journey which I am still travelling along to this day. So it's back to my debut. I had just turned six on June 4th, the new football season started on the 18th August so it was into Anfield for me first game, at the Anfield Rd end. I can't really remember anything at all about the game, all I remember was the atmosphere. It was magical. No singing and chanting in these days, just continuous clapping and plus, of course, the famous rattle. The noise they made when thousands of people was rattling them was deafening. The attendance, and don't forget lads this is the Second Division, was 49,344, not bad for a Second Division side. Not bad? Fuckin amazin'! Even though we lost the game 3-2 to Huddersfield Town, me dad Harry was not happy at all on our journey home but he soon forgot about that and started goin' on about Billy Liddell. He scored both of our goals. The loss didn't dampen me dad's spirits, he was there every home game, taking me with him. I just knew then that I was born to follow our beloved redmen. Me and me dad didn't realise it at the time but the manager of the opposition was none other than our soon to be saviour Bill Shankly. How weird was that for my debut. What makes it even more weird is that Shankly came to Anfield in 1951, the year I was born, but refused the job because the board insisted on picking the team. Shanks said "Thanks but no thanks."

Anyway, me dad took me to every home game for the next five months. I was really loving it. Then disaster hit. I get a bad injury. It just came from nowhere. It was about 8 o'clock in the morning, me maa shouted up to me "come on lad it's time for school" but I just couldn't move my body. My groin felt like someone was sticking a knife into it. I'd never felt pain like this before. Plus the sweat was just pissin' out of me. I was soakin' wet. Me maa shouts up again "Gerry, I won't tell you again lad. Get your arse down here. Now!" I tried to shout back but nothin' would come out. I felt so weak.

Me maa finally came up to the bedroom screamin' and shoutin', as she opened the door she just looked at me and said "Oh Gerry. You look awful. I'll have to get the doctor out". He finally arrived a couple of hours later. He just pulled the blankets back and pressed on my groin with his finger. It was just like getting stabbed. The doctor just looked at me mam and said he needs to go to hospital straight away. It was serious - rheumatic fever. So shortly after the ambulance arrives to take me to Alder Hey Hospital. It was nearly five months before I was well enough to come home. Two months totally bed ridden and about three months riding a stationary bike. Me mam and dad were really concerned as the doctor said I'd got it bad. A lot of kids died in the late 40's, early 50's but it looks like I had beaten it. Worry over (for now). I was back home and after a week or so I was starting to feel near enough back to normal. I couldn't wait to get back to Anfield to watch our beloved redmen. But it didn't last long.

About six months later, bang, just like the last time, it came out of nowhere. I went to bed feeling ok, no problems, then early hours of the morning, bang, I woke up in total agony. Me dad comes rushing into my bedroom. All I remember him saying is "Oh no, not again", the next thing I'm back at Alder Hey but this time, it was much more serious. Alls I remember is me mam and dad standing at the end of my bed looking at me, me maa crying, me dad with his arm round her trying to comfort her. Standing next to me dad was a priest, then me dad just broke down, I was just lying there sweating so bad. The nurse kept drying me off with a towel. Then the priest started doing all these hand signs. I didn't have a clue what he was doing. The next thing me mam and dad said "we have to wait outside son, you need to rest." The nurse gave me a tablet and dried all the sweat off me, I was so weak. The pills eventually kicked in and I was asleep.

When I woke up me mam and dad were beside me. They'd stayed all through the night. Apparently those hands signs that the priest had made were my last rites. Me mam and dad were so happy to see me wake up. They told me the doctor only gave me a 10% chance of making it through the night. He said if I do somehow make it through, I would have a good chance of making a full recovery. And that's the way it worked out. I was seven months in Alder Hey and it was much more difficult than the first time, the pains were unbelievable, the slightest movement of my legs and the pain was unbearable. I just had to lay there dead still. And finally, after seven months of pain and hundreds of hours on the stationary bike I was allowed home. I couldn't walk comfortably for six to eight weeks after I got home, but slowly and surely I got back to something near normal. Big Thanks to Alder Hey Hospital. Just as importantly I was finally back supporting our beloved redmen.

After seeing about six or seven games in the '57-58 season and the first four or five of the '58-59 season, I was back full-time. I fucking hate being out injured, now I knew how the players feel when they couldn't play. Me dad said to me "I'm taking you to every home game this season, without a doubt". We had finished fourth last season, but as usual me dad was so confident and his confidence seeped into me, and it's still in me to this day. Hence, the title of this book, In My Blood. After 21 games we were really struggling, winning only nine of them, five draws and seven losses. It wasn't looking good at all. Then it finally happened. The arrival of the proper Special One (smoke it Mourinho), the one and only Bill Shankly. No one had any idea how the bold Bill Shankly was going to improve this very, very average side. But we know now quite simply, in my mind, if there was no Shanks, there would have been no famous and admired Liverpool Football Club. He totally changed the whole outlook of the club. This time he was in total control, picking the team, buying the players and telling everyone "what a toilet Anfield is". But he could sense something special, especially in the fans. 40,000-50,000 every home game.

He had a vision and told the fans, "I will make this 2nd division side into a side that will be champions of England, and also conquer Europe." But it didn't start well. His first game in charge was at Anfield against the mighty Cardiff City, from the Valleys. After a 4-0 drubbing Shanks knew he had to change things big time. He got rid of 24 players, but he kept the backroom staff. Ian St John arrived from Motherwell, Scotland for about £35,000. Then he signed a colossus - Big Ron Yeats, again from Scotland. This was the start of the Championship winning side. After finishing third in the league, a slight improvement on last season, it still wasn't enough to take us back to the big league, League Division 1, as only two teams got promoted to the First Division. Alongside St John & Yeats, my all-time idol, Sir Roger Hunt had signed after coming out of the army, just before Shanks took over as manager. Roger scored on his debut against Scunthorpe. We finished the season third yet again but Shanks told everyone it wouldn't be long before we get there. True to his word, the bold Bill was right. Our beloved redmen stormed the Second Division in 1961/62,

winning it by 8 points which was quite a margin as it was only 2
points for a win back then.

THE SHANKS

FINALLY, AT LAST! We were back in the big league. I never missed a home game all that season and that was before I was ten years of age. Thanks to my great father Harry. There was some party in our house! Me dad was in heaven. We were back! I just couldn't wait for the new season to start. I'd been going in the Anfield Road end with me dad and his mates but now the Boys Pen beckoned. I just fucking loved it. Looking at The Kop swaying everywhere, with the rattles going off. There was no chants or songs in them days, just cheering, clapping and rattles. I was only a foot away from being in but there was a big fence in front of me. I think I watched the world famous kop more than I did the match. It was incredible. The noise, the banter.

There was no fucking way that big fence was going to stop me from being a Kopite. I'd seen a couple of kids climbing up the fence at the back of the pen and crawling onto the girders, so I thought, the next game, I'll have some of that. As usual I paid my 9d (4.5p in today's money) so expensive! Anyway I'm in the pen, so I made my way right to the back where the kids from last week were. I'm up the fence in seconds and onto the girder. I dropped down to The Kop with 28,000 other Kopites. Now I'm one of the family. Wow. It felt magical. After a few months the bizzies got onto me and the others, putting one bizzie at the top of the pen, and another on the other side, in the Kop. But where there's a will there's always a way and I found it. Simple. I just got a couple of lads that I knew to start a bit of commotion, you know, a phoney fight or something. The bizzie fell for it hook, line and sinker. He made a move towards the kids, I was just behind him, and as he moved towards the kids I was gone up the fence like a fuckin monkey, laughing me cock off. The busy was going nuts. But I still had to drop into the Kop, with the other bizzie waiting for me. I just looked at him and he shouted "get down now soft lad, your goin' nowhere. Ill 'av you today. I've been waiting for this." I just shouted back at him "we'll see copper". I must've been on the girder for about 15 minutes, but this bizzie was so confident. I couldn't drop back into the Pen as the other bizzie was back at his post, just as he was waiting in the Kop. He was trying to wind me up. Looking up at me and laughing. "You're going nowhere today lad". He'd been after me for about four months now. I was just praying for Liverpool to score into The Kop end because I knew that was my only chance to drop in. We scored and the bizzie just got sucked into The Kop going wild. I think he ended up about half way down. I dropped down and shouted "smoke that copper" and to make it even sweeter, when I dropped into the Kop, I landed on a ten bob note (50p in today's money). Get in, ten bob. It was only 9d to get into the Boys Pen. 12d was a bob (a shilling) so it worked out, I could pay into the Boys Pen for the next 11 games. Happy Days.

The FA Cup was the next game. The third round, which was so special in those days, it was a massive competition back then (but purple nose Fergie soon put an end to that, much more about that later in the book). It was away to Wrexham. I'd been begging me dad for about three or four months now. Anyway me dad comes home from work on the Friday night about 6 o'clock and soon as he walked in the door, he just looked at me and said "I want you in bed nice and early tonight lad". I said "Wa? What av I done now?" He said "Nothing lad. But I don't want you being tired in the mornin' coz I'm taking you to Wrexham for your away debut. So get your scarf, your rosette and of course, your rattle ready, ok?" Wow. I was buzzin' like a bee. "Thanks dad. I love ya. I love ya" He said "I love you too son so get yourself off to bed and I'll see you in the mornin'." So it's off to bed. I don't think I slept a wink all night. I could not wait. Wow, the world famous FA Cup.

The morning finally arrived. I looked out of the window. There was thick snow everywhere, and more was coming down. It must've been 18 inches high, no exaggeration lads. Me dad says "I don't think we'll be going to Wrexham lad, I think the match will get called off". I was fuckin gutted. But thanks to all the local Wrexham people who came out in force and cleared the pitch, the game went ahead. So it's off we go, my very first away game. Buzzing. I get me wellies on, me scarf, me rosette and me rattle, I just loved turning that rattle. All the young lads had them. Anyway it takes us nearly two and a half hours to drive to Wrexham (do it in less than an hour now). The snow was so bad, we couldn't drive more than 15-20 miles an hour all the way. We finally arrive and in we go. The atmosphere was magical. I think at the time the FA Cup was on a level to winning the league championship. It just had that aura about it, worldwide. I'm afraid to say that's all gone now. That purple nose twat Ferguson and Manchester United Football Club refused to play in the FA Cup, so his team could play in the World Club Championship but it turned out very, very bitter for him as his team got well and truly destroyed. Anyway back to my away debut. My all-time idol Sir Roger Hunt opened the scoring about 20 minutes in, then Kevin Lewis made it 2-0, and then in the last minute, Jimmy Melia made it three. The atmosphere was amazing. Redmen bouncing everywhere. It was a boss drive home with me dad and his two mates, Ted Rattigan and Dougie Wilson, fellow committee members of Liverpool FC Supporters Club. I am so proud to say that my late great father Harry was one of the founder committee members.

We got back to the Supporters club at about 7.30pm. The snow was still coming down really heavy. Me dad gets his usual large Rum and a bottle of Mackies. He gets me my usual, a packet of crisps and a glass of lemo. Then it was time for me dad to take me home, drop me off and pick me maa up to go back to the supporters club. I'm shattered. Drained. I went straight to bed. Took my wellies off and my skinny little legs were badly chapped. A red raw ring all round my legs. They were so, so sore. Me maa put some cream on them and it really did the trick. I was asleep in no time, dreaming of my next game. I just couldn't wait for my next away game. I'm one of them now. A travelling redman, one of the massive family. And I'm loving it. Back to the league. We're up and down. Winning, losing, winning, then it's the fourth round of the

FA Cup. I'm praying we get a team not so far away, like Blackburn, Wigan, Preston, Burnley, Bury and my prayers were answered. We get Burnley away. I'm delighted. We drew 1-1. Kevin Lewis scoring. It was a good journey home, an hour and a half or so, so it was back to the supporters' club, our usual quick drink, then back home to drop me off and go to the club with me maa. The replay was much harder than we thought it would be, although Burnley had a top team at the time having won the league a couple of years earlier. We were 1-0 down after about 15 minutes, but bang on half time, the Saint, Ian St John, makes it 1-1. It stayed that way for the 90minutes, so it went to extra time. It was very, very tight. Then in the last minute, Liverpool get a penalty. The 58,000 crowd erupted, then up stepped Ronnie Moran to smash it into the net at The Kop end. The Kop went mental, with me directly behind the goal, about two thirds of the way up, standing on a barrier waving me scarf and rattling me rattle. I ended up near the front. It was mayhem, but beautiful. Get in!

So I waited in anticipation for the draw of the fifth round of the FA Cup which was usually on the radio at Monday lunchtime. My dreams are soon dashed. We got drawn against Arsenal away, at Highbury. I'm gutted as there is no way me maa would let me go to London. "You're only 11 lad, no chance!" so that was that, I had to listen to it on the radio. Of course me dad went. It was horrible listening to it on the radio but the main thing is that our beloved redmen won 2-1 to send us into sixth round, with goals from Jimmy Melia, in the first half and the winner from the penalty spot just after the hour mark, Ronnie Moran making no mistake. So it's into the quarter-final of the world famous FA Cup at home to West Ham United. It was a very, very tight game but yet again Sir Roger nets again with only 10 minutes to go. The atmosphere was incredible. We were nearly there. Only Leicester City stood in our way of reaching the final at Wembley. But sadly at Hillsborough (of all places) we came unstuck against our old bogey team Leicester. They had already beaten us twice in the league, 3-0 at Filbert St and 2-0 at Anfield and we lost the semi 1-0. It was a very, very long and sad drive home. No one uttered a word for ages. I was having a little cry in the back, then me dad said "Gerry, don't feel down lad, it's only our first year back in the big time." We finished a respectable 8th in the league and Shanks told us it wouldn't be long before we started winning trophies. And boy was he right.

Here we go, 1963-64 season, we become champions of England. My hitchhiking days are about to start. The opening game of the season was at Blackburn Rovers. We win 2-1, Ronnie Moran scoring from the rebound after his penalty was saved and the winner coming from Ian Callaghan in the 75th minute. For the following home game against Nottingham Forest I'm bouncing in The Kop with 28,000 other redmen. I pay me usual 9d for the Boys Pen, up and over, job done. Bizzies going nuts as usual (fuck them). We were halfway through the season, winning 13, drawing 2, losing 6. We are still right up there as everyone was beating each other. Then my very first time hitch-hiking. After a 0-0 draw at Anfield with Port Vale in the fourth round of the FA Cup, we went to a midweek replay. Me dad says "Look Gerry, you can't go to the game at Port Vale. Your maa is goin' nuts. All's you are doin' is bringing trouble to the door. Sacking off school, always fighting and getting into trouble with the police." I went to school not very happy at all. At dinner time and I just said to myself "Fuck it, I'm goin'." So after dinner I goes back to school and after about ten minutes I says to the teacher "I don't feel well. I need to go to the toilet". The teacher says "Go on but don't take all day". So I just stays in the toilet knowing eventually the teacher would send someone out to find out what was going on. A few minutes later one of the lads out of my class comes into the toilet and said "The teacher goin' nuts. He said to get your arse back in there now". So I said to the lad "Go back and tell the teacher that I'm spewing up everywhere". I knew the teacher would come out to check on me so I just drank about two pints of water out of the tap and watched out for the teacher coming. When I saw him coming I just put me fingers down me throat and started spewing up as he came in. The teacher said "I think I'd better send you home. I'll get one of your mates to walk you round as I know you only live round the corner". The teacher fell for it hook line and sinker. Soon as we walked out I said to the kid "Give it ten minutes and then go back to school". So that was it. I was off, thumb out, got picked up and away I went.

I got to the East Lancashire road at about 1.30pm. There was four other young redmen, all under 15, waiting with me but it didn't take long to catch a lift, probably no longer than half an hour. A Bedford van with four redmen in it. What a touch! All the way to Port Vale. We get there nice and early, a good few hours before the kickoff. I had enough for a portion of chips. That'll do me. I was buzzing. A little bit nervous though. As I knew when I got home I was in for a terrible hiding from me maa (so what), but I just didn't care. I'm with the travelling redmen. Had no ticket. Bunked in no problem, simple jump over the turnstile, piece of piss. We were 1-0 down with only 10 minutes to go and up popped the jolly Roger to make it 1-1. 90 minutes up, onto extra time. It stayed that way until the 118th minute. Me dad's idol Peter Thompson bagged the winner. The travelling reds were buzzing. Got a lift back with the same lads in the Bedford van. They lived in the Old Swan area so it wasn't too far away from Liverpool 8. After about a 20 minute jog from Old Swan I was home.

I got to the door of the house and gave it a knock. Me ass was gone, I knew what I was going to get. As soon as I walked in me maa just started slapping me everywhere. She got so violent, calling me for everything, that me dad had to pull her off me. Me dad had never hit me. But me maa? Wow! She would've gone to jail if that would've been nowadays! It didn't do me any real harm though. It was off to bed then, no tea, nothing. The next day I had more to come as I knew I was in for six of the best, the cane, across the palm of my hand. Boy did that sting for hours, but it was worth it to watch my beloved redmen. It was straight home after school as I was grounded again. Me maa gave me my tea and said "Straight to bed after you've finished". No telly for a week! I was fucking gutted. I tried to blag me dad, "Please dad. I'll be good". But he just said "You know your maa lad. Sorry. No can do." So it's off to bed, it was a double bed which I shared with my two brothers Billy and Bimbo. Fuck me it's only just turned 5 o'clock and I'm in bed.

I could hear the telly with my brothers laughing at the cartoons. All I had was a packet of cards. No Playstations, Laptops, mobile phones or anything remotely like that. Just a packet of playing cards. But they have seen me right over the years. More about that later on in the book. Seriously though, you young redmen today are so lucky. The nearest thing we had to a mobile phone was two tin cans, one with the lid and other a hole in the middle, with a long piece of string connecting them together. Shouting down the can "Now then. Can you hear me?" Believe me it worked. Well, sort of.

The week dragged for me. Me dad tried to blag me maa after about three or four days but me maa said "No way. It's a week". I couldn't wait to see the reds again now. We were at home to Sheffield United. Me dad took me to the Liverpool Supporters Club, gave me money for the game, my usual in the pen, up and over, piece of piss. The game was brilliant. We thrashed them 6-1. Two from the jolly Roger, one from Peter Thompson, and a glorious hat-trick form Ian St John. Back to the supporters club, me dad was buzzing and so was I. But it didn't last long. I'm soon back in trouble with the police. But this time it was big, big trouble for me. I was on my way home from school and I saw this Lambretta Scooter on its side. So I pulls it up, the key was still in it. So I kick started it and away it went. Not very far though. I only got round the corner and bang a bizzie car blocks me in. I ran like fuck. But this fit bizzie caught me. I'm nicked. Taken and driven away. I'm dreading seeing me mam and me dad, especially me maa. I'm in the police station, then me mam and dad came to pick me up. Me maa battered me as soon as we got out of the police station. Me dad was going nuts as he had never in his life been in trouble with the police. And here's me, my 2nd time in court in nearly 18 months.

The first time was for a theft of Dinky toys off a wagon that was parked up in Edge Hill train station. It was really funny how we got nicked. Me, our Billy, Our Bimbo and three other mates from school had climbed over the train station wall two nights on the run, about 7 o'clock, then we went back for a third night and all seemed ok. So it was onto the wagon, take the tarpaulin off so we can get at the boxes. We grabbed a box each with about fifty or so Dinky's in it. The next thing, we hear police whistles going everywhere. They'd been hiding behind the other wagons, watching us. They started legging us everywhere. It was like something out of a Benny Hill sketch, fucking hilarious. I got a £1 fine in court.

So it's off to court for the second time, this time for the scooter. I'm thinking I'm only going to get a bigger fine, a fiver or something, or probation or something like that. But no, the magistrates sentenced me to attend a detention centre. It was probably the equivalent of what we call community service today. I got sixty hours, 10 days at 6 hours a day, 1 day a week. You have probably guessed it redmen, the day was Saturday! Ten o'clock in the morning until 4 o'clock in the afternoon. I'm absolutely gutted. That is me well and truly fucked. I'm going to have to miss about eight games. I had to attend the detention centre at Nile Street, at the back of the old cathedral, Liverpool 8. I'm in bits. I'm going to miss loads of games. The detention centre itself was bollocks. A couple of hours in the gym, then an hour or so polishing wooden floors in the centre, then making these fucking stupid moulds of the pope, or jesus, or something like that. Then the bell goes, its 4 o'clock. I've got me pumps on ready and I ran like the wind, all the way from the bottom of Parliament Street, to Lodge Lane, jump onto the 26 bus (bunked on of course) all the way to Anfield, getting there about twenty past four. That's when they opened the gates to let people out who wanted to leave early. A little jib past the lone steward on the gate and I'm in. So right away I shouts to the first kid I seen "What's the score lad?" "4-0" he shouts back to me. It finished 6-1 so at least I saw them score two and the same thing happened for the next five home games. But it's right back to home and away for the rest of the season, apart from that London, it won't be long though (I reckon I've been to that London between 200 and 250 times).

There were ten games to go in the league. We are about 5th or 6th but only four or five points off the top spot. Then we hit a beautiful purple patch, seven straight wins. Yes seven, wow, me and me dad are buzzin', but as usual me maa is goin' nuts. "I blame you,

Harry" she would shout. "All's he's done (me) is get into trouble the last year or two and you still take him to all the games". "Give over Elsie" he would say back to her. "Our beloved Liverpool Football Club plus the messiah Mr. Shankly are on the verge of winnin' the league title for the first time since 1947". Me maa says "It's your fault Harry. All's I've heard from you and Gerry the last five years or so is Shankly this, Shankly that. At the end of the day lads, its only 22 people kickin' round a piece of leather." They don't understand lads do they?

Anyway my next away game is at of all places Hillsborough, the home of Sheffield Wednesday. Cunt of a place to hitch-hike to in those days. Over the snake-pass and the Pennines, but thankfully I'm back in me dad's good books but I'm sure he knew if he didn't take me I'd hitch it there anyway. I know he didn't like me hitch hiking, nor did me maa, but I was hooked. I just had to go. I hated missing any game, I still do now to this very day. So it's off to Hillsborough with me dad and his mates. Loads of travelling redmen there as usual. But we are 2-0 down with only about 20 minutes to go. We get a corner. Me, me dad and his two mates are no more than 3 yards away from the corner flag. Peter Thompson comes over to take the corner. Me dad shouts "Come on Tommo, put it on the Saint's head". I swear Tommo just looked straight back at me dad "I'll try me best Harry, I'll try me best". And what did he do? Just that! St John, 2-1. Less than 20 minutes left. I felt so proud Tommo talking to me dad. With only 2 minutes left to go up steps Willy Stevenson, a fabulous player from Scotland, who Shanks had rescued from a team in Australia, to make it 2-2. A point kept us right up there in the mix. Me dad was very pally with Tommo, as he used to go to watch the players train at Melwood regularly.

Anyway, it's off back home to Liverpool. Our journey home was, I don't really know how to start! It's so weird. The roads were really bad for driving, we nearly died! Yes, Died! Untrue or what? 45 years later the Hillsborough disaster happens, where I lost my boy. This is so hard to write this, as the tears are just dripping out of my eyes. We will come back to this much, much later in the book. Anyway back to the journey home. We're on the snake pass, pissing down, then it happened. It was like watching one of them old fashioned movies on the telly, where the car skids on the bendy roads and ends up screeching to a halt with basically one wheel over the edge of a big drop. Fuckin' scary believe me. I'm nearly thirteen at this point, I had no fear at all as a rule but I was screaming and all sorts. I will never forget that trip. It was so scary but so funny in the end. As we came to a halt I'm in the back with Ted, me dad's mate. Eventually we all scramble out of the car. Everyone is shaking like a leaf. Eventually we get our shit together, more so me dad's other mate. He actually shit his pants. He had to lash his bills (underpants) and wipe his arse on the grass verge.

We finally put the car back from the edge and onto the road and off we go again. Me dad says to me "Say nothin' to Elsie (me maa) when we get home or she will 'av a go at me ok?" "No probs dad" Mind you it didn't take long for her to find out about it. The next night in the Liverpool Supporters Club she soon found out. As normal when we gets home from Sheffield me dad has one drink with me and his mates in the Supporters Club and drops me off at home and takes me maa back to the Supporters Club. I couldn't wait to go to school on Monday, so I could tell all the lads about me dad talking to Tommo and all that. Anyway the next morning me dad gets me out of bed for me breakfast and he says to me "O what a laugh we had last night after we dropped you off, me and your maa". Me dad said he had a word in the compere's ear (he's the guy who presents the acts on stage etc) just before he was introducing his next act. So the compere asks over the mic "As anyone lost a pair of bills?" Me dad said his mate went bright red, just stood up and done one!

Anyway back to the next game. Ipswich at home. We are still right up there. As normal I ran like the wind and gets there with eighteen minutes to go. Finishes 6-0. Happy Days. Next up it's Fulham away where we lose 0-1. No chance for me to go there this season, maybe next year. My community work is over now. No more 20 minutes for me. Next game I'm in the Boys Pen about half one, it's fucking chocka everywhere outside. Massive queues, 52,000 inside, turnstiles close about 2.15pm. Over 1,000 locked out. But I'm in the pen, and as usual I'm waiting for my moment to come so I can jib over into the Kop. As usual that twat bizzie was watching me like a hawk. I managed to get half way up but he was on me. Smashing his baton onto the fencing where I'm trying to get up. The bizzie was smiling at me and shouted up "Not today sunshine". I just stared back and said "We'll see copper." Five minutes to kickoff. The players come out. The Kop go fuckin mental. Everyone surges forward. We're gonna win the league. Bouncin' everywhere. I took my chance and I'm up and over in the blink of an eye. He sees me and tries to chase me. But there's no way he was catching me. Well too fast for him. I was gone. Shouting to him "See ya Copper". Fuckin hilarious, I was pissin' myself laughing. So I gets to my usual spot, roughly two thirds of the way up the Kop. It was incredible because I don't know whether it started this game, or a few games before but this was a real, real first. Nobody, no fans anywhere in the country sang or chanted. It was just waving the rattles and clapping. If memory serves me well, the first song we sang, I think, was 'She Loves You' by The Beatles, which we changed to "We Love you, yeah, yeah, yeah".

Anyway, back to the game. The Kop could smell the title. We just had to beat these Manc twats United and then we would only need a maximum of 4 points from our remaining five games. We destroyed those Manc bastards, 3-0 on the pitch and about 30-0 on the terraces. Leathered them, tormented them to death, as only us scousers can do, ha-ha. Burnley next up. Same again 3-0. Here we go redmen, it's Arsenal, at Anfield. A win will guarantee us the title. Didn't sleep much the night before, nor did me dad. We just couldn't wait for the morning to come. It finally does. Me dad says "This is it lad. This is what Shanks promised. We're gonna win the league today". I couldn't wait to get there. He drops me off about 1 o'clock at Anfield, then he went back to the Liverpool Supporters Club to have his usual two or three Rums before the game. As you can imagine it was mental outside Anfield before the game. Every turnstile chocka, queues everywhere. I'm in the queue for the Boys Pen, there's only about five or six kids in front of me, then the turnstile just shut. Full. Fuck me its only 1 o'clock. Two hours to go till kickoff! Loads and loads of lads were trying to bunk in everywhere, the Kop, everywhere. Coppers running round chasing people. It was nuts. Couldn't keep me out though. A leg up and I stood on this big kids shoulders at the side of the Boys Pen, straight into the Kop, another kid was right behind me, we were in. The Kop chanting "Champions, Champions." It was electric. Then the roof, believe me, nearly came off the Kop, St John scores to make it 1-0 after about 7 minutes. The Kop went more mental than I've ever seen before. Arsenal just looked shocked. All of their players staring into the crowd, chanting "We love you Liverpool, we do. We love you Liverpool, we do". It was awesome. Alfie Arrowsmith, so vital in the run in, makes it 2-0. Me dad's idol Peter Thompson bags 2, then my idol makes it 5-0. There was still half an hour to go. The scenes were incredible. The Arsenal players looked visibly shattered. Heads down, mumbling to themselves. I think our beloved redmen had a bit of pity on them, and just strolled through the rest of the game in 2nd gear. Final whistle goes, our 6th title secured. It seemed like the whole stadium was on the pitch. Everybody hugging and kissing each other and singing "We love you yeah, yeah, yeah." Then to a man everybody started chanting "Shankly, Shankly, Shankly". Then he appeared at the front row of the Main Stand, just above the Kemlyn Rd, directly above where the players come onto the pitch. I had never seen grown men cry in my life. I was just 13, and then I went as well. Tears of joy everywhere. Oh my god. What a day.

I've experienced so many different emotions. I can't remember the exact time we got out of Anfield, the game finished at 20 to five, as there was only a ten minute break at half time back then. I'm sure it was gone 6 o'clock by the time we got out of Anfield. Shanks paraded the trophy with the players from the Main Stand. Then the Shanks raised his arms and spoke. Everybody went quiet. He said to his disciples "This is just the start of turning Liverpool Anfield into a Bastille, a fortress." I finally made my way back to the club to meet me dad, it's about a six or seven minute run. There must be about half a dozen pubs on the way down to the club, everyone dancing outside the pubs all the way down, people dancing in the street. I gets back to the club and the whole club were dancing on tables and stools, me dad included, it was boss. Then me dad sees me and comes running over. "We've done it lad, we've done it, we've done it". He was hugging me so hard it hurt, but he loved Liverpool and he loved me. Tears of joy everywhere. "Come on son, I'm taking you the bar." I says "Wa?" He says "It's time for your first bevy. A pint of lager shandy". Wow. It just kept getting better. Then me dad says "Come on son, were off home now. There's a big party goin' on in our house. Your maa an your four aunties have sorted it all out. We're gonna 'av some night."

We gets home to Ivy St were the party was ready to go. Loads of scoff. Chicken, Pork, Lamb, sarnies, all sorts, and of course, a giant pan of scouse. Me maa and her sisters not only sorted the scoff, the kitchen was packed to the rafters with beer, whiskey, vodka, rum. You name it, it was there. There was at least 60 or 70 people there, probably more. Mostly family, aunties, uncles, cousins, big family. The party was amazing. I forgot to say about the game that it was the very first televised Match of The Day highlights, on BBC1 at 10 past 10. Me, me dad and loads of our uncles and cousins went into the living room to watch the highlights. Don't forget, no one had ever seen highlights of the game before. You lads today you take everything for granted, Sky Sports, Live matches, fuck me you can even pause live telly now, nothing anywhere near that at all back then, you lucky bastards! (only messin' lads). It was just incredible, just try and imagine it for the very first time. As soon as it was finished, it was back to the party, everyone singing and dancing, loads of Beatles music playing. I'm having more than a few shandys now. I'm dancing away when all of a sudden me legs started to wobble a bit. Me head started spinning. Wow. What the fuck is going on here. I just remember going white and started spewin' everywhere. The next thing I know me dad is carrying me up to bed. I was comatose, goneski, or whatever you want to call it. I finally awoke at about 8 o'clock in the morning to the Beatles on the record player. "She loves you, yeah, yeah, yeah." The party was nowhere near over. Still chocka. It went on well into the next night, not far off midnight I should imagine. Eventually everyone was done in. It's back to bed for me. I was ill for days after. But fuck it. It was more than worth it. My first of many hangovers. What a party. What a day and a half. I'm in heaven. Our beloved Liverpool Football Club, Champions of England.

The pre-season flies by. Here we go. Shanks is telling everyone "just watch us go now" and what a historical season it turned out to be. As for me at the start of the season, the same dance as usual, pays me 9d in the boys' pen, up and over, no problems. I think the copper who had been trying to stop me had had enough. His replacement didn't fare much better than him. I was just simply too fast for him. Simple as that. I hitch hiked to more or less every game, apart from London, this season. The season starts early for us as we are in the first round of the European Cup. Away to a team from Iceland, Reykjavik. No problems, 5-0 away, Gordon Wallace being the first ever player to score for Liverpool in a European cup tie. So it's off to the league we go. The first game is at Anfield. Funny enough it's against Arsenal, the team we beat to secure the title in the last game of last season, into the pen, usual up and over. We win 3-2, a great game. Next up, midweek, away at Leeds United. It was one scary hitch hike. I was in school and me maa said "No way are you going to the match tonight, there is no way. You get your ass back home straight after school." Anyway about half past 1 in school I decided "Fuck her, I'm goin'". But I was thinking "4 o'clock after school, that's pushin' it that, to get to Leeds in time for kick off." So I decided to get off early using the "Sir, I feel sick" stunt I pulled earlier. Once I was in the clear that was it, I was gone. Running again all the way to Walton Hall Park, it took me about half an hour. But it didn't take me long to get a lift. Only about 10 minutes. A wagon pulls in. He was going to Birmingham. So he dropped me off at my old hitch hiking spec, Haydock Island. As usual fucking loads and loads of young redmen were looking for a lift, probably 12-15. I saw a kid I knew from Huyton, John Donelley. I said "Alright lad. Me and you together. ok?" He says "Sound Gerry". After about an hour and a half or so we get a lift. There was still at least 10 other redmen waiting for a lift. It's getting harder to catch a lift now. A big Rover pulls up. Me and John are right on him "Goin' anywhere near Leeds mate?" He says "All the way lads, jump in". John jumps in the front seat, I goes to get in the back seat and sees this huge golden Labrador dog. The driver says "It's alright lad, get in. He's very, very friendly." Fuck me, I didn't realise how friendly he was. Anyway I gets in and we're off, driving for about half an hour. All of a sudden the driver puts his left hand, while steering with his right hand, and started playing with the dog, giving him a German Tank! Fuck that. I went "Ay mate. Fuckin pull over now, you sick cunt, or I'll take your reg and phone the bizzies". He went fucking white. He went "No, No, No, No". He finally pulls over and starts telling us to get out. We couldn't get out fucking quickly enough. He was a big cunt as well. He just drove off dead fast, putting his lights out so we couldn't get his reg. So we're walking along, just outside Huddersfield, on an A road. We soon gets a lift. A Leeds fan living in Huddersfield going all the way to the game. Got there about quarter to 7. Plenty of time. Kick off was half 7 if memory serves me right. In we go. Fuckin gutted though. Paid for a change. Dead hard to jib in at Leeds. Full length turnstiles, no chance of a jump over, obviously. Cunt of a night. Got spanked 4-2. Tried to get on one of the coaches home. But no joy. All the drivers are well and truly clued up now with the hitch hikers so it was a long night hitching home. Didn't get home till about 2 in the morning. Fucking gutted. I knew I was going to get smacked all over the place in the morning by me maa but what the fuck. What a twat of a start to the season. After the first eight league games, we only win 2, lose 5 and draw 1. Champions? Fuck me. We certainly weren't playing like a team of champions. The game that hurt in that eight game run was against the blurts, Everton, at Anfield. They absolutely destroyed us 4-0 and it could've been more. I never went out for days. Plus I'd lost all me pocket money betting on my beloved redmen. Stupid cunt. Giving the blue bastards 3 to 1 I was. It's me own fault. I thought I was buying money. Ha ha. Mind you, only lost ten bob. That's the equivalent of 50p today, but not the same at all. With 50p today, what can you possibly buy? Maybe 2 cigarettes, but back then, in the good old days, or some say the bad old days, ten bob would buy you fish and chips five or six times over. Yes, five times at least so just do the maths.

Back to the games, I'm fuckin sick as we're struggling in the league, but things get much better. We go on a really, really nice run of 14 league games, staying unbeaten, winning nine, drawing five. That's more like it redmen. In between that run, we had the third round of the FA Cup. It was West Bromwich Albion away at The Hawthorns. I went with me dad as it was getting really hard work hitch hiking, maybe forty or fifty kids at Haydock Island, so as you can imagine, murder, cars just wouldn't pull over. So it's off we go. Only an hour and a half journey, just down the M6, with West Brom's ground, The Hawthorns, being not even 10 minutes from the motorway. Nice and handy for getting off. We win the game 2-1, with goals from who else but my idol Sir Roger and St John. Then disaster. Winning only four of the last thirteen league games. Finally finishing in seventh position. Not good enough for us that. But the FA Cup and the European Cup keeps our hopes alive for the rest of the season. Next up is the FA Cup fourth round, Stockport County, at Anfield. Piece of piss we thought, but they gave us one hell of a game. Holding us to a 1-1 draw, Gordon Milne scoring a rare goal within the first 5 minutes. Anyway, I think it was Wednesday night the replay. I've already pulled me sick trick a couple of times so I needed another way to get out of school. As normal, me and me two other brothers, Billy and Bimbo, got up for school. So off we went. But I had a mate who was boss at forging signatures, so I got him to write a letter for me, saying that I had a touch of the flu, but would probably be back in school tomorrow, and signed it Harry Blayney. They fell for it hook, line and sinker. I've got loads of time to waste now as it's only going to take me a couple of hours at the most, so I decided to go to Sefton Park for a few hours to watch people fish (I like fishing), mind you there wasn't many people there as it was freezing. I end up leaving there and getting to Haydock for about 3 o'clock. As usual, it's fucking chocka. Finally, I see me old mate John Donnelly. "Hello lad. Me and you again?" "Is right Gerry" he says. Got a lift pretty quick, was there about three quarters of an hour. Wagon driver, fuckin love them me. Most of my lifts all through my hitch hiking days were from wagons. I think the drivers just liked a bit of company, driving all day on their own. Anyway, we get there really early. The driver took us through that twat of a place, Manchester, not far from Stockport. I think it was about 5 o'clock when we got there, to the ground. You should've seen the travelling redmen. It was boss. Everybody buzzing. Singing and dancing, all singing Beatles songs of course. With "We love you yeah, yeah, yeah". It was magical. The rattles were rattling, the scarves were waving, and singing "We're gonna win the cup". Every game it just seems to be getting better and better for me. I am loving it. Me and John bunked in yet again. Mind you, we had to because we only had 2 bob between us ha-ha. The game itself was easy. We win 2-0 with goals from, yes, you've got it, Sir Roger Hunt. It wasn't just the win that was boss, it was the travelling redmen. They never stopped singing and dancing all the way through the game. I am so proud to be a part of this beautiful massive family. Getting home was easy. We got to the coach park and jibbed on a coach. It's getting harder though, as I said before. Most of the coach drivers are on it now so you've got to wait for exactly the right moment or you're fucked. Anyway I ended up getting home about 11, 11.30. As I said before, the teacher at school was easily blagged with the letter. But as usual me maa wasn't very happy at all. She knew right away when I didn't get home till after 11 that I'd hitched it again to the match. So the normal, a few slaps, loads of verbal. "Get to bed, and by the way, your tea's in the dog". Me dad had this great big Alsatian, he loved the allies me dad.

Anyway, back to the European cup. After beating Reykjavik and Anderlecht, of Belgium, next up it was Cologne, from Germany, in the quarter finals. What an epic. Three games, yes three games. A 0-0 draw away, and then the same score, 0-0 at Anfield. Then it was the decider, at a neutral ground. It was held in Rotterdam, Holland. Me and me dad and all of his mates were listening to the game on Radio World Service, with full commentary of the game. Its fucking funny looking back at about six or seven of us all gathered round, listening to this little radio in the living room of our two bedroom house. All on the booze, me an' all (shandies of course). Fucking nerve rackin' or what. If memory serves we go 1-0 down after about 15 minutes, everyone's heads went down, swearing and all sorts. But less than 10 minutes later, it was bedlam. About six or seven of us jumping up and down, beers getting knocked everywhere, tables, chairs, etc, but we didn't give a fuck, because the Saint, Ian St John had scored to make it 1-1. We had no sooner settled down, everyone breathless, then the one and only, Sir Roger Hunt was at it again, to make it 2-1 to the mighty reds. Half time whistle goes. It didn't take long for a German to equalise and make it 2-2. Fucking gutted. The 90 minutes are up and its extra time. It was horrible listening to it on the radio, so nerve racking. No goals in extra time. Fuck me, it's down to a toss of a coin. Yes, the toss of a coin. No penalties in them days. Big Ron Yeats our captain stood alongside the Cologne captain and the referee, with the rest of the players huddled round waiting for the toss. And to add to the drama, it was incredible. The referee tosses the coin into the air but it lands in the mud, not on heads, not on tails. Fuck me. What's going on? We're listening to the commentator on the radio, and we just hear "I don't believe it. He's got to toss it again. It's stuck in the mud". He tosses it again, the next thing we hear is the commentator saying "Big Ron Yeats is throwing his arms up in the air with delight. Liverpool have won the toss. We are through to the semi-final of the European Cup". We went absolutely mental. Tables, chairs, glasses, everything. "Get in. Get in!"

In the semi-final we are to play against the giants of the day, Inter Milan, from Italy. I'm really looking forward to that one. Back to the FA Cup and it was Bolton Wanderers away. Nice easy drive up the Lancs. Went with me dad and his mates. Ian Callaghan got the only goal of the game, which took us through to the next round against Leicester City, our bogey team. But bogey teams don't last forever. They held us 0-0 at Leicester and we were really, really confident of beating them at Anfield in the replay, but as usual, with them, it was a very, very tight game. The Jolly Roger scores with about 15 minutes left. 1-0. It was a very uncomfortable last 15 minutes but the bogey team had finally been put to rest. That'll do us redmen. We get Chelsea in the semi-final, at Villa Park. The whole of Liverpool is bouncing, dreaming of getting to Wembley, one game away. Only Chelsea stand in our way.

The drive down to Villa Park with me dad and his mates was boss. Loads of cars beeping their horns, flags and scarves hanging out of the windows, and don't forget the rattles. Looking back now, rattles? Fucking crazy. We get there early. Me dad and his mates, Dougie and Ted, fancy a few beers before the game, as you do. I get my couple of shandys and then it's into the game. The atmosphere was incredible. Nearly 70,000 packed into Villa Park. The travelling redmen as normal were giving it loads, singing "We love you Liverpool we do, we love you Liverpool we do, we love you Liverpool we do, oh, Liverpool we love you". It brought a lump to my throat. Very emotional. The game itself was very tight for the first hour. Then after about 65 minutes, Peter Thompson, me dad's idol, scores to make it 1-0 to our beloved red men. We were well in control. Chelsea had to start taking risks so it was no surprise to all of us red men when Willie Stevenson made it 2-0 from the penalty spot with 10 minutes to go. The final whistle goes. We are there. A date at Wembley to play Don Revie's Leeds United. Without a doubt the most ruthless, dirtiest side I've ever seen in my life. Anyway the journey home to Liverpool was magical as always. People dancing on top of cars, horns going off, the usual. Me dad told me maa before we left for Villa Park "Elsie, if we win, get your glad-rags on girl. We're going to the Cabaret at the supporters club. Me and our Gerry will get back from the match at about half past 7, I'll drop Dougie and Ted at the supporters club, then I'll pick you up and drop Gerry off". Boy was I buzzing lads. I've got the highlights to look forward to as well – it was fucking brilliant to watch it again. Finally I fall asleep with a big smile on me face. I just couldn't wait to go to school on the Monday morning (can't believe I'm saying that! I fucking hated school) but I was so looking forward to showing me mates the programme and telling them all about the game, as you do.

Anyway it's the final at Wembley. I'm dead nervous as I'm

thinking me maa won't let me go to Wembley as I'm still only thirteen, but I was hoping me dad would talk me maa into it. As it happened he did, no problem. I'm made up but that soon changed. The whole city had gone wild, everyone trying to get tickets and transport to go to Wembley. It was incredible. People selling everything they had: old cars, jewellery, anything they had to get the money to go. But it wasn't as simple as that. Those cockney touts charged the earth but according to me dad, some of them went home not very happy as loads of them got battered everywhere, all their tickets taken off them, plus the cash. Fuck them. Anyway, a few days before the final, me dad says "Gerry, it's near on impossible to get tickets or hire a car. Everywhere's booked up." Then came the words I was dreading to hear. "Look Lad" me dad said. "I don't know how to tell you this but I don't think you will be able to go to Wembley. It's only 3 days away and we have only got 3 tickets between 6 of us. Shanks gave me one, and we got the other 2 off the season tickets. And as for the car, as you know lad, the clutch is on the way out". It was a big car, a Vanguard-Engine, took six or seven people in no problem. "We can't go in that, we'll never make it to London" he said. "The only car I could get on hire was a Ford Consul in yellow of all colours." He said "We'll be like sardines as it is, not a very big car at all".

I said "Can't you take a chance going in our car dad. Please, please dad".

"I'm sorry la, it's just not possible", he said, "Your ma said there's no way you're getting' in that car with 6 or 7 of us. It's too dangerous. And don't even dream of it Gerry, don't even dream of it. Do not try to hitch hike there".

I was fucking gutted, but what could I do? Me dad was as well but he said I could watch it on the telly. All the family were coming to ours to watch it so it was going to be a boss day. "You can drink whatever you want lad, never mind the shandys, have a proper pint if you feel like it," adding "listen lad, Shanks has told us that there will be loads more Wembleys in the future". Anyway on the morning of the game me dad is ready at about half 5 in the morning. He calls me over and gives me a really big hug. He says "I'll give the reds a big cheer for you all game lad". And then he was gone. I'm in bits, tears running down me face. Straight back to bed for me, gutted. It still hurts me to this day. Anyway you should've seen all the streets round by our house, street parties all over the place, it was magical. I've never seen a street party like it. Loads of young girls flashing their red knickers. Our house was chocka with me aunties, uncles, cousins, about 40-50 relations in total. I was so nervous as the game was starting but it just seemed to fly by. After ninety minutes it was 0-0. Then all of a sudden The Jolly Roger was as it, yet again. Get in. 1-0. But then out of nothing, that fucking Billy Bremner, the dirty little bastard, scores to make it 1-1. But with less than 10 minutes of extra time to go, up popped the Saint, Callaghan went past the full back tight to the dead ball line but managed to whip it across for Ian St John to score a spectacular diving header which turned out to be the winner. Everyone was going crazy. Bouncing everywhere. Dancing up and down in the streets. The FA Cup has finally come to Liverpool. I couldn't wait for me dad to get home.

The party in our house was chocka. As usual The Beatles were playing on the record player, everyone having fun, pissed up of course. Then about 12 o'clock, maybe a bit later, I hear a car beeping outside. I just knew it was me dad and his mates. I'm out of the house in a flash. Big Hug. "Get in" he said, "I told you we'd win it". Then I'm right in his ear "Tell me all about it dad. What were the travelling redmen like? Did you see Shanks?" He said "Gerry, it was incredible. You were never out my thoughts throughout the whole ninety minutes and extra time." Then he said to me "By the way, I've got a really nice surprise for you in a few weeks. I hope it makes up for not going to Wembley". Then he looked me straight in the eye and said "Are you ready for this?" I said "Ready for what". "I'm taking to Melwood to watch our beloved redmen train, and you will meet our god, Shankly." WOW. I couldn't believe it. I was going to meet the great man himself. I'll tell you what, it was the best possible consolation prize.

Before that there was the small matter of the first leg of the European Cup semi-final at Anfield, against the best team on the planet at that time, the mighty Inter Milan. What an atmosphere.

I know I've said it many times before - "What an atmosphere", but this was really special. I've never seen anything like. It was so special. I got to the ground nice and early, just about managing to get in the Boys Pen, it was chocka everywhere. Same dance as always, up and over into the Kop. It was so hard to describe to you, The Kop was in full throttle all game, chanting "Go back to Italy". The whole ground. It was deafening. We destroyed the best team in Europe 3-1 with goals from the Jolly Roger, Ian Callaghan and St John. It could've been 5, having two goals disallowed, one from St John, which probably was offside, just, but no way that Chris Lawler's (the Silent Night) was offside. Everyone was very confident, but Shankly was very wary of the Italians, and he was right to be wary. So it's off to Italy. Then disaster. They beat us 3-0. Well, they never, the referee did. He was an absolute fucking disgrace. Shankly was going absolutely nuts, telling everyone "that Spaniard (the referee) has cost Liverpool a place in the final of the biggest club side competition in the world". The referee never did another game in his entire life. He was banned for taking a bribe, believed to be £5,000 cash, a villa in Italy and a new Fiat car. If that was to happen in today's football, Liverpool would've gone through, banning Inter Milan from the competition, for god knows how long. But that was then, and this is now. It left a bitter taste for years, even now actually. We should've been the first English side to win the European Cup.

That's it, season over. But not mine. A couple of days later I'm off to Melwood with me dad to watch the mighty redmen training. It was mainly the reserve players as most of the first team were away on their holidays, but Peter Thompson, me dad's idol and Sir Roger were there. Thompson seen me dad as he was training and shouted over "Alright Harry, nice to see you again". I was loving all this. Then Shankly blew his whistle and the training was over. All the players made their way to the showers while Shanks picked up a big net and started to gather all the balls together. He was only about 15 yards away from us when he shouts over "Harry, I'll be with you in a minute son". Wow. Over he comes and says to me dad "Is this the famous Gerry you have been telling me all about?"

Me dad says "It certainly is". Then Shanks said to me "Look son, it wasn't possible for you to go to Wembley this time, but don't worry, this the only the beginning. We will be going to Wembley many, many more times." Then the great man said "I've got to go now Harry, I'll see you soon son". Then he looked at me and said "You too Gerry son". He called everyone son. I was buzzing for weeks on end. Me and me dad with the Shanks? Boy I couldn't wait to go to school to tell all me mates about it. I was buzzing all the way through the summer break

By the 1965-66 season I was 14 so there was no way I was missing out on London this season. I didn't care if I get a few slaps off me ma or the teachers at school, London here I come. The first thing I do is look at the fixture list to see who our first game in London is against. It's West Ham away. I'll come back to that in a few minutes time. The first game of the season, it's our bogey team, Leicester City away. I get to Haydock Island for about 10 o'clock in the morning. It was chocka. Took fucking ages getting a lift. It's getting really hard hitch hiking now. I don't think it will be long before I start going on the coach. Anyway we beat Leicester City 3-1. Great start to the season. Five games later it's West Ham. Really looking forward to going to London. Me dad said he was going to take me to London but something came up, or should I say something came out. Another brother was due to be born. So Friday night I'm off to the East Lancs. I get to Haydock Island for about midnight. Not too many kids there really. Only about six or seven. A nice change. We were only there for less than half an hour I reckon, and then we got a lift. He took us to Birmingham and dropped us on the A5, then we got another lift from a wagon, all the way to London. I think it was about 7 o'clock in the morning by the time we got there. Wow, London. It was pissing down, but it didn't bother us. We went into this small cafe, got a cup of tea and a bacon sarnie, and stayed there for a couple of hours, playing pinball and just wasting time waiting for the match.

Then it's off we go to Upton Park. No problem bunking in.

What a great game it turned out to be. West Ham had a really, really good side. With Bobby Moore, Geoff Hurst and Martin Peters all future World Cup winners but we ran riot, winning 5-1. The travelling redmen were bouncing everywhere. After the match we go back to the coach park trying to bunk on one of the coaches or get a lift. I saw a few lads I knew so me and me mate Johno just got on their coach with them, walked up to the back and hid under the seats. The coach drivers always counted to make sure the same number that came down were on to go back. No problems, he pulls away from the car park, then we're up from under the seats sitting with the lads. It was a great journey home, everyone singing "We're gonna win the league, we're gonna win the league, ee aye addio, we're gonna win the league". I think we got back to Liverpool at about half 12, yes half 12. It took about six or seven hours to get to Liverpool from London in those days. We got dropped off at Lime Street and I walked home to Liverpool 8, Ivy Street. I was dreading going home to the house. I knew there wouldn't be a problem with me dad, it was me ma I was worried about. I knocked on the door, knowing full well me dad would be waiting up for me to make sure I got in safe.

He opened the door and says "Are you alright lad?"

I said "Great dad, but I'm tired and I'm hungry. I bunked the coach home dad".

Me dad says "Your ma has left you a bit of scouse in the pan there". Then he said "Look son, me and your mam really hate you hitching it to the games. It's really, really dangerous. I know you can look after yourself son but it's your maa, you know what she's like."

I says "I know dad. And it's getting harder and harder. I think it's time for me to start going on the coach".

As it happened there was one running from the Fantail Pub in Kirkby. I was more or less brought up in Kirkby. As I told you earlier on, I've got loads of aunties and uncles, me ma having something like 11 brothers and sisters, or something like that. Anyway, as I said I was more or less brought up in Kirkby, because me favourite auntie, Cheeky, lived there. Her proper name was Alice, but me ma told me she was a hard faced little bastard and that's where she got the name from. She also had nine children, all born in Kirkby so I was down there a lot. Also my favourite cousin, Colin, known to everyone as Snap lived there. Without a doubt he's the Arthur Daley of Kirkby. He had his finger in many, many pies. Loved him. His dad George was one of the first people selling scarves & rosettes all over the country at football grounds, but not only football grounds, he used to do the rugby finals, where he used to make loads of money, he said more or less fifty years ago, but still to this day, the family still sell scarves, flags and loads of other memorabilia outside the grounds.

Anyway, back to getting what turned out to be my second to last hitch ever. My last hitch was a nightmare, but we'll talk about that in a few minutes. Not really looking forward to Sunday morning. I just know me ma will have a right go at me. Boy did I get a really nice surprise. I'm expecting the slaps to start coming straight at me as soon as she laid eyes on me, but no, she just looked at me straight in the eye and said "Look lad, I'm sick to death of fighting with you, I slap you silly, I ground you, but it still doesn't seem to work. From now on you can go the match on the coach. We are dead happy you are not going to hitch hike anymore. But I am telling you straight now lad, If you bring any problems to the house, from the police, school, fighting, anything, I mean it Gerry, and you know when I say that, you won't be able to sneak out of the house to go to the match 'cause I'll nail the windows down in your room and I'll put a lock on the outside door so there is no way out. It's up to you now lad". Then as she turned away she just started muttering "That Shankly has got a lot to answer for. He's got you and your dad brainwashed". I thought to myself, "Just me and me dad? He's brainwashed fifty-six thousand other redmen who go to the match!" That was it. No more slaps off me ma, didn't hurt anyway, but I've really got to calm down.

But trouble just seemed to follow me round. I just hate being told what to do. I was sick of the words "Get to the headmaster's office" for six of the best with the cane. Boy did that sting. So I must try harder to keep my fucking big mouth shut otherwise me ma will definitely keep her word. Just two or three days later, me ma has the new baby, our Alan. That's four of us now. Anyway, back to the games. Halfway through the season, 21 games played. We are right up there in the mix, winning fourteen, drawing three, and losing four. The next five games, we beat Fulham, draw with West Ham at home, then lose 2-1 to spurs. Next game up its 'The People's Club' (people's club my ass). The Toffees or the blues shite, that's what we call them. Boy did we give them a good walloping. 5-0. Won a nice few bob (probably £1) off me Evertonian mates. Back to Europe, preliminary round, first leg away to the mighty Juventus, of Italy. We lose 1-0, but Shanks is really, really happy. He was telling everyone "Don't worry, we will destroy them in the second leg at Anfield. The Kop will petrify them again. Just like they did to Inter Milan last season". As usual, bold Bill was right. He said "No bottle them Ities, never 'av had" (run away, run away, run away, that's what they done in the war). He didn't like the Italian sides Shanks, he just didn't trust them. And he was dead right. He even made sure that all the food we would needed while in Italy was brought with the team, so the Italians couldn't fuck around with it. Shanks, as good as his word, watched as we beat Juventus comfortably, no problem. 2-0, winning 2-1 on aggregate. The Kop was on form at the final whistle. They sang "Go back to Italy, Go back to Italy, Go back to Italy, Go back to Italy" to what I think was an opera song. It was magical. Anyway back to the league. We go on a decent little run, winning seven, drawing one, and losing two. Top of the league, and looking really good. Next up in the European Cup was Standard Liege of Belgium. No problem at all, 3-1 at home, 2-1 away. Then a fabulous run in the league, winning seven and drawing one of eight games. We are running away with the league now. There is only eleven games left. I think we are eight or nine points clear, playing absolutely fabulous football, brilliant to watch. Don't forget lads it was only two points for a win so on today's football, we would be probably more like sixteen, seventeen points clear.

Oh writing this next piece really hurts me. Next up it's Fulham away, which turned out to be the very last time I hitch hiked to the match. I know me ma said she would kill me but I just couldn't miss the game and couldn't sort a coach to go. What a fucking nightmare. Without a doubt, one of the worst moments of my life. We had just moved house from Toxteth, Liverpool 8, up to Huyton. I was nearly fifteen then. Back to the hitch, I got to Haydock at about midnight, fucking mental. Must've been about thirty or forty kids. It took us way over two hours before we got a lift. I thought "Fuck this, this is definitely me last hitch. Too much like hard work this." Eventually we get a lift. Fucking big wagon. Lovely. The driver was a scouser, well more or less, he was from Birkenhead. Really nice guy. His name was Harry, the same as me dad. And what a touch, he was going all the way to London. He had to take a break from driving, so we pulled in on the A1 at Cannock, just outside Birmingham. An all-night Cafe. All the wagons used to stop there. We ordered two teas and then the wagon driver says "Aren't you hungry boys?" We both looked at him and said "We're starvin', but we've only got about 6 bob between us". The wagon driver says to the server "Give the boys a bacon sarnie each, I'll pay". We were fucking made up. "Thanks mate". Then he says "Look lads, I've got to get an hour or two sleep now, so I'm gonna go back to the wagon. Give me a shout in two hours, then we'll be straight off to London". As he was leaving the cafe, he shouts to the server "Give the boys another cup of tea if they want one later". Wow. What a really nice fella. He was only young, maybe about twenty five, thirty. He was a redman but his work meant he couldn't get to many games. Five minutes before we were due to wake him up I had this terrible feeling so I said to me mate "What do you think of the driver?" Me mate says "Sound, why?" I says "Don't you remember the Labrador fella?" He says back "Oh fuck this Gerry, let's get off before he wakes up". Then I said "No, he's alright. He must come to this cafe all the time as the server greeted him with 'What you having Harry?' And then I said "Anyway, how the fuck can he try anything as there is a fucking big console between the driver's seat and the passenger's seat. He would have to have six foot long arms". So we go and wake him up, then we're off to London. He dropped us off at Enfield. (Not Anfield.) As we got out he said "Take care lads" and threw us half a crown. Enough to buy us both

In My Blood

a portion of chips and a sausage between us. We get to the game, easy to get in. No problem. Twat of a game though. I'm sick. We get beat 2-0. Back to the coach park to try and bunk on a coach. No joy at first. Got caught a couple of times trying to get on. It was right on top now. The coach drivers would check everyone getting on. Luckily, I had a mate who was on one of the coaches, and he knew how to open the boot from the inside of the coach. Anyway, he gets it open and four or five of us are in like a flash. Fucking bumpy ride but it was ok. Fuck me, we are three quarters of the way home, at Keele services in Stoke. The driver pulls over for a little break. Me mate opens the boot for us and we are out. Really cramped up to fuck. Shit, the driver sees us getting out in his mirror, comes off the coach screaming and shouting at us. "Are yous fucking mad. You could've died in there. Now fuck off and don't even try to get back in." Fair enough.

We walked away. Then just like the two times before, it hit me like a lightning bolt. Fuck off. Me legs went. The pain was immense. I knew what it was right away. That bastard rheumatic fever had come back. This fella was getting out of a car, noticed me on the floor and came running over. "Are you alright kid?" I said "No mate. I need to go to the hospital I think." He said "Just stay there, I'll bring me car over and I'll give you a lift home." He was going to Halewood. I told him the score about my illness so he took me straight home to Page Moss, Huyton. He knocked on our door, me dad answered and came out and had to carry me in. I was in agony. Me dad thanked the fella over and over, and so did I. Then me dad carried me back out to his car and took me straight to the hospital. The doctor came over and just prodded me groin with his finger. The pain was unbearable. Felt like he was sticking a knife into my groin. The he just looked at me dad and said "Sorry Mr. Blayney. The fever is back." So that's me out for the rest of the season. Injured again. I'm devastated, but what can I do? Fuck all. We win the league with about three games to spare. We get to the final of the European cup winners cup. It was held at Hampden Park, Scotland. Obviously me dad and his mates went, and there's me on that fucking stationary bike again. Me dad comes into see me after the final, but sadly we get beat 2-1 by Borussia Dortmund of Germany. That's it, season over. But it's ok because we are champions of England again. Get in there. After three or four months I was well enough to come home. There was only five or six weeks left before the start of the season. I can't wait. But hopefully that's the end of my rheumatic fever days. Full recovery, never to come back again, hopefully. Thank God for that. I really do hate missing games being out injured.

It was a really hard time for the family at the time. I had only just come home from hospital, then one of our brothers, our Billy, gets rushed to Whiston Hospital with pleurisy. He'd had asthma since birth but it was touch and go if he was going to make it. He was really, really ill. Then there was the new baby, our Alan, fuck me it was a nightmare for me mum and dad. Visiting me or our Billy every night. I really can't describe how bad I was feeling. Obviously me dad visits me every night. Then one night he came in and said "I've been to Melwood today to watch the Reds train. I had a little chat with Shanks and told him about you being back in hospital with rheumatic fever. Shanks told me to tell you that he was asking about you." Wow. That was boss. The Shanks asking about me. A couple of weeks after that I'm home and I'm feeling great. They were long months them. The strain was starting to show on me mam and dad's faces but they never gave in. I was so lucky to have such good parents. Ok, me ma could be very cruel, but nine out of ten times I deserved it. I hadn't missed a league game since that injury and I was determined not to miss a single game the next season, to get the full forty-two league games in.

The season starts. I've just left school now and it's just job after job after job after job. The day I left school, I'll never forget it. There was about three or four lads waiting to see the headmaster for our final report. I'd just been in and got mine so I was just waiting for the other lads to go in. I just lit a ciggie up and the teacher came rushing over screaming. What a dog she was. She was at least 6 foot 5 and ugly as fuck. She shouts at me "Blayney, put that cigarette out now". I just blew smoke in her face and said "Fuck off Mrs. Cross. My school days are over." Boy did she look like a man. Then I just walked out with the swagger of a scallywag. I just didn't like school at all. I was so happy I was leaving. I actually started work fifteen minutes after I walked out of the school gates. Seriously, I started a job, now don't laugh lads, as an order boy in a big grocery store. It was two minutes' walk from the school, St Saviours, Canning St. I had to deliver all me orders on a bike. One of those bikes with the big baskets on the front. I lasted about three or four days. On the last day, it was freak weather. Pissing down, torrential. So she sends me out on the bike, gives me a Macintosh and a hat to keep the rain off. I must've looked like a right wally. Fuck that for a lark. I just said to the woman, the owner, "This is not for me love. I'll call in in a few days for me wages."

The next day I got another job right in the centre of town. The fruit market in Queens Square. 4 o'clock start in the morning. But then we were finished at 12. £4 ten shilling a week. Sadly I was only there two weeks as I got sacked for robbing a hand full of Kit Kat chocolate bars from a shop we were delivering to. Within a year I must've had about fifteen or twenty jobs. Milk man, Coal man (fucking hard work that), I even worked down the mines in Cronton for about five weeks. Then I got a job on Dock Road making these big sails for the ships on the dock. I'd been there about a week. I didn't like it at all. The building I was working in had the painters in white washing all the walls. So the gaffer of the painting firm came over and started talking to me. He was only young, about 35 or something. He asked me did I like working there. I just told him I fucking hated it. Then he said to me "Can you paint?" I said "I suppose so. Why?" He said "I need another lad because that little prick over there hasn't got a clue. He's getting sacked, so there is a job here with me if you want one." The money was well better so I said "Yeah". So I started work for him and I'd been there about three days when we got a job painting a school. Anyway one day I'm up the ladder painting the top of the guttering, then the boss shouted up "You've missed a bit there lad". I shouts down "Where? I can't see from where I am". He says "Just stay there and I'll come up and show you". So he comes up the ladder and he's right behind me, literally pressed up against me. I shit myself. "Whoa whoa whoa, what's going on here!?" "I'll pay you. I'll give you extra". I said "Get to fuck." And that was the end of that job.

Anyway back to the football. It was not a good season at all. We finished fifth in the league, knocked out of Europe early doors then knocked out of the FA Cup by the blue shite from across the park. Well as I said my hitch hiking days are over now so onto the coaches. Firstly from Kirkby, with my favourite cousin, Snap, Colin O'Brien, and a big black kid named Joey Magabee. Game as fuck him. Could have a good fight. There was also another kid Tommy Kinsella plus another few game lads. The coach used to leave from The Fantail Pub, just up the road from where I was going from, The Johnny-Todd. One of the games, Sheffield Wednesday, comes to mind. One of my very first tastes of football violence. We win the game 1-0 thanks to Peter Thompson, then on the way back to the coach park, there was about five or six of us all buzzing about the win. All of a sudden about fifteen or twenty Sheff Wed skins came from nowhere. Fuck me you should've seen Joey Magabee go. Fuck me he knocked about three of them out then we all got stuck in and they all ran away like the cowards that they were. Boy did that feel good. Don't fuck with us, we've got balls. Then every away game there was running battles everywhere. The violence was really kicking into the game now. Everyone was at it. I only missed one game all season, Leeds United away. I so wanted to get the forty-two in, but forty-one wasn't bad but couldn't as that fucking Scooby Doo (flu) meant I was in bed for three days. Anyway the next season was soon upon us.

By 1967-68, for some reason or other, the Kirkby coach was no more. So I started to go with Crown Coaches which left Liverpool from just over the road from Lime Street Station. Boss coach, boss driver. His name was Wally. He used to let me go for free as I would go round with a hat on the coach and have a whip around for him, making sure he would get a nice drink out of it. Happy days. I got to know this kid on the coach. He was about 22, 23, about six or seven years older than me. His name was Lenny Woods. As far as I'm concerned, he is probably the greatest Liverpool fan ever. He is a living legend alongside Bobby Wilcox, and my other life-long redmen, big Phil Aspinall, and big Dave Penno. I still see Lenny every away game today. What a redman Lenny is. I don't believe there is a man alive that I have seen at more games, especially in Europe. FACT. I thought I would just give you a mention mate. See you at the next game. Anyway the coach was boss – same crew every week. Happy days for me. All over the country for fuck all. Bunking in at most of the games, even snatching the odd turnstile. Took £30 at Sunderland. It doesn't sound a lot but it was. Thirty £1 notes was a big wad. I was working all week for just over a fiver so that was about six weeks' wages. I'd never seen so much money. Done a few more, one at Wolverhampton, £18, then £20 at Southampton. But the coppers soon got onto it. They put a copper on each turnstile. Soft twats. Only had a copper on the outside. So I just paid in, think it was Carlisle, I'm not sure, then snatched it from the inside, disappearing into the crowd. Turnstiles were getting snatched all over the country by everyone. It seemed everyone was at it. It was so easy. As long as you could run. And boy could I run like the wind, remember? Finally the penny dropped. The dozy copper finally put a copper on the inside and one on the outside.

Look, I am not really proud of what I was doing but that's the way it was. I didn't take me long though to find another little earner. No pinball machine or juke box was safe. Funny as fuck when I look back at it. A small screwdriver worked a treat, every time. There was a time at Leeds, probably the hardest ground in the country to bunk into. It was one of the first grounds to have full length turnstiles, meaning it was impossible to jump over and very hard to double click. So it looks like I'll have to pay in. Didn't matter though as about half an hour before we go in we were all in the pub right outside the ground called The Peacock. There was a nice big juke box in the corner. The pub is chocka with scousers singing and dancing everywhere. Perfect. It was a doddle. Just bent down, screwdriver out, get the cash box open. A few kids noticed I was trying to get at the box. I said "Fucking take it easy lads. You'll bring it on top. The box is nearly full. There is plenty for all of us. Just keep dixie". In other words keep an eye on the manager on the bar. So out of me pocket I pull this sock. I carried it everywhere. Filled it up, not sure, about £15-£20 worth of change. Then I said "Here you go lads". They are right in there, falling over each over and everything. Then the manager gets on it. He jumped over the bar comes rushing over to the juke box. Fucking hilarious it was. I was gone. But there was no way I could go into the game with that. I'd have probably got nicked. So I had to find somewhere to hide it. Just behind the pub there was a big hill with a football pitch on it. I dug a hole by one of the goal posts, buried me sock, and off I go to the match. After the game I just went back and dug it up. Happy days. A few bob in me pocket and our beloved redmen win 2-1 thanks to goals from Chris Lawler and Bobby Graham. Not long after that we signed Tony Hateley, a big centre forward who was by far the greatest header of a ball I've ever seen. Unbelievable. We signed him from Chelsea for £96,000 which was big money in those days. He was a really big headed guy. Apparently when he signed he said to the rest of the side "I've been signed to pull you lot out of the shit". I believe Tommy Smith went nuts and wanted to rip his head off.

As I said before, the violence at the games was getting worse. But we didn't give a fuck. There was a main firm of skinheads in the Kop, a big firm, with the leader being a kid named Kelly. But I was not going to be a foot soldier for anyone. There was only about eight or ten of my little crew, but all were game as fuck. Thinking back now it was crazy. My right hand man was a big fucker, Andy Fisher (The Fish). We had some balls me and him. We used to infiltrate their fans. The first time we done it was at Arsenal. Straight into the North Bank with all their skins. We were just about half way up, mingling with all their skins, giving our best cockney accents. "Fack off you scouse bastards" and shit like that. Then I gave the fish the wink. Let's go. Fuck off, butted two or three each. Blood and snot everywhere. Then it was right on our toes. Right down to the front, onto the running track behind the goal, along the stand and right into the travelling redmen. The away supporters weren't in the Old Clock end then. No. The away supporters were to the right of the North Bank. It was boss. All the redmen were cheering me and the Fish as we dived back in. Some buzz. Don't forget, I was only seventeen and I didn't give a fuck. Gave a fuck about the result though. We got beat 2-0. Fucking long drive home on the coach.

The '67-68 season wasn't going so well. We went out of Europe in the third round to Ferencvarosi, the Hungarian champions. They beat us 1-0 away and 1-0 at Anfield, becoming the first European side to win at our place. Then we went out of the FA Cup in the quarter final after three games and two replays. But a game that comes to mind was in the third round of the FA Cup, away to Bournemouth. It was so funny. There was a row of turnstiles then a big wooden gate with a small door in the middle. I just walked over and tried the handle. Fuck me. Low and behold, it opened. No one was about inside for about twenty yards. There was a cafe and it was chocka. So I started shouting to all the kids outside "E R Lads. A shilling each to get in here". Loads of them came running over. I probably collected about a fiver or something in ten minutes. But then it came right on top. Bizzies chasing the lads everywhere. I often look back and laugh at that one. Then there was a game at West Brom and before it there were loads of birds knocking about so I get chatting to them, as you do. I copped for one of them. She was about my age, sixteen, seventeen - Little Mo. She had jeans on with an M on one cheek and an O on the other. Anyway, after the game she came to meet me at the coach park before I left for Liverpool. I'm kissing the gob off her at the back of the coach. All the lads at the back of the coach are perving out at us. I got her to give me a Jodrell Bank. The back of the coach were going mental, screaming to get her tits out. Fucking hilarious. Another game comes to mind, away to Arsenal. We are getting beat 1-0. A really horrible night, it was pissing down. I think there was about half an hour to go and Roger Hunt scored to make it 1-1. As the ball went across the line it started to thunder and lightning. In a flash the travelling redmen were chanting "Shankly has spoken" as though it was Shankly who had made the thunder and lightning. Pure scouse humour at its best. But it was another poor season for us, finishing third in the league. The best thing about the season was the signing of Emlyn Hughes (my mate) who we'd signed from Blackpool. What a player. Shanks told everyone "This boy will captain England one day" and as always, the Shanks was right. Much, much more about Emlyn later in the book.

1968-69 saw us start badly again – winning three, drawing two, and losing two. Tony Hateley, after a fabulous debut season where he scored 27 goals and while my idol, Roger Hunt, hit 29 (for a total of 56) got a bad injury and didn't play for most of the season so Shanks had to go out and buy a new striker. He buys a young kid, only 18, from Wolverhampton Wanderers. His name was Alun Evans for £100,000, that was a record fee for a teenager back then. Shanks had remembered him from the season before when he played at Anfield when he was only 17. He'd had a blinder, giving big Ron Yeats a right roasting. He scored in The Kop end and that prompted his strike partner Derek Dougan, a Wolves legend and a great character in to parade Alun before the Kop. If that wasn't enough, Dougan dropped his shorts and mooned the Kop. He never even got booked. Funny or what. But The Kop ended up having the last laugh as we won 2-1.

Alun Evans made his debut at home to Leicester City and we win 4-0. Evans scores. Bogey team? Not anymore. Then the next game, of all people, his away debut was at Wolverhampton, the club we just signed him from. Just before the game a big firm of Wolverhampton skinheads were right up for it. And boy did they get it. The redmen were taunting them as they were running away with the sound of "We're not afraid of the big bad wolves, big bad wolves, big bad wolves". It was hilarious, we were laughing our cocks off at them. What a game though. We destroyed them 6-0, with Alun Evans bagging two, Roger Hunt two, and Peter Thompson two. A boss trip home. A bit later on in the season Alun Evans drives back down to Wolverhampton to visit his parents. He ended up going out to a nightclub with a few of his mates, then apparently about four or five Wolves fans started giving him grief.

Then one of them shoved a pint glass straight into his face. He had to have loads of stiches. He was out of the side for a good few weeks. He got back in but he was really struggling, his confidence had gone. I blame a lot of fans for this. As you probably know, crowds can be really cruel. The last thing a good looking young lad needs is a gobshite shouting at him "fuck off scarface". I know exactly how he was feeling as the year before I'd got a leather cutting knife pushed straight into my face. It was shaped like a half moon, and as sharp as a Stanley blade. It happened as I was working in a leather cutting factory on Wilson Road, Huyton, just opposite the famous Huntley and Palmer Biscuit Factory. I'd only been working there a couple of weeks. I was sixteen. This cunt, he was twenty-one, seventeen stone, a big cunt. I think I was eight and a half stone soaking wet. He was the charge hand of the factory. A horrible cunt. Anyway we get into an argument, the next thing I know the blood is squirting everywhere out of the left hand side of my face. My legs go. The next thing I know I wake up and I'm in a hospital bed with my left arm up in the air in a sling. All sorts of tubes were sticking out of it. I'd lost about four pints of blood so needed a blood transfusion. My face was cut from just under my left eye (he'd only missed my eye by half an inch) then all the way through to my top lip. After about a week in the hospital the nurse said "Your bandages are coming off today, then you can go home." Then she says to me "I think it would be better if you go to the toilet on your own and take the last layer of bandages off". So I went to the toilet, started to take the bandages off in front of the mirror and as I got to the last layer and pulled it off I nearly fainted. It was so noticeable. My confidence with the girls was gone. And believe me, I was banging for England. Copped for a bird every week in town, at either Reece's nightclub, just at the bottom of Bold St, or the famous Mardi-Gras Club, which I liked better. The first six months was so hard for me. I was very conscious of the scar. I even had a strip of plaster on it for months on end. That's when I decide to grow a 'tache to cover some of the scar up. The 'tache has never been off my face to this day and I'm 60 now. I really did feel for Alun Evans and boy did I take it out on a fellow redman. It was away at Burnley. The travelling redmen were bouncing as usual. I was bouncing with my little firm. Then half time comes. I just hear this kid about ten yards behind us screaming about Alun Evans as the players are going off at half time, calling him all sorts. Then it came. He just shouted "Fuck off you scar faced cunt". Wow. That was it. He was a bit older than me. A big cunt, but a big divvy. All mouth with his six or seven cronies to back him up when it goes off. Anyway I just walked straight up to him, never said a fucking word, and just butted him. Bang… I must've butted him about six or seven times. I made a mess of his face. I've never seen that big divvy again since. Fuck him. He got what he deserved.

Anyway we go went in the first round of the UEFA Cup, now known as the Europa League. We lost 2-1 in the first leg away to Atletico Madrid, then back at Anfield we're getting beaten 1-0 with just over ten minutes to go. We needed a miracle. We needed to score twice just to take us to extra time. The Kop was magnificent, willing the redmen on. Chris Lawler pops up to make it 1-1 and with only three minutes left my mate Emlyn Hughes scores. He went fucking berserk. No wonder we called him crazy horse. What a player. Extra time no goals. So it's down to the toss of a coin. As the ref tossed the coin you could hear a pin drop. It was so nerve racking. The despair. Bastard. We lose the toss and were out of Europe. The FA Cup was no better. That fucking bogey team Leicester City again. I thought we'd sorted that. We do all the hard work, getting a draw away, but fuck it up at Anfield. Their skinheads were game for the violence after the match. Not many of you young redmen reading this book will know the nickname of their firm. What a fucking name. They were called The Flower Pot Men. Anyway back to the game. At Anfield we lose 1-0. But the worst of it was my all-time idol Sir Roger got subbed. He just took his shirt off, lashed it at the bench and walked down the tunnel. A bad, bad day that was. We're going great in the league. Nip and tuck with Leeds United. But we draw three and lose one in the last four games, finishing second. So close but no cigar.

So it's on to the next season, 1969-70. Fabulous start to the season, winning seven and drawing two of the first nine games, but it soon started to go wrong, winning one of the next seven games. One of the games was at Nottingham Forest. They are a really big firm of skinheads. But my little firm, about eight of us with the Fish (Andy Fisher) were on form. Done them like kippers. I love watching them run away. So it's back to Europe. Shite again, going out in the second round to Victoria Setubal. Then disaster in the FA Cup quarter final. Watford away. Everyone is convinced we are going all the way to Wembley but sadly it wasn't to be. We lose the game 1-0. Their big centre forward, Barry Endean, scored the only goal. After the game, The Shanks told all the press "That's the last straw now." He always said he was dreading this day, but he knew it would come sooner or later. He had to break up his first great side and build another one. We finished fifth in the league. The Shanks said "I need to replace at least four of this great team as they are coming to the end of their careers. But none of you fans ever forget this. These players have been a credit to Liverpool Football Club, dragging them from the Second Division to becoming Champions of England. Not once, but twice. They also made Liverpool history by becoming the first Liverpool side to win the FA Cup, which all the Liverpool fans have longed for for many, many years". Shanks said "Sadly, I'll have to break this side up". It was the same for the fans as they knew Shanks had to do it. Nothing lasts forever.

My all-time idol Sir Roger Hunt was the first to go. At the time I was eighteen and working in a factory on Wilson Rd, Huyton Industrial Estate. I got home from work about half five I suppose. Me tea, as usual, as well as The Liverpool Echo, was waiting for me. I sat down to eat me tea and picked the Echo up. I was fucking gutted. The back page headline read 'Roger Hunt Signs for Bolton'. I was ill. I just got up from my seat, pushed me tea away and said to me ma "I'm going to bed. I don't want no tea. Don't wake me up." All I could hear on my may up the stairs to bed was me ma shouting at me dad "He's not right in the head Harry. He needs to go and see a doctor. This is not normal." Anyway I went to work the next morning. The manager was one little prick. He knew how much I loved Liverpool Football Club and my idol Roger. He just kept taking the piss out of me, and he was a blue by the way. My job was really hard graft. I stood on a loading bay stacking 50 gallon drums, empty of course, onto a flat-back wagon. One, two, three on top of each other until the wagon was full. The drums are about three feet high and the same in circumference. Not that heavy but by two or three o'clock in the afternoon? Fuck me it was like lifting three times the weight. I ended up with arms like Popeye. Anyway I'm stacking the wagon, taking the drums off the conveyor belt but then it got jammed up, drums falling everywhere. The manager was going fucking nuts, shouting "Turn it off you stupid fuckin' idiot". So I turned it off. Then he comes walking up the conveyor belt shouting "You Blayney. You are fucking useless, just like your poxy team. Fuckin useless". I just said to myself that enough was enough. Don't forget I am only just eighteen. He must be in his thirties. As he comes to the top of the landing bay I just threw the head in. Butted him. Fuck off. Hilarious. He went tumbling down the conveyor belt. I just fucked off quick thinking he's bound to get the bizzies in, but no he never. So dead cheeky, I just went back the next morning. There he was just standing there with his eye in a sling. He looked at me and said "Blayney, you're lucky I'm not getting the bizzies in. I've already given your wages to your mate so fuck off before I do get the bizzies".

It was around this time that I started singing in the clubs around Manchester. I used to play amateur football on Sunday mornings, then after the game we would go for a bevy in Long View Labour Club in Huyton. They always had a group on called The Quotations. Also a few people out of the audience would get up and have a turn. I was in my element as I had won loads of singing competitions as a kid. After all the singing was over they always had a stripper on. After the stripper had finished she made her way to the table I was sitting on. She said to me "You've got a very good voice. Have you ever thought of giving it a go on the night clubs?" I said "No I just do it to have a laugh with the lads. I enjoy it" Then she said "Look I can get you an audition in a nightclub in Manchester where I strip at the weekends" I thought why not? "Yeah, I'll give it a go"

So the weekend comes and she picks me up and takes me to Manchester. It was about midnight when my audition was due. The club was fucking chocker. I loved it and so did the audience. I got a standing ovation. I got booked for three nights a week, £6 a night for singing five numbers. It took about twenty minutes. I did a couple of Tamla Motown numbers, a Beatles song, then I would finish with a Rolling Stones number. I can take Jagger off to a tee. I love the singing, especially afterwards when loads of young birds come up to me asking for my autograph. One girl asked me "You're from Liverpool. Do you know the Beatles?" I told her a little porkie pie (lie) and told her that John Lennon was my cousin and he would come up to my mam's house every Sunday that he could in his big white Rolls Royce and have his Sunday dinner with us. What a buzz I was having! I also got booked for three nights in Stoke at a club called the Torch. But I was getting a lot more money in there, £20 a night, again for five numbers. A pint of beer was between 12 and 15 pence in them days meaning you could get seven pints for a pound. Times that by twenty, which would work out at the equivalent of around £300 a night today.

I was really beginning to believe I was going to be a popstar. But as always, I fucked it all up. One day I travelled to Risley Remand Centre to visit a mate who had been nicked for shop lifting. Anyway on my way up there I stopped at this shop to get him some magazines, sweets n that. The shop sold all sorts, record albums on vinyl, so I just stuck about a dozen up my jumper inside my coat, but the shop assistant saw me and phoned the police, giving them my car registration number. The police pulled me over and nicked me for robbing the albums. They also found a small piece of cannabis, enough for about two joints. They kept me in custody and I went to court the next day. I got remanded in custody for seven days. When I got to court again I was fined £10 for robbing the albums and £20 for being in possession of cannabis. While I was locked up for them seven days I missed two nights singing at the nightclub. The stripper who got me the auditions was going mental, mainly because of the cannabis. Don't forget, this is 1970 and cannabis was looked at in the same way as smack or crack is today. So that was the end of my singing career. Well it was good while it lasted, but I'd just have to do all my singing in the Spion Kop now instead.

★

Anyway back to the reds. As well as Roger Hunt leaving, so did St John, Yeats and Lawrence. Shanks knew he had to do this but it broke his heart but the replacements he brought in more than compensated for the players that went out. In came Ray Clemence, a magnificent 'keeper, as valuable as any goal scorer. He made so many wonderful saves, winning us games and silverware everywhere. Then came the big Welsh dragon, John Toshack, from The Valleys, Cardiff. What a fucking debut he had, against of all people, the blue shite from across the park. The Kop just fell in love with him straight away, and of course me as well. But the game itself didn't start very well at all. We were getting beat 2-0, with goals from Joe Royle and Alan Whittle. Owww. I can see it now, watching it in my head again. My favourite derby game ever. Even better than beating them at Wembley twice. It was just incredible. I'll never forget that game. As I said there was less than twenty minutes to go. We are attacking The Kop end. Stevie Heighway, another who we had just signed, from of all places Skelmersdale (some player, absolutely brilliant), pulls one back for us after a brilliant run down the left flank, tight to the byline. Roger Kenyon, the blurt, tried to scythe him down. Stevie was far too quick for him, skips past him, into the box and scores from one the acutest angles you've ever seen. Get in. The Kop went wild. Game on. The Heighway was at it again. Down the same flank, skips past the defender and puts in a great ball for the debut boy big John Toshack. Big John leaped like a salmon above everyone and slammed a magnificent header into the back of The Kop net. Now it's Desmond. 2-2. Game on.

Heighway was ripping the Everton defence apart. They had

three players booked, all for fouls on Heighway. Everyone just knew the winner was coming. And it did. No surprise who made it. Yes it was Stevie Heighway. With five minutes to go, he flew down the flank again, leaving defenders in his wake, puts in a great cross which Toshack flicked on with his head for the incoming Chris Lawler to volley the winner into the back of The Kop net. Game over. Smoke that you blue nose twats. What a full back Chris Lawler was. He played an incredible 546 games for our beloved redmen, scoring 61 goals. Incredible when you take into account that he never took free kicks or penalties. The noise of The Kop at the final whistle was greeted with a song I will love forever. It goes something like this "Stevie Heighway's always running, John Toshack is always scoring, then you hear the Kopites roaring, Toshack is our king". Fucking magical. Every hair on my body is tingling. Couldn't wait to see my blue nose mates to get paid. About a fiver all together. Get in! I was only on about £7 a week ha-ha. But sadly our form in the league was up and down, drawing far too many games. Seventeen all together, ten at Anfield. We finally finished fifth.

The FA Cup was looking good. After beating Aldershot, Swansea City and Southampton, we draw Tottenham at home in the quarter final. They hold us to a 0-0 draw. So it's off down to that fucking London again on a Wednesday night for the replay. We left with Crown coaches as usual from opposite Lime Street Station. We got to London about half 7 in the morning. Can't remember much about the day but I'll never ever forget the match and the violence outside White Hart Lane. We won the game 1-0 and have a guess who scores? Heighway yet again on target but then came the violence. Fuck me it's been getting heavy now for a couple of years but I've never seen anything like this. There was literally over a thousand, yeah, over a thousand skinheads. Maybe even fifteen hundred. They were going nuts. Running battles everywhere as we came out of the ground. So as we're coming out the ground I thought "Fuck me we're gonna have to be on our toes here lads". There were thousands of them. Charging towards us. I got a few digs in but all of a sudden, fuck off, right on the jaw. Down I went.

I managed to get up and do one as four or five of them were trying to kick my head in. Fucking lucky me. Then as I got away from them I saw about four or five of my boys about 500 yards away from the coach. All of a sudden about twenty skins come running after us.

So we got on our toes, then fuck me from nowhere about twenty of Kelly's mob appeared. Fuck me they shit and got on their toes. But I managed to grab this little red headed twat. I had him in a headlock. We marched him back to the coach with us. He's crying like a little fucking baby. "Please scouse, let me go, let me go". So we gets on the coach with the redhead still in the headlock, telling him "You're coming to Liverpool with us". Again he begs me "Please scouse, let me go, let me go". I just gave him a slap with the back of me hand (as you do). I'd sorted out with Wally the driver that we'd lash him out just as we get onto the M1. He was like a little fucking girl. I just put my face into his and said "Shut it you cockney bastard. You're coming with us to Liverpool." Then I said to him "If you can sing three or four Liverpool songs we'll let you go". I had him singing 'You'll Never Walk Alone'. He hardly knew the words. It was hilarious. Then as we are pulling onto the motorway he was screaming with fear. He actually pissed his pants with fear as he saw the sign for the M1. He started screaming "No,no,no". Then Wally, the coach driver pulls over onto the hard shoulder. I dragged him to the front of the coach and Wally opens the door. I booted him up the arse dead hard and he ran like a rabbit. The whole of the coach was in stitches. Fucking boss journey home. Didn't get home till about five o'clock in the morning.

In Europe we were having a great run. We get revenge on Ferencvarosi of Hungary in the first round, then beat Dinamo Bucuresti in the second round and then in the third round we get Hibernian from Scotland. For some reason the coach wasn't going so we all went on the train. It was my debut on the train. It was bouncing. Lenny Woods, Bobby Wilcox, big Phil Aspinall and big Dave Penno from Kirkby were all present. There was another kid, Billy Edwards, a bit on the fat side, but game as fuck when it came to violence. We won the game 1-0 thanks to a John Toshack goal. What a brilliant signing by Shankly that was. The final whistle goes. We start to leave the ground and just as we are walking out there is about 200-300 of their skins wanting to kill us. We just stopped in our tracks and looked at each other, about eight or nine of us, and I said "Fuck this lads. Let's just do one back into the ground. We've got no chance". There was building work going on at that end of the ground. Loads of bricks and pieces of wood everywhere. I picked up a big piece of wood and so did a few of the other lads. Their skinheads seemed a little stunned and backed off a little bit, then they just ran at us. They were only about twenty five yards away from us. I said "Just lash the wood at them and then do one back into the ground". So that's what we did and got on our toes. But Billy Edwards was too slow and ended up getting stabbed in the stomach with a pig stabber. Apparently the doctor said to him "Good job you're a bit on the fat side otherwise you would've died". It was the fat that saved him.

The football violence was getting really out of hand now. Lots of weapons involved. Knives, Stanley blades, fucking scary. Anyway we get the mighty Bayern Munich in the quarter final. First leg at Anfield. Alun Evans had the game of his life. An absolute blinder, scoring all three in a 3-0 win. Evans absolutely destroyed the greatest centre back ever, the great Franz Beckenbauer. I'll always remember the headlines in the Liverpool Echo, on the back page. It read "Blonde Bomber Blitzes the Germans". We hold them 1-1 away to put us in the semi-finals to play our great rivals of the late sixties and early seventies, Leeds United. First leg was at Anfield. In the Kop. There was fucking mayhem outside. It was a very, very physical game, as it always was against Leeds United. Without a doubt, and I've already said this, they are the dirtiest side I have ever seen in my life. Fucking animals. They had some great players as well though. Billy Bremner, 'Bite your Legs' Norman Hunter, Big Jack Charlton, but the dirtiest little bastard of them all was little Johnny Giles. A snidey little bastard. Always at it off the ball when the ref wasn't looking. Anyway they beat us 1-0 at Anfield with a goal by Billy Bremner. The return leg at Elland Road was really,

really bad. There were running battles everywhere. The game itself was horrible. Leeds just sat back with ten men behind the ball and held us to a 0-0 draw. Fucking gutted. The coach got bricked on the way out. Fucking nuts them Yorkshire in-breds.

Next the FA Cup semi-final. What a draw. We get the blue shite, Everton, at Old Trafford. I was so nervous before the game. Only Everton stand in the way of me making my Wembley debut. Please, please reds, let's have it. I'm praying to god (and I don't even believe in god). It was mental. Just try and imagine. 60,000 or so scousers inside Old Trafford, and about 10,000 or more locked outside. The fucking Mancs didn't know what had hit them, especially the touts. They won't learn will they? Loads of the touts got their tickets snatched from them by the redmen, and the blueboys. Touts getting chased everywhere and stripped of every ticket they had plus whatever else they had, cash etc, just for a bonus. One Liverpool kid had snatched a good few tickets from a tout. We saw him running, the tout trying to chase him but he got kicked to fuck by everyone else. Then the kid just started to walk along with us. I've seen him loads of times at the match but I can't remember his name. He said to me "Have you all got tickets lads?" He was a lot older than all of us, about twenty-eight I suppose. I said "No, we just need one". There was four of us. He said "Here you go lad. 'Av one on me and the tout I've just robbed". Happy days. In we go. The atmosphere was brilliant. Reds and Blues together. No problems at all. (Not like today). The game kicks off. The nerves start kicking in. Everton score. 1-0. Fucking sick. It stayed that way 'til half time. In the second half we are well on top with all of us redmen willing them on. Then it came. The Blonde Bomber Alun Evans makes it 1-1. Not long after Brian Hall puts us into the lead, 2-1. Everton are throwing everything at us, then a header by Brian Hamilton of Everton was on its way into the net but Ian Callaghan blatantly handballed it to keep it out. The Evertonians were going fucking nuts, no penalty. Every Liverpool fan and Everton fan was convinced it was handball but the referee Clive Thomas never saw it. Then the final whistle. Get in. Wembley here we come. It was really amazing with all the redmen chanting "We're on our way to Wembley," and then taunting the Evertonians with "You're not, you're not". But what a disappointing finish in the league, fifth yet again. But the signs were there for all to see. Shanks's second great side was nearly complete. So it's off to Wembley for the FA Cup final against Arsenal. A brilliant journey going down there on the coach. But it all turned sour. We were so in control of the game and then it all went pear shaped. Lucky, lucky Arsenal. The game finishes 0-0 after ninety minutes so it's into extra time. It only took two minutes of the second half when the brilliant Steve Heighway put us in front to make it 1-0. But somehow Arsenal score twice to shatter our dreams. I remember walking out of the stadium. I was literally vomiting everywhere. I was like a zombie, stunned. I got back to the coach and we started making our way home to Liverpool. What a horrible, horrible journey. It took me weeks and weeks getting over that defeat.

On to 1971-72 and as I said before the signs were there that we have got a very good side. As always the Shanks only made one big signing. Fuck me, some signing. A certain Kevin Keegan signed for £35,000 for Scunthorpe of the Fourth Division. There was a real buzz at the club. Shanks was telling everyone "Wait while you see this kid". As always Shanks was right again. Just twelve minutes into his debut he scores against Nottingham Forest. He actually mishit it but they all count. He went on to form an uncanny partnership with John Toshack. The Kop just loved him instantly. Not only did he score goals, he ran his socks off. We love 100%ers us redmen. He worked so hard to make himself a better player. His energy was unbelievable. Non-stop for ninety minutes. That was the last piece of the jigsaw. Now for the start of the Shanks's second great team. You could just see it coming together. Most of his signings were really starting to gel now. Big Larry Lloyd replaced Big Ron Yeats. He was similar to big Ron. A great player, but not as good as Ron. Alec Lindsey was settling in very nicely. Shanks had actually signed him as a midfield player but decide to play him at left back. As always Shanks was right again. He said "Lindsey could open a tin can with that left foot of his". The new goalkeeper Ray Clemence was amazing. Then there was the immergence of Phil Thompson, plus the irresistible Steve Heighway. And in my opinion, the second greatest Liverpool player ever, me old mate Emlyn Hughes, the greatest obviously being King Kenny. But to all you young redmen under the age of thirty five-forty, he was so vital to this great team. He had everything: pace, power, tackling, and he read the game superbly. He probably ran more than Dirk Kuyt did. His nickname was Crazy Horse. He could play anywhere across the back and in midfield. I got to know Emlyn really well over the years, so did me mam and dad. He had many a drink with Harry and Elsie in the supporters club. Such a genuine, nice guy. He just loved our beloved Liverpool Football Club, just like me and you boss redmen reading this book. Much, much more about Emlyn later on in the book.

Back to the games. Despite all this promise we went out of the FA Cup in the fourth round at Elland Road, 2-0 to Leeds. We were really struggling in the league and looked way off the pace, then it just clicked. What an incredible end to the season. Then out of nowhere we won thirteen and drew one of the last fourteen games with two games left. There is only one point between us, Leeds United and Brian Clough's Derby County. The two games left couldn't have been any tougher. One of them was Derby County away. It was absolute mayhem at the Baseball Ground. Loads and loads of fighting. Bastards them Derby skinheads, they were always well up for it. Their leader was a big black kid. Boy did we have some run-ins with his mob over the years. There were loads of redmen there with no tickets trying to bunk in. Loads and loads of them got nicked and taken away in those big black police vans. The bizzies were really heavy handed, especially these two bastards on the horses. Unbelievable. Just galloping into the fans. They did not give a fuck. I'm telling you lads it was fucking scary. Loads of fans injured. They didn't give a fuck. Anyway the game turns out to be a nightmare. We lose 1-0. There was murder everywhere. Getting chased outside. I thought "Fuck this violence lark. It was a bit of fun at first but now it's mental. I think my skinheading days are coming to an end".

Leeds United only drew their game. It was so tight, one point between the three teams with only one game left to play. Leeds were playing away at QPR and Derby had already played their last game when they played us, think they were on a beach in Spain at the time. Fuck me I remember our game like it was yesterday – away at Arsenal. Over the years they have caused us big heartache, more than any other team, even to this day. Much more about that later on in the book. The game itself was so tight but we were well on top as it came near to the end. Loads of Liverpool fans had transistor radios listening to the QPR v Leeds game. QPR were winning 2-0. Everyone was made up. Even though Leeds pulled it back to 2-2, we only needed a 1-0 win to secure the title. The travelling redmen were doing their utmost. Non-stop chanting. Willing them to get the goal. I'm not sure how long there was to go but it must've been no more than ten minutes or so. Toshack and Keegan teamed up and scored. You can imagine what the crowd was like. Then disaster. The goal was disallowed for offside. That was so hard to take after the unbelievable run we had been on. It finished 0-0. That was one bastard journey home. Twat ref. Season over. Derby won the league without kicking a ball, imagine that today! But all the signs are there for next season. Couldn't wait for it to start.

At the start of the 1972-73 season, every red man was buzzing. We could just smell it. It was coming. The team had gelled so well the last two seasons. As usual the Shanks made only one big signing, Peter Cormack for £110,000 from Nottingham Forest. He made the team complete. A much underestimated player. Excellent in the air, he was also a brilliant passer off the ball. We get off to a flyer in the league, winning four and drawing one of the first five games. We beat both the Mancs, City and Manure, both at Anfield, beating City on the opening day of the season 2-0, then destroying Manure 2-0. The Kop was in full force chanting "We're gonna win the league, we're gonna win the league, so now you gonna believe us, we're gonna win the league". There's no better feeling in football than watching my beloved redmen destroying the Mancs, that's what it was like, even in those days. Then again, it was just as sweet beating the blue shite. My coach days were finished. It's time for the train for all the London games and drive to rest as I've just bought my very first car. A Triumph Herald convertible. It cost me £30. It was about ten years old, maybe more, but what a runner. It got me and me mates all over England until it finally died.

One game comes to mind, half way through the season, I think it was away at West Bromwich Albion. Perfect little drive. About 85 miles approximately. We got on the East Lancashire Road just by the Yorkshire Imperial factory. About two hundred yards up the road I see this kid hitch hiking with a Liverpool scarf on. I pull over and say "Get in kid, all the way to West Brom". He was a bit younger than me, about seventeen, eighteen I suppose. Low and behold it was only a young red legend in the making. It was Marty, also from Huyton, who eventually got the name The Pyjama man. One funny man. He wore just pyjamas all over for the European away games for about twenty-five, thirty years. People just took to him. Even the Russian bizzies thought he was funny as he stood in this little fountain orchestrating the Liverpool fans to sing. If you're reading this book Marty it was a pleasure ok. Love you redman. More about Marty later on in the book. By the way we drew the game at West Brom 1-1 thanks to a Phil Boersma goal. That was in between a really good run of six wins and four draws. Believe me young redmen, we Kopites could just feel it. The side is now complete. Shanks's second great side. And Shanks was telling everyone, as he always did, that this team was going to sweep everything before them. And as I've said before and I'll say many times again in this book, without Bill Shankly there would be no Liverpool Football Club as we know it today, one of the greatest club sides ever. Sorry red men I'll correct myself. THE GREATEST CLUB SIDE IN THE HISTORY OF THE ENGLISH GAME. (fact). One for Rafa there lads.

Back to the games. We're flying in the league. It's about half way through the season but we go out in the fourth round of the FA Cup at Maine Road to Manchester City, after a 0-0 draw at

Anfield. But we are flying in the UEFA Cup after beating Eintracht Frankfurt, AEK Athens, Dynamo Berlin and Dynamo Dresden. So it's into the semi-final against Tottenham Hotspur. Two legged game, the first leg at Anfield. It was a very tight game but we scrape it 1-0. For the away leg we get the train to Euston station. Wow there was running battles everywhere. Then at the ground it was worse. I'm thinking to myself "It's getting too heavy for me this lark. I'm going to drive everywhere from now on, just need to get myself a better car." It was really heavy, ambulances flying everywhere. We managed to keep away from the trouble and into the ground. It was a great game. 0-0 at half time and then it came, Stevie Heighway. Ten minutes into the second half. Fucking get in. Tottenham threw everything at us and equalised to make it 1-1. The atmosphere was brilliant from both sets of fans. Then they scored again to make it 2-1 on the night. It was a very nervy last five minutes or so, I'm not sure but I think they even hit the post. But we survived and the final whistle went. Yesssssss. Get in. We're through on the away goals rule. Our very first European final is in the bag. Back to the league. With only three games left we are top of the league but it is very tight. Only a couple of points separating about three or four teams. So it's off to Newcastle United. Fucking nutty fans them. The travelling redmen were in full force as usual. Kevin Keegan opens the scoring. As you can imagine the travelling red men went mental. Then it all went quiet. Fuck me. They equalise a couple of minutes later. Then they score again to make it 2-1. We huffed and puffed, battering them but sadly no way through. Final Whistle. We leave the ground making our way to the train station when all of a sudden a fucking big crew of Geordie skins come running after us. I was gone, on my toes, the usual, run like the wind job. Thank God I can run fast as would they fuck give up. They were catching me. I must've been only twenty yards from the station and they were ten yards behind me. Wow. Just made it. There were four or five redmen form Huyton standing in the station pissing themselves laughing as I came scorching into the station. But I had the last laugh on them. I took a nice few bob off them on the way home playing cards. And when a say a nice few bob I mean about £300–£400, so it was a really nice consolation after losing the game. The day turned out really good in the end as the teams in contention for the title all had bad results as well. So it's not so bad. We take four points from the last two games, a 2-0 win at home to title contenders Leeds United, with Cormack and Keegan scoring the goals. With other teams slipping up again, we only needed a point from our last game at Anfield against of all teams, our old bogey team Leicester City. Oooh the game was horrible. It dragged and dragged and dragged. Then that was it. Final whistle. The goalless draw was enough. My beloved redmen are champions of England yet again.

There were parties all over the place. Everyone buzzing. You know the buzz redmen. The buzz that only our beloved Liverpool Football Club can provide. Some people say it's better than sex, watching the reds win a trophy. Listen lads, anyone who knows me knows I love my sex as much as any man, if not more, and I assure you redmen in my eyes sex doesn't even COME close to Liverpool winning a trophy. Simple as that. Oh by the way, the buzz lasts a lot longer as well. Two weeks later with league title nicely secured it's the first leg of the two legged UEFA Cup Final against Borussia Monchengladbach. What a night. It was absolute magic. We just blew them away. They were lucky it was only 3-0. Two goals from Kevin Keegan in the first half and a towering header form big Larry Lloyd. I ended up in St Helens that night at the Plaza Nightclub. All the young birds loved the Blayney boy's chat, a different one every week. Modest cunt aren't I? (Hope your enjoying this book Chap. Just asking a redman legend in the making). The second leg, no way I could go. I'm just 21. I'm working in a factory in Rainhill so it was impossible to get the time off. I haven't even got a passy yet. It's so easy for you young redmen travelling all over Europe now. There are so many different ways to travel. Back in our day, I think only one plane would go to each place as it was so expensive. Anyway as you all know now, after one all mighty battle in Germany we hang on by a thread. They destroyed us really. 2-0 up in no time. But somehow we hung on, winning the UEFA Cup 3-2 on aggregate. All thanks to a superb penalty save from

Keeper Ray Clemence in the first leg at Anfield. Wow. What a season. Champions of England and our very first European trophy with many, many more to come.

That was a glorious summer as I went about winding up all my Evertonian mates and collecting my bets. It was just heaven but I was fucking sick of all these shit jobs I've been doing so I decided to go and do a bit of graft down on the south coast. Went to Bournemouth first. Fucking loved it. The usual summer resort, nightclubs bursting with sexy young birds. I was in my element. The season was soon upon us and no-one on earth could've predicted what was about to happen. As usual, all the redmen are dead confident and Shanks, as only Shanks could, was telling everyone how good we were. I also had a surprise. I knew this day would come sooner or later, as I never like to wear them stupid condoms. Every time I would put one on I would lose my hard on. Anyway I'm living in a flat, my very first flat, 209 Tarbuck Road, just around the corner from the notorious Huyton Park Pub. Boy there are some great redmen who've bevvied there for years, lots of them good friends of mine. 'The Huyton Baddies' - that's what the flag says. All over Europe that flag has been. Anyway back to the flat. I'd only been there a couple of days when I copped for a bird and took her back to my flat. Fuck me, a couple of months later I get a knock on the door. It's the girl's mother. She was quite nice about it. She just came straight to the point and said "Look lad, you've got my daughter pregnant. I know you don't love her and she doesn't love you but she is keeping the baby. So you will have to get together with Patricia and sort out what's going on". Wow. Me a dad! Sick really because Patricia was a decent enough girl. I'd only seen her for a couple of weeks, which is a long time for me to see a bird. Normally I'm just right in and right out, if you know what I mean lads. Anyway, we have a good chat and decide that, with me being in and out of work, it would be better for her if she tells the dole that she doesn't know who the father was as she would get money from them. I told her I would throw her a few bob when I could. My ma loved her, trying to talk me into marrying her. I said to me ma "Are you real? I'm nowhere near ready for any of that lark!" Anyway she has a baby boy. Fuckin' ringer of me. So as us men do, I had a look at his little thing, or should I say not so little, just like his dad!

Patricia used to take Peter up to me ma's every Sunday, me maa used to spoil him to death. Buying him everything, as this was her first grandson. I used to see him every other weekend at me maa's. Then when he was about five I started to take him fishing. Then when he was about seven Patricia met a guy, fell in love and got married. He was a really nice man so I had to tell Peter "You are a very lucky boy, son. You have two dads now, so I won't be seeing you as much in the future as I have to go and work away, but never forget that if you ever need me, just tell your mum and she will phone me". I'll come back to Peter later on in the book.

Back to the start of the season. Not a bad start. Winning five, drawing three and losing two. Not good enough though. One of those games was away to Leicester City and The Flower Pot Men. What a name. They get some stick from the likes of the Chelsea Headhunters and The ICF (Inter City Firm) form West Ham. I think our nickname at the time was "You scouse bastards". The Leicester skins were well up for it again. As I said last season, fuck all this fighting lark, but it was hard to get away from it. It was rife. Every firm wanting to have a go at us. As we were getting off at the end of the game, there were three of us. I can't remember who was with me. We were parked up about half a mile away or so from the ground, then from nowhere about twenty-five skins came chasing us. We got legged everywhere. But I was far too fast, I was gone, and so were my mates. Next game up it was The European Cup second round against Red Star Belgrade. They beat us 2-1 at their ground and then beat us by the same score, 2-1 at Anfield. Those two goals they scored are two of the best goals I've ever seen at Anfield both from about thirty yards. Clemence had no chance. Back in the league, we are in about fourth place, only four or five points off the top. Then we hit a brilliant run, going twelve games unbeaten, winning nine and drawing three. It's looking really good. Peter Cormack fitted in straight away.

Next up it's the FA Cup. First up was Doncaster Rovers, a

Third Division side. Boy they gave us an almighty scare. They were beating us 2-1 at half time but thanks to Kevin Keegan scoring both goals, we got out of jail. We were really lucky to get a replay but we didn't underestimate them at Anfield, winning comfortably 2-0, thanks to Peter Cormack and Steve Heighway getting the goals. In the next round we get a really nice draw, Carlisle United at Anfield. Fuck me, we nearly slipped up again, drawing 0-0. Thankfully no problems in the replay. 2-0 – John Toshack and Phil Boersma scoring. Then we beat Ipswich 2-0 at Anfield, Hall and Keegan scoring. The redmen are buzzing. A quarter-final away to Bristol City. You could just feel it. It was coming. The sniff of Wembley. We got to Bristol a bit late. The traffic was at a standstill. There was only about five minutes to go before kickoff but believe me, it kicked off big time outside the ground. I'm telling you lads it was scary. Most of their skins were not your normal skinheads. Mostly men in their forties or even fifties. Fuckin' lunatics. They did not give a fuck. Even fighting with the bizzies. The bizzies just did one in the end. They shit themselves. We got in the ground and there's loads of fighting inside. Fuck me you could feel the hostility. We win 1-0 thanks to Big John Toshack, but without a doubt it was one of the worst scenes I've ever seen at a football game. Then on the way out, it was just fucking mayhem. Bizzies on horses getting bricked by the Bristol lunatics. It was pure relief just getting back to the car.

In the semi-final I was fucking sick as we get paired with our old bogey team again, yes Leicester City. In the league, we'd suffered a dip in form after such a brilliant and we were now a good few points away from the chasing pack. But after winning only one, drawing five and losing two in the last eight games we finish second in the league to champions Leeds United. So the FA Cup was our last chance of silverware – the semi was at Old Trafford and it was a very nervy game. It finished 0-0. So it's down to Villa Park for the replay. The travelling redmen are there in their thousands as usual, cheering us on. We could just smell it. We knew we were going to Wembley. It was very nervy again. 0-0 at half time. Getting a bit worried here. But the nerves disappeared in the first minute of the second half. Kevin Keegan scores. Get in. Redmen going mental everywhere. Then Brian Hall makes it 2-0. They pull one back to make it 2-1. They were throwing everything at us, but we broke away and the Welsh Dragon, big John Toshack, scored to make it 3-1. What a buzz. You know the one lads. The one that only the reds can provide. It was crazy on the journey home. Horns going off, scarves waving.

I couldn't wait for Wembley where we would play Newcastle United. Their centre forward, Malcolm McDonald, was telling the whole of England what he was going to do to us in the final as he had scored a hat-trick against us on his debut two seasons before in a game when Tommy Smith missed a late penalty and we'd lost 3-2. Anyway this big bandy legged centre forward talked a good game but that was all. He never got a touch the whole ninety minutes. It was glorious just watching him trudge off the pitch at the final whistle. The travelling redmen were giving him a torrid time. The game itself will go down in history as one of the most one-sided finals ever. We absolutely destroyed them. Unbelievably they got to half time at 0-0. How they got in at that score I'll never know. Alex Lindsay had hit a screamer from the left from about twenty-five yards. It flew in. But for some strange reason the referee disallowed it. That just made the reds even more determined. One way traffic. Then it finally came. Just on the hour. Kevin Keegan. Brilliant goal. Wembley was rocking. Ten minutes later the brilliant Steve Heighway makes it two. What a player this kid is turning out to be! Absolutely brilliant. Then with just two minutes to go Keegan put the icing on the cake after a brilliant move to make it 3-0. As Keegan turned away in triumph, the commentator says "Newcastle have just been undressed, STRIPPED BARE" I just love watching it again on the video. Game over. The cup belonged to Liverpool. Happy days.

With the season over it was back down to Bournemouth with me old blue nose mate Tommy McDonald. My best mate, still to this day, over forty years later. We decided we'd had enough of Bournemouth so Tommy said to me "Do you fancy going to Bognor Regis Butlin's holiday camp? It's fucking boss on the camp.

Loads of birds everywhere from all over the country". I was in my element. So many birds. It was like shooting fish in a barrel. They just love me and my scouse chat. Plus my modesty of course.

Then right out of nowhere, every Liverpool fan in the world was in complete shock. The messiah, the one and only, The Shanks had had enough. Just like that. The city was in mourning. He said "I've done my job. Now it's Bob's turn " meaning Bob Paisley. When asked in an interview on television how he felt when he decided that it was all over, he said he felt like James Cagney in an old gangster film called Angels with Dirty faces. If you haven't seen this film lads, do yourself a favour and find it. A superb film. Shankly just loved the old gangster movies, especially Cagney. Anyway he said he felt like Cagney at the end of the film when he'd been sentenced to death by electric chair. Anyway, everyone was just in shock. It was just so hard to understand. No more Shanks. But thanks to the Shanks, this was only the beginning.

ARISE SIR BOB

B OB PAISLEY RELUCTANTLY took the job, saying "How can I replace the Shanks?" Fuck me, he more than did that! But as I've said before, if there had been no Shanks, there would be no Liverpool Football Club. But typical Shankly, he left us one big signing at the end of the season – Ray Kennedy. Shanks signed him from Arsenal as a striker. Kennedy had a formidable partnership with a player named John Radford. They had won the double for Arsenal in the 70-71 season and what a superb signing he turned out to be. One of the greatest Liverpool midfielders ever.

The next season felt so strange without Shankly. But as the saying goes, life goes on. First up is Luton Town away. We win 2-1 thanks to Tommy Smith and the irresistible Steve Heighway. The first four games we win three and draw one. Then Ray Kennedy makes his debut away at Chelsea. What a dream debut. Although playing in midfield rather than upfront, he popped up with the opening goal after twenty minutes or so. Phil Boersma scores two to make it a very comfortable 3-0 away win. What a brilliant move from Paisley. He turned an inside-forward into one of the best midfielders we have ever had. Kennedy went on to make 384 appearances, scoring 72 times, he had a superb left foot and was a joy to watch. I went on the train for that game. Best move I've ever made. I'd heard there was a load of card games going on, on the rattler. I'm not a bad player, actually I'm pretty good. Far too good for the lads on the train. It turned out to be a very fruitful couple of seasons for me. I won fuckin brewsters, like taking sweets from a baby. That's when I got to know the Scotty Road firm. All younger than me. I'd be 23, they'd be 17, 18 maybe. There was also a firm much older than me, all in their early thirties, a firm from Huyton with loads of good redmen. Anyway back to the journey home from the game. I was sniffing round the train for a good card school, walking round from one carriage to another. Loads of 2 bob games but they're no good to me. Then bingo, it's Christmas. I sees this card school. It was the lads, no not lads, the men from Halewood. I just stood there watching for about twenty minutes, half an hour, about fifteen hands or so. I just couldn't believe how bad all four of them were. There were five pound and ten pound notes going in all over the place. I thought to myself "There's only one place all them notes are going, right in my bin".

I said "Alright lads, any chance of me joining in?"

"As long as you've got a few bob lad. This is no two bob game. We don't want you coming in with a tenner".

I just pulled a little wad out, about a hundred quid. As I sat down for the first hand, the one that was doing all the winning said to me, "I hope you're better than these three, lad!" I just smiled at him and thought, "I'll show you how good I am". He was the best player out of the four of them but sadly for him he was nowhere near my league. All he did was bluff, bluff, bluff. When he threw in a big bets, everyone just folded. I had him well sussed. Happy days. I took just over £700 on the way home. They were definitely grafters, not workers. Mind you I don't mind who I take money off in a card school. £700. Wow. I think the average wage was about thirty, forty pound a week. I gave me ma a few bob. Everyone was happy. How good a day was that? Our beloved redmen destroying those Chelsea Rent Boys 3-0 and £700 in me bin. But the season didn't go as well as everyone expected, winning only twenty games, drawing eleven and losing eleven, finishing second in the league. Out of the FA Cup early doors, fourth round away to Ipswich, no good in the league cup, going out to Middlesbrough at Anfield. We also went out of the European Cup Winners' Cup in the second round losing to Ferencvarosi on away goals after two draws. I was glad the season was over. But as always I looked forward to the next season.

★

By 1975 I finally had my passport and I was determined to go to

Europe this season and what a season it turned out to be! First up was Queens Park Rangers, away at Loftus Road. Train job. As normal I'm hoping to find a nice card school, so it's my usual cruise along the carriages, looking what's happening. Loads of two bob games as usual but then I saw something I liked. Here we go. Fuck me, some dough on this table. Five young redmen playing. They were all a little bit younger than me. About 17, 18, 19 maybe. It was a little firm from Scotty Road. Over the years I got to know a lot of young redmen from Scotty Road, many more than the six I was about to play cards with. Their names were Jase, Jim S, Brian P and Brian K plus Jamo (blue nose cunt, but a nice guy). The last guy was Denny D. Anyway, I watched them for a while. They were all shite apart from this Denny kid who was quite good. I say "Alright lads, any chance of me joinin' in?"

"How much dough 'av u got lad?"

I just took me little wad out and said "About £150 ok?"

They said "Yeah, that's sound, it's three card brag. £1 in and £10 maximum".

I said "That's sound with me lads, let's play cards".

I didn't get involved in the first few hands but this kid Denny was cleaning up. He must've had a monkey in front of him (£500). If you don't know the rules of three card brag, you can bet without looking at your cards (a blind bet) so if I have £1 blind, the next fella can also put £1 in blind, or if he looks at his cards it will cost him £2 to bet, and so on. Anyway I had noticed this Denny D character always looked at his cards. He either folded or if he had a good hand he would pay £2 to bet. But when it was his turn to deal he would always pay the £1 blind. I was on him straight away. I knew he was at it. And boy was I going to teach him a lesson. Here it comes now. It's Denny's deal. So I watched him like a hawk. Bingo. I've fuckin got him. Thanks to my five uncles who taught me to play cards and how to spot a cheat. So I just let him deal, saying fuck all. The first kid bets £2 blind. The next one looks and folds. The next two call the bet blind so it's down to me. I just had a look and I've got a really good hand, a pair of queens. That's absolutely massive in a five-handed game, where the other four players are blind. I'm probably about 85% favourite to win the hand. After a few more bets there's just me and him left. And he raises it to £5 blind which means I've got to put £10 in. Blind my ass. He knew exactly what he had. So I just carried on, carried on, carried on even though I knew his hand was going to beat mine. Now I'll explain. There must've been £300 in the pot. I just knew the worst hand he had would have been a flush, meaning three hearts, three spades, three clubs, but it will probably be a run, meaning eight, nine, ten or nine, ten, jack – something like that.

He started to get a bit cocky and said to me "Ooohh you must 'av a big hand". I said "We'll see won't we". He says "Ok I'll call your blind." I said "Ok lad, on one condition." He says "What?" and I said "I'll fuckin tell you what lad. I watched you for the last half an hour or so and you have been planting hands when you deal. Do you think I'm fucking soft lad?" He went the colour of boiled shite. I said to all of his mates "Look lads, I've got a pair of queens here. How fucking strong is that against a blind hand? I'll tell you how strong. It's about 98% to win every time." Denny just looked at me and I says "We're swapping hands". He says "No". I says "We fucking are lad. You're on top, and I'll even tell you what you've got (roughly). You've got 7,8,9 - 8,9,10, or 9, 10, J, or something like that". His mates just looked at him and I turned over his so called blind hand and low and behold, what did he have? 9, 10, J. I just took the money. It was fuckin hilarious. "You fucking twat" all his mates were shouting at him. He took a nice couple of slaps. But I took the money. The Blayney boy strikes again. I still buzz on that story today. I like the Scotty Road lads, and they like me (apart from Denny of course). We became really good friends over the years, especially with Jase, Jim S, Brian P and Brian K. I've had many a good bender with Brian K and his mate who was always with him, Charlie. Fuckin' nuisance him. Keeps you out all night.

I bought myself a nice E type Jaguar with the winnings. It was a right bird puller (not that I needed one). We've just signed a new left back, the one and only Joey Jones (my mate, got to know him really well). Even though he only made 97 appearances with the Reds, scoring three times, he will always be a legend to me and all the other redmen. Much more about Joey later. I'm not sure what away game it was, we were on the train so it must've been a London game. So as normal I'm looking for a nice card school. Didn't take me long to find one, a load of lads from Huyton, the same lads that I took a few bob off at Newcastle last season. I got to be really good friends with a few of them, but one or two of them didn't like me because I was taking all their dough. There was Joey D, Dava P, Gerrard C and Big Aso. Joey accused me of cheating so I said "Ok lad you can deal all the time if you like". "That's fair enough" he said, but as normal, no problem. Took about £250. It really was like taking sweets from a baby. They were really bad players who didn't have a clue. It was getting really hard now to find a decent game. My reputation was getting around as a card player. So I thought fuck it, I knew it wouldn't last long anyway, so I decided that would be my last train journey for a while and I'd drive everywhere instead. I've got a good car now, the E type. It will take me all over the country, down to London no problem.

It was not a very good start to the season, we got beat 2-0 at Queens Park Rangers and drew 2-2 at home with West Ham United but don't worry redmen, things got better. Much, much better. I was really looking forward to the draw in the UEFA Cup. It comes, my very first away game in Europe. Fuck me, I didn't even need my new passy as we got paired with Hibernian of Scotland. Back to the league. We're hovering nicely in third or fourth place. But then it's back to Europe. We get Real Sociedad from Spain. I didn't manage to make that one, or the next one, against Slask Wroclaw. We won 2-1 away in the first leg and 2-0 at home in the return game. Next up is my first plane journey watching the reds. Dynamo Dresden. The game finished 0-0. Can't remember much as I was drunk as a skunk. I was a bit afraid of flying so I drank half a bottle of Southern Comfort. Think it was straight in and out. There was only one plane going in those days. I think I was sitting with Ritchie Harrison and Eddie London. Eddie's dead now, topped himself about 2006, if I remember rightly. In the Semi-final draw we get Barcelona. I'm more or less certain it was in and out again and I was drunk as a skunk again. All I remember is the redmen going nuts when John Toshack scored after about fifteen minutes. The game finished 1-0 so it was back to Anfield for the second leg. The game was very tight, 0-0 at half time. Then of all people, Phil Thompson scores at the start of the second half. Barcelona pull one back but we hung on to book our place in the final. We all ended up in town after the game. We ended up in Gatsby's or the She Club, or maybe the Pezz. What a fucking hole that place was! It was famous for your shoes sticking to the manky carpets, they hadn't been cleaned in years.

Back to the league. Fuck me what a season this is turning out to be. Already in the UEFA Cup final and still in with a chance at the title, with nine games to go. We win the first five games, beating Birmingham, Norwich, Burnley, Leicester and also the blue shite at Anfield with a very late goal from David Fairclough (super sub) in the 89th minute. The whole of Anfield shuddering to its foundations, everyone going mental. We just all know that feeling. We just knew we were going to win the league. And that's what they were all singing for about fifteen minutes after the game "So now you're gonna believe us, so know you're gonna believe us, so now you're gonna believe us, we're gonna win the league". So it's down to the last game of the season, away at Wolves. A week before the Wolves game, there was the small matter of the first leg of the UEFA Cup final against FC Brugge at Anfield. What an unbelievable game. We were 2-0 down at half time, and it was looking really grim. But never write off the mighty reds. As Andy Gray found out in 2005, you Manc loving cunt. Back to the game. In a sense, it was very similar to Istanbul. The game turned on its head, just like in Turkey, all within six minutes. Firstly Ray Kennedy pulls one back just on the hour. Then two minutes later, Jimmy Case makes it 2-2. The crowd were going mental. The Kop was deafening. Then a couple of minutes later we get a penalty. Up steps Keegan, no problem, 3-2 in front. And that's how it finished.

So it's back to the last game at Wolves in the league. A draw is no good to either team. We needed to win to guarantee us the league and they needed a win to avoid relegation. What a day, what a night, incredible scenes. I was with the Huyton lads; James,

George, Mikky and Click. We had a really good day. We stopped in a little town called Dudley, just outside Wolverhampton, to get something to eat. Then we went in the bookies. James had a nice little bet up on the horses, backing the last two winners. The first horse won at 4-1, Sneakers Delight, and in the last race of the day, at 5 o'clock, Sneak Thief romped home at 10-1. So his little £10 double paid £550. A great start to the day. Then it's off to the game. We get there at about quarter to six. It was mayhem everywhere. Just a mass of red and white. There must have been 20,000, maybe 30,000 redmen there. It just got too much for the bizzies and the stewards. The turnstile attendants just got off. Everyone was diving over. The atmosphere was incredible. I bumped into my dad and my brothers Billy and Alan. I think our Alan was only 11. It's a day he'll never forget. The game starts. The tension is mounting. Then fuck me, Wolves score. 1-0 half time to Wolves. We were really struggling. We'd actually done well to get to half time at only 1-0. The half time break was horrible. People just muttering to themselves. Fuck me, we can't throw this away after such a fabulous run in the last nine games. The teams come out for the second half and believe me, the travelling redmen did their job, and more, to lift the boys. Time was running out though. There was only fifteen minutes left and we needed to score twice. The first one came thanks to Kevin Keegan. We were throwing everything at them, everything. There was only five minutes left to go. Then the big Welsh Dragon did the business yet again. Every redman in the stadium as one, started chanting, "Stevie Heighway's always running, John Toshack is always scoring, then you'll hear the kopites roaring, Toshack is our king". We had only just calmed down then it was game, set and match as Ray Kennedy scored to make it 3-1 in the last minutes. The pitch got invaded with scousers chanting "Champions of England", and in two weeks' time it was off to Bruges for the second leg of the semi-final. I couldn't wait.

Back to me new car, the Jaguar E type. A couple of days after the Wolves game I drove down to Bognor Regis. I met my best mate Tommy Mac, blue nose cunt. He said "Wow, nice car lad". It was a beautiful sunny day so we had the roof down on the car. I said "Jump in Mac, I'll show you what it can do." Boy was it fast. Without a doubt the fastest car I've ever driven. Got it up to 155mph. Took my breath away. It was about 4.30pm. We were about thirty miles away from Bognor so we decided to have a bit to eat before we went back. So we pulled into this little town centre, Horsham. We parked in a big car park at the side of the town and went for a wander. After we finished eating we walked through the town back to the car when I see a television shop. The telly in Tommy's flat is on the blink so we went in to have a look. As we walked in we noticed the woman was cashing up. She put the takings for the day in a night safe bag and put it behind the counter. Then she asked if we needed any help. I says "Just browsing love." She says "Ok, I just need to go to the toilet before I lock up. If you need me just shout me". Me and Tommy just looked at each other and said "Let's go". Tommy grabbed the bag and just as we are about to leave the shop, the woman came back (some piss that). She started shouting and chasing us through the little town, shouting "stop thief, stop thief!" People were trying to trip us up and whatever but somehow we managed to get away.

We hid in a cemetery behind a headstone. We could see the car park were the car was parked. We must've hid behind that headstone for about an hour. It felt more like three hours. Then there was only my car left in the car park. It must've been about 6 o'clock. So I said to Tommy "Look, they are looking for two people. So I'll walk down to the car on my own and you walk along the bushes and I'll pick you up, ok?" So I walked down to the car really casual, got in and started it up. I pulled up at the barrier to pay the attendant as there was a big barrier which he had to raise. He was shaking, literally shaking. Then in front of me, about twenty yards away, I saw these two CID police walking towards the car. I threw a fiver at the attendant and says "Keep the change lad" and he put the barrier up. The two CID came running towards the car. I just revved it up and up and drove. They shit themselves and dived out of the way. I tell you lads it was the most amazing thing I've ever been involved in. It was like a Steve McQueen movie or something. As I pulled away Tommy Mac came running out from the side of the bushes towards the car and literally dove full length into the car. Incredible. We were laughing our cocks off. I just put me foot down and we were soon on a dual carriageway. I'm doing about 125mph, then way back in my mirror I saw this fucking police bike. A Triumph 750. So I just banged me foot to the floor. Must've been doing 150mph. I'd left the bike, he was way behind, then I turned off down the country roads. Fuck me, roadworks. Temporary traffic lights. I was boxed in. Cars coming towards me and cars stopped behind me. There was a big field to the left and a big field to the right. I looked at Tommy and said "We're fucked here lad". Then the copper on the bike arrives. He comes over to us and I swear on my late great father's life, I just looked at the copper and said "Can I help you officer?" He just looked at me and said "You're nicked smart arse". Then the usual "Anything you have to say..... blah blah blah".

The next thing a big van arrives to take us to the police station. We get charged and banged up in a cell for the night, in court in the morning. Tommy is already on probation as he got in a bit of trouble the year before. I hadn't been in trouble for a good few years. So I said to Tommy "We'll tell them I grabbed the bag, it's not worth both of us being found guilty as you may face a small jail sentence. Me, I should only get probation or maybe a suspended sentence". So we both agreed, more Tommy than me though. Anyway Tommy gets bail, I get remanded in custody. Can't believe it. Our solicitor said there would be no problem both of us getting bail. The lying bastard. Fucking gutted. Now I was going to miss the game the following week, the second leg of the UEFA Cup final but what the fuck can I do? It's my own fault.

Anyway, I got a shock when I got to court – six months! I was not looking forward to it at all. They send me to an open prison called Northeye, in West Sussex. Could've done one dead easy but why? I've only got six months. With good behaviour (me with good behaviour?) I will be out in four. I'd only miss the first two games of the new season, so it's off to jail for the first time. I knew it would come one day as what I'd been getting up to wasn't quite legal. Anyway, I was a little bit wary as I'd never been to jail before but I had fuck all to worry about. I couldn't believe how easy it was. It was a joke. Like a fucking holiday camp. And being a scouser, I took full advantage of it. You can get everything in there. Everything apart from sex! Weed, booze, anything you wanted really. Mind you there was a bit of sex going around but I wasn't tempted – dirty bastards.

I don't think I mentioned it earlier but I played a bit of football. Top scorer for three seasons at school, then I played amateur for about three seasons. I wasn't brilliant but boy could I score goals. They had a football team in jail which played in the local league. All our games were at home for obvious reasons. They had a really good team. The two strikers were really shit hot. A black kid from Basingstoke, and a kid from Bournemouth. The kid from Bournemouth was due out in two weeks' time so for the first time in about six or seven years I was back in the gym – circuit training. Fuck me, I was spewing up after every session for the first week or so. Mind you what could you expect after the last six or seven years just boozing, birds and drugs. I got named as substitute after a good training session. I was nowhere near fully fit so I was more than happy to be on the bench. Anyway, watching the game, of all teams we were playing, it was the local Police team. It was half way through the season, the bizzies team was top with us, Northeye, were a point behind but with a game in hand. With only about twenty minutes to go we were getting beat 2-1. Enter the Blayney boy. I was only on the pitch about three or four minutes when a lovely through ball found me. I was on it in a flash. Get in Blayney. Desmond. 2-2. Game on. This bastard centre half, a big mountain of a man, was kicking fuck out of me every time I got the ball, and giving me loads of verbal as well, shouting "fuck you, you skinny scouse cunt, I'll bury you". Anyway I picked the ball up with my back to goal and turned him like a kipper. Then he hacked me down. We both squared up to each other. The ref booked both of us, giving us a free kick just outside the box. The free kick came in, he was marking me but I left him, the big slow twat. I'm in and just as I smash it towards the corner of the net I shouts "smoke that you prick". But low and behold the ball hit the bar and came back to me luckily, bang, 3-2. There's only about six or seven minutes left. Anyway this bizzie is up me arse again so I turn round and say to him "Eh you, you fucking big divvy, this is the last time I'm warning you. Do it again and I'll deck you". Next time I pick the ball up he's at it again. Hacks me down. I'm up again in a flash and grab him by the neck. We're both rolling round punching each other. We had to be separated. We were both sent off. So anyway, the game finishes and that puts us top of the league. I'm due out in about three weeks' time. So hopefully we can win the league before I get out. Sadly I found out a few weeks later that they lost the league to the bizzies by one point, losing the last three games. Boy did they miss the Boy. 33 goals in 15 games. Ian Rush or what?

★

Anyway I'm out and I need to buy a new car as I had a really bad crash in the E type just after I got out. The crash was horrendous really. I was so lucky. It happened at the back of the Butlin's camp in Bognor. I hit a solicitor. Both cars were write-offs. It was my fault. I'd been drinking all day and night. How I passed the breathalyzer I'll never know. But somehow I did. The bizzie couldn't believe it, snatched the bag off me and made me take it again. He said "Now this time blow in it properly". So I did with the same result, so he had no option but to let me go. I walked home to mine and Tommy's flat. Only a five minute walk. I got in and just collapsed on the bed. When I woke up in the morning I felt rough as fuck. I looked at Tommy Mac and said "Tommy I had a horrible dream that I smashed the E type up". I rushed over to the window to see if it was there, then my nightmare became a reality. The car wasn't there. It had really happened. Fuck me. £700 gone. I was sick as a pig. Anyway back to the games now.

I only ended up missing the first game against Norwich City at home. I got out the day before we played West Brom away. As always I was really looking forward to the new season. I needed to get a new car. I bought it with a couple of friends, the Huyton lads, between us. It was a yellow Mazda. Lovely car. Got us all over the country all year round. And a few games abroad as well. We had a great start, winning five and losing one of the first six games. I just felt this season was going to be really special. But how the fuck can our beloved redmen do better than last season, winning the double. But boy we did. What a season. Every redman I knew was feeling the same buzz. Looking back we just knew we were going to be champions of Europe. We just felt invincible. We cruised through the first couple of rounds against Crusaders of Ireland, scoring 11 goals and conceding none, but got a much tougher opposition in the quarter Finals, St Etienne of France. They were a really, really good side. Technically very gifted. Fuck me they gave as good as they got. The away leg was first up. I drove with four lads from Huyton; George Queen, Micky Dunn, Paul Robbo and a guy I formed a really nice friendship with, James Queen. We had a good drive to France, but sadly we get beat 1-0. We played really well. Stevie Heighway hit the inside of the post. I just wasn't our night.

On the way back we stayed the night in Lille. We got booked into a hotel, had a nice shower and then out for the night for a nice bevy. It's only about half past ten so I'm on the lookout for a little bit of ooh la la. The bar we ended up in was pretty lively, but not many free birds available. Loads of couples but the bar itself was boss. I love my music and the bar owner had the most amazing album collection I've ever seen in my life. Just try and visualise it, a big bar and behind the bar there was a built in cabinet shall we say. I estimated he must've had about 5,000 albums. Unbelievable. Absolutely incredible. You name it. He had it. Every classic you could think of. The Beatles, The Rolling Stones, Pink Floyd, Fleetwood Mac, Genesis, The Who, The Kinks and so on. Anyway it's about 12 o'clock and the bar owner wanted to close up as there was only us five of us and a school teacher left in the bar. So he put on a Rolling Stones number, Jumping Jack Flash. That was it. I was up, strutting my stuff. I do a mean Mick Jagger. I was singing in the clubs in Manchester in 1970, 71. I used to get £6 for a twenty minute gig. I'd sing five numbers, couple of Stones numbers and a few Drifters numbers from Motown. A pint of beer them days was about 3 bob. 15p in today's money. So it was a few bob. Back to the bar. The owner was loving me doing me Jagger so he decided to take the towel off and phoned upstairs for his girlfriend and her friends to come down and have a drink. It turned out he was a Liverpool fan and his favourite band was the Stones. What a night we had. We finally left the bar at about 4 o'clock in the morning. I was absolutely bladdered. Slept like a baby. Then we drove back to Liverpool in the morning.

Back to the league and the FA Cup, and we were doing well in both - right up there in the league and into the semi-final of the FA Cup against the blue shite from across the park. With seven or eight games to go in the league, there's nothing in it at the top, a couple of points separating about three or four teams. Everyone is buzzing after a nice nine game run, losing only one. The return leg of the European Cup against St Etienne is up next. What a night! Very similar to the Inter Milan game in 1965. Amazing scenes before, during and after the match. Just incredible. That feeling. You know the one redmen. It's hard to describe the feeling when Davie Fairclough scored what turned out to be the winner. For sure I'll take those memories to my grave. Next up it's the semi-final against the blue shite at Maine Road in Manchester. All us scousers invaded Manchester. Redmen and Bluenoses having the crack. No trouble whatsoever. Sadly we can't say the same today as those bitter blue bastards turned snide after the Heysel disaster. All English clubs got banned from Europe, stopping Everton going into the European Cup. All us older redmen know that there was no fault in our amazing travelling redmen, it was those Italian shitbags, attacking some young reds, then when the reds fought back they ran away. With that and the state of the stadium (equal to a third division club in England), they were the two reasons for the disaster. The cowardly Italians and the organisation of the game itself. Anyway back to the semi-final against Everton. It was a really nail biting game. It finished up 2-2 so it's a replay back in Manchester four days later. Same as the first game. The atmosphere was amazing. Reds and Blues mingling together, no problems at all. Again it was a really tense game. Our beloved redmen went 1-0 up thanks to a Phil Neal penalty. Everton were throwing everything at us but we stayed strong and hit them on the break in the 88th minute, as Jimmy Case netted. Then just to rub the salt in, Ray Kennedy made it 3. Game over. Redmen bouncing everywhere. On the short thirty-five mile journey home down the East Lancashire Road there were people hanging out of windows everywhere. All sorts going on. I got home and it's into town, ending up in the Pezz – what a dive, but I always copped off in there. Woke up in the morning with a big smile on me face. There is surely nothing better than waking up with that great feeling of beating the blue shite in a semi-final, and also having a very sore knob. What a night!

With only six games to go now, we are right there on top, but only a point or two ahead. Then we beat Ipswich and that shite from down the East Lancs, and follow that with two draws. That left only two games to go. We only needed a point now to be Champions once again. And it came against West Ham United at Anfield. A 0-0 draw was enough to clinch the title. At the final whistle the pitch was well and truly invaded. That one and only feeling kicks in again. Fucking magical. I had a nice few bob to come back off the bookies in the morning. Just on £1,000. The bookies arse was gone. Apart from my nice win in the league, I'd got a bet going for Liverpool to win the league, the FA Cup and the European Cup. If it went in we are talking in the region of £25,000 coming back to me. So fucking unlucky (them Manc twats!) but I still collected about another £3,000 from the double, the European Cup and the league. Next up is the semi-final of the European Cup against FC Zurich away in the first leg. We just flew in and out so not much to write about apart from the fantastic result. We won 3-1. Phil Neal scores two and Steve Heighway got the other. Got well and truly walloped, drunk on loads of bevvies, but mainly drunk on emotion. We are almost there, the final of the European Cup in Rome. Then it came. We cruised through the second leg at Anfield, winning 3-0. Fucking boss night in town as usual.

There were a few weeks to go before we play the first of our two cup finals, first up being them horrible pathetic blue eyed boys from down the East Lancs road. Me and every other redman were convinced we were going to win the treble, but sadly, after outplaying the Manc bastards for 80 percent of the game, we lose. I honestly can't remember being more devastated at the final whistle of any other game. The players were lying on the turf. Shattered. They gave so much yet got no reward. That's football, sometimes the best team loses.

So three days later it's off to Rome. What an unbelievable day and night. I'm so proud to say I was one of the 40,000 redmen that invaded Rome on the 25th May. It was simply just a mass of red and white everywhere. The scouse banter was at its best. Banners waving everywhere. We all knew that there was no way on earth that we wouldn't be taking old big ears back to Anfield with us. The flight to Rome was boss. Everyone singing their hearts out. All me Huyton buddies and all the Scotty Road lads, my very good blue nose mate Ritchie Harrison was there along with a kid named Wanna. Anyway we got to the hotel, checked in, had a quick shower and were out on the town.

The capital of Italy, it wasn't up to much to be honest. Just eating houses everywhere. Spaghetti, Spaghetti, Spaghetti. Anyway we decided to have something to eat. Guess what we had? Yeah you got it, Spaghetti. Carbonara for me. It was bellissimo. Then we noticed on the next table there were two of the Italian stars from the national team, Mazola and Grazianni. Some players those two. Anyway most of us decided to call it a night as there wasn't much going on in the clubs. Mind you it was a Tuesday night, so everyone's up in the morning. Most of the lads said they were off to do a bit of shopping, or should I say, shop lifting. I still felt a bit fucked the next morning so I told all the lads "I'm gonna have a few hours kip. I'll meet you at the nearest beach" It was really hot. Apparently the beach was only about 10 minutes' walk. I finally got up at about midday, had myself something to eat, went outside the hotel and jumped in a cab and said to the driver "The beach mate". He just looked at me and says "Que?" I gesture to him with my arms as if I'm swimming. He says "Si, ok". We were driving for about 10 or 15 minutes so I said to him "How much longer?"

pointing to my watch. He says "No problem, soon, soon". 10 minutes later and we're still driving. I said to him "What the fuck are you playing at lad? Where are you taking me?" He just looked at me and smiled. In the end I just said "Back to the hotel". We got back to the hotel about half an hour later. I said "How much?" He says so many million Lira. I worked it out and it came to about £70. I said something like "Go fuck yourself" and threw about a tenner or something like that at him. I got out of the cab and the driver was right behind me screaming and shouting. The next thing all the other taxi drivers are out of their cars and surrounding me, pushing and shoving me. What the fuck could I do? I'll tell you what I did. I butted four of them, then punched the other three. Only messing lads. I had to pay the Italian bastard. I went back into the hotel and asked where the nearest beach is, the receptionist says "It's a five minute walk at the back of the hotel". I just burst out laughing. She looked at me and said "Why you laugh?" I said to her "I've just had to pay a taxi driver £70. He drove me everywhere, apart from the beach". She just smiled and said "Taxi drivers give Italy a bad name". I wonder why I thought. I walked to the beach and as she had said, it took me about five minutes. I found my mates and told them what'd happened. They all started taking the piss out of me, giving me loads of stick. Especially my little mate, Wanna from Scotty. "I thought you were clued up" he was shouting at me, laughing. We had a really good day at the beach but a couple of the lads got burnt so I had a good laugh at them.

So it's off to the game. Amazing scenes everywhere. You could feel it. I know it's easy to talk with hindsight but believe me, the best supporters in the world just knew it was our time. And so it turned out to be, thanks to a glorious team performance. The first goal was absolute quality. The Kirkby scallywag Terry McDermott, boy could he drink but boy could he play. He was an integral part of this great side, scoring many, many great goals. Jimmy Case was at fault for giving the ball away for them to draw level. A misplaced pass let in the brilliant Sorensen, who still had an awful lot to do, but he smashed it home from a very, very tight angle. Clemence had no chance. Fuck me the nerves are going. 1-1. We were under so much pressure for the next 10-15 minutes, but then we got hold of the game with more than a little help for our amazing travelling redmen. Then the goal came. From of all people, Tommy Smith. He got on the end of a cross from Stevie Heighway and scored a thumping header. The travelling redmen were going nuts but that was nothing compared to the third goal, a penalty after a brilliant run by Keegan, going past a few defenders into the box and getting hacked down. It was a definite penalty. No doubt about that. Phil Neal stepped up and scored. So that made it 3-1 with only six minutes to go. They were a beaten team. The final whistle went and within seconds the whole pitch was invaded, covered in the red and white of the travelling redmen. Champions of England and now Champions of Europe. I was that drunk later on in the night I can hardly remember what happened in the town. But I'll always remember the game. Anyway it's time to fly home. The airport was chocka with redmen dancing and singing, most of them still drunk on emotion. It's time to board our plane. As we are going through passport control I noticed my mates passy was hanging out of his ass pocket. So I dipped it and put it into my own pocket. As my mate Wanna got to the passport control, he couldn't find his passy and starts shouting round "Has anyone found my passy?" We are all through the other side laughing at him and shouting "Don't worry lad, there will be another plane tomorrow, so get your arse down to the British Embassy as soon as you can". He just went white and started to walk away. Then I shouted "Wanna, here's your passy lad" pissing myself laughing. I said "I thought you were clued up lad" laughing my cock off. "That's what you get for laughing at me over the taxi rip off". Everyone was taking the piss out of him. A kid from Scotty getting dipped? So it's on the plane and it's home we go, back to the bookies to collect my winnings again, thanks to my beloved Liverpool Football Club. We headed back down to Bognor Regis for the summer season to get a few more notches on my bedpost. The summer flies by. I had a boss time.

As always everyone is commenting that it is going to be a great year. We just seem to keep getting better and better. Kevin Keegan had left us at the end of the last season as he wanted to move abroad to Hamburg after six great seasons with our beloved reds. He scored exactly 100 goals in 321 appearances. Every single redman was gutted. How the fuck are we going to replace him? The great Bob Paisley made what is probably Liverpool's greatest ever signing. The fans soon realised that we had an even better player than Keegan, King Kenny Dalglish. Without a doubt Liverpool's greatest ever player. We got £500,000 on Keegan and paid only £440,000 for the King, with £60,000 left in the bank. It didn't take him long to settle in, only 7 minutes actually, scoring on his debut at Middlesbrough. A world class player without a doubt. Paisley had also signed Graeme Souness, another brilliant player (Twat of a manager though). Souness was without a doubt one of the hardest players I have ever seen. He took no prisoners. Ferocious in the tackle, he was the complete midfield player. He would walk into any of the greatest Liverpool teams. We got off to a good start to the season, losing only one of the first twelve games. Paisley's other signing of this season was a certain Alan Hansen. The nearest thing I've seen to the great Bobby Moore, captain of the England world cup winners, and also the magnificent Franz Beckenbauer of Germany, the greatest player in his position ever, in my opinion. Paisley paid a mere £100,000 for Hanson. Those three signings went on to be Liverpool legends. What a manager Paisley was. But for me the Shanks was the man who made it all possible.

We were back in Europe and got East Germans Dinamo Dresden, first leg away. Just in and out. A great result, we win 2-1. The second leg was at Anfield and we won 5-1 with a very rare goal from Alan Hansen after fourteen minutes. Up next it's Benfica of Portugal, away leg first. In and out job again. A very good result, winning 2-1. The return leg was no problem, winning 4-1. Next up was the FA Cup and we go out at Chelsea, losing 4-2. I'm fucking gutted. I was even more gutted getting off the train at Lime Street. I found a card school on the train. The usual watch for half an hour or so and then got involved. Easy money for me I thought, but no. This one kid didn't have a fucking clue. But he had the luck of the Irish. I ended up losing over £200. I don't know how his luck held out, but it did. The jammy twat. But that's what happens sometimes when a bad player gets lucky, that's poker. Back to the league, things aren't looking too good, about eight points off the top. But we finish off in style, winning ten and drawing two of the last twelve games, it was a brilliant finish to the season but just not good enough. We finished second to Nottingham Forest. The European Cup was our last chance of silverware. Next up we get Borussia Monchengladbach. First leg away. I wanted to drive but most of the lads wanted to fly, so fly we did. It was a really hard game. We were getting beat 2-0 with only two minutes to go and then up popped Davey Johnson (my mate, more about Davey later) to make it 2-1 giving us a good chance in the return leg. We made no mistake at Anfield. Absolutely destroyed them 3-0 to put us in the final again, to be played at Wembley against Brugge of Belgium.

Without a doubt this was the most boring final I've ever watched in my life. Brugge just had ten men behind the ball for ninety minutes. Boring bastards. But after sixty five minutes, King Kenny was put through inside the box with a brilliant ball from Souness. As the goalkeeper tried to cut his angle down Kenny just chipped it over the advancing keeper and that's how it finished. 1-0, the mighty reds securing the European Cup for the second year in succession. Wembley was bouncing. The mighty reds had done us proud. After the match I travelled down to Bognor Regis, it was only about an hour and a half drive. I'd been seeing this bird Kim, fucking gorgeous little thing. I really liked her, and had been seeing her for about three months. Wow, that's a long time for me. But I got in a little bit of trouble and had to get out of Bognor fast. I really liked Kim so I said to her "I've got to go, but you can come to Liverpool with me and we'll get a flat". She loved me Kim and said "Let's go". She was only nineteen and I was about twenty-seven but it only lasted a couple of months. As usual, it was my own fault. I couldn't be happy with just one woman, so she fucked off back down to Bognor. I didn't like living with a bird. I'm far too young and virile for that malarkey. Too many oats to sow.

Then disaster hit me. I'm in town one night with my mates. We get in an argument with these Evertonians. It turned really nasty; bottles and chairs getting smashed everywhere. It ended up with nine people getting nicked for grievous bodily harm and causing an affray. I knew I was going to jail. I was thinking eighteen months, two years at the most. But no, that prick of a judge gave me four years. I nearly fainted in the dock when he said four years. Fuck me it wasn't even my fault as I was only trying to defend myself. The first couple of months was a nightmare. But what could I do. I just had to try and make the best of a bad situation. And boy was it bad. This was proper jail, not an open prison. It was nothing like today with tellies, laptops and phones. Fuck me that's not jail. I was locked up for twenty-three hours a day, every day, banged up in a little cell, and I mean little. I think it was 8ft by 8ft. A pair of bunk beds for two people, no toilet, just a plastic pot to piss in. It was inhumane. Mind you they did let us have a small radio. That fucking Walton Jail, known locally as the Big House, was not a nice place to be in, but it got a lot better after the first year. I got moved to a jail in Lancaster. It was Lancaster Castle, an old castle turned into a prison. It was a lot more relaxed there. I got to work on a farm outside the jail a couple of days a week. My job in the jail was as a clothing changing assistant in the bathrooms. In other words, people used to come in to get a bath once a week (yes, once a week). Me and another kid, Frankie Finn, from Scotty Road, got on really well, he wasn't a big football fan but I let that go. Frankie had been in and out of jail all his life. He was a loveable rogue. He was doing six years. He really helped me through the dark times.

By now I'm really missing watching our beloved redmen but with a bit of luck I could be out in four months if I got parole. I should get it as everything is going for me. A job to start when I'm released, and a place to live with my family. But no, I get the knockback. I got a six month review, which means if I stay clear of trouble then I will be released in six months' time. Twenty-three months altogether that would make it. However, it's hard to keep out of trouble in a place like that as 75% of the inmates were in for sex related crimes. Mind you I had some satisfaction from messing with those pervy bastards. As I was saying before I was working in the clothing exchange where everyone came in once a week to have a bath and change their underwear. I stood behind a big open hatch and as the screws brought in the cons for a bath I would change their gear. 1 Shirt, two socks and two pairs of underpants. When it came to the beasts (sex cases) I'd say "What size shirt" to the perv and he would say "size 15 shirt". I turned to my assistant and say "shirt size 18". Then with a pair on tongs that I had been supplied with I picked out of the dirty washing basket underneath me the dirtiest pair of underpants I could find. Then gave him two pairs of dirty socks for his two pairs of dirty socks. This prick started shouting for the screw. The screw just came over and said "Come on bollocks, back to your cell". Then came one of the best moments I've ever had in jail. The screw brought this new nonce in for his bath. The dirty bastard had just been given a poxy six years for sexually assaulting a 6 year old girl and a five year old boy, using a screwdriver. The dirty sick bastard. The screw who brought him in was a decent enough guy. He more or less dragged him into the bath house, put him by the bath and said "You've got 5 minutes. Hurry up you dirty bastard". Then the screw comes back to us and says "Look lads, this bastard is one bad, bad man." He just gave us a wink and said "I'm going for a smoke. I'll be back in five minutes". Me and Frankie just looked at each other and said "Let's do this fucking nonce". So we filled a metal mop bucket with hot water and crept into the next bathroom, I stood on the bath and looked over, and there he is playing with himself. Frankie passed the bucket up to me. I lifted it up and shouted down to him "Alright nonce!" He looked up and I lashed the red hot water all over him. You should've heard the fucking screams. I just wished the mother and father of those kids could've heard those screams as well. Fuck all happened to us over that. The screw covered it for us, saying he slipped or some shite.

My parole review was coming up now. I was so fucking nervous. The screw who let us do what we did to the nonce was a nice guy. He said "I've done my best for you Blayney in my review to the parole board. Good luck lad". I went to the board and yes, get in. I'm out in twelve days' time. I had just missed the whole of the 1978-79 season, missing us being crowned champions yet again, but I am going to see the last six games of 1979-80. I'm home but with no money and no car things look grim, but a few good mates from my past threw me a few bob to get me back on my feet. My first game back was against of all teams, the blue shite at Goodison Park. Fucking great result. We beat them 2-1 thanks to goals from Phil Neal and Davey Johnson. We had already gone out of the European Cup in the first round against Dinamo Tbilisi. The governor in the jail wouldn't give me time off to go! Arsenal knocked us out of the FA Cup in the semi-final, but we had a great chance of the league title. So with six games left we win three (including Everton), and draw two to seal the title with a game to go. We sealed it against Aston Villa at Anfield, winning 4-1, leaving the last of the season academic. The title was won. Fucking get in.

A SEASON ON THE BENCH

I WAS NOW IN BAD NEED OF A HOLIDAY after all the shit in the last couple of years. So me and my mate Billy Swan from Huyton decided to go to Spain for a couple of weeks in the sun, but it didn't turn out to be much fun. After being there for a couple of days we both fancied a little smoke. You know, a little bit of hashish. So we walked down by the seafront to try and get one. We meet this fella and he says "You want buy hashish?" I say "Yeah. Ten grams, how much?" He says something like a tenner, "Come with me to my car round the corner". He gets in the car and opens the glove compartment, takes a bag out and passes it to me. I say "Thanks" and pay him. Me and Billy just go to walk away and all of a sudden, there are police cars everywhere. Both me, Billy, and the Spanish guy are lashed to the ground, cuffed and thrown into the back of the police van. What a fucking nightmare! They took us to a police station and took me and Billy up to an interview room. I've never experienced anything like what was about to happen in my whole life. Me and Billy are thinking we will get an on the spot fine or something like that. 10 grams is fuck all. But no, these two CID coppers were shall we say not very nice people. I've never been so scared in my entire life. They sat me on a little wooden chair and took Billy over by the windows. I think we were three floors up. They sat Billy down in a similar chair, then they both walked back over to me. One of them stood right behind me and one directly in front looking down on me. He starts screaming in Spanish. I didn't understand a fucking word that he said but I can see the aggression in his face. I look up and say "No speak Spanish". He glares down at me and says "No comprende bastard?" Then the next thing I know I'm smashed in the side of my head, chair knocked over, me on the floor. Fuck me this is getting heavy. I was getting scared. They did this three times to me as Billy sat there watching. He was as white as a fucking sheet. More and more shouts come my way. "Nombre, Nombre, Nombre". I didn't have a clue what he wanted to know. Then bang again in the side of the head. Then I just thought on my feet, or should I say on my arse. As I'm spread all over the floor I just started clutching my heart and saying "Can't breathe", giving it loads. Then I was giving it convulsions all over the floor. They shit themselves, fell for it hook, line and sinker. What a fucking actor.

They sat me down in a proper chair and gave me a glass of water. They just kept looking at me saying very mildly "Tranquillo", meaning relax. Then they walked over to Billy. "Fuck me what next?" I'm thinking. Then the door opened and another prick came in. He just looked straight at me and said, in English "You are in a lot of trouble my friend". Then he says "Watch" and points to Billy and the other two pricks. They pick Billy up out of his chair, open a big window, push Billy right over to it, grab him by his legs and started dangling him out of the window. Fuck me I nearly fainted. Then they dragged him down again next to me. Then the English speaking prick says "Look boys, you are fucked. We need to know who you work for. You tell us and you can go free today. You don't tell us and you go to jail for a long time. Possibly two or three years before you even go to trial. So tell me your boss's name." I said "We are both self-employed. No boss". He says very angrily "You think I'm stupid?" and gives me a slap. "You big drug dealer. Tell me boss's name". "I only tried to buy a smoke for us." I said. "No" he says "Taxi driver who sell you ten grams says you say if it is good you want to buy 20 kilo. Now tell me name of boss". Me and Billy just looked at each other and thought "What the fuck is happening here?" Eventually they took us down to a cell, which was more like a cage, with five other people in it. One was a bird, rough as fuck though. I think she was nicked with receiving 'swollen' goods.

Anyway three days later the poxy consulate representative came to see us. He says "How are you lads?" We just looked at him and said "What the fuck's goin' on lad? We've been locked in here for three days, twenty-four hours a day. For fuck's sake get us out of here." The smell was unbelievable. Fucking foul. The consulate says "You need a lawyer". We say "For a poxy 10 grams?" He says "They don't believe you. They say you are dealers, but don't worry. It will take a bit of time as everything in Spain is so slow. Maybe a few weeks. In the meantime, you will be getting moved in a day or two, to Alicante Jail".

Wow, this jail was so old. It was like a big old castle with a guard on each of the four corners, an M16 machine gun in hand. Fuck me, scary. Apparently no one had ever escaped from there. There were a few tries but they all ended up with the convict getting shot dead or badly injured. I don't like the look of this. Anyway, me and Billy ended up getting put in a dormitory with about three hundred other cons. Underneath the dormitory there was about a hundred cells, each with two people in. Then there was the under 21's wing, about eighty, a hundred or so, making it around five hundred prisoners in total. The dormitory was huge. It was like a massive Aircraft hangar, like a big dome, with three lines of steel bunk beds. No fucking mattresses or sheets. I'm not joking lads, it was untrue. Maybe out of the three hundred beds or so, there were fifteen or twenty with mattresses on. So as the screw opens the big steel doors, he just pushed us in and then closed the heavy metal gates behind us. We just sat on the first bed that we saw. I remember saying to Billy "Is this a fuckin' dream lad?" So we just sat there for a few moments trying to take in the environment around us. It was almost like a dream. Anyway, the next thing we know, this little Spanish guy comes walking over towards us. He stops at the bed and says "Hi, you English?" I says "Yes, yes". Thank fuck for that. Someone to talk to, to see what it's like in here. I said to him "My name is Gerry. What is yours?" He just looked at me and said "My English is no good". In other words, he could speak as much English as I could speak Spanish. Not a lot. The lad was a bit younger than me, twenty-five, maybe twenty-six. His name was Martius Monsuzat Moya. I just called him 'M'. We just clicked me and M. A really nice kid. Locked up for fuck all really. He went to the docks one day, as he had been doing for about six months, to look for a day's work on a fishing boat. Some days he got work, others he didn't. It took a couple of months for us to communicate properly but in the end we could talk. He had been in the prison two years and three months awaiting trial for robbery with violence. What happened was he got a job fishing for the day but the boat owner wasn't very happy because they had had a bad day's catch. Not so many fish. So when M asked him for his day's wages the guy said "Half days wages today. Fish no good". M says "I say to him Gerry, 'I worked hard all day. You tell me you pay me so much and then you want to pay me half'. So I grab him with my knife and take out his wallet. But only I take what he promised me and gave him the wallet and the money back. Then I got off. The next thing I know the Police arrest me then the boat owner tells the police 'He no work for me. He just come on boat and rob me with knife'. Then he shows the police his wallet and he has emptied it so that was enough to get me locked up in this shit hole". Anyway within half an hour he had us sheets and a mattress. Unbelievable.

Night time comes, first night in there. Time to try and sleep. But M told me "Anything valuable you have, you wrap it up in your clothes and put it under your mattress and sleep on it so that no one can rob you. Yes?" So I say "Ok". Finally I get to sleep, then when I wake in the morning I pull the mattress up to get my jacket with my gold necklace. At first as I pull it out everything seemed ok. But then when I put my hand in my pocket, fuck me, no gold necklace. I went fucking nuts. Screaming everywhere. "What bastard has robbed me?" Then M comes running up and says "Gerry, problem? What problem? What problem?" I explain, more with hand gestures than language, what has happened with my gold chain. He says "Tranquillo, tranquillo" meaning relax. He told me to "sit, sit". So I sat down. He just walked away. Within ten minutes he came back. He looks at me and says "Open" gesturing to me to open my hand. Then he dropped the gold necklace back into my hand. I said "Thank you, thank you my friend" Then I say "Nombre, nombre, who take?" M says "No say. You have necklace so forget now".

I felt so sorry for M. He had been there for two years, three months and still hasn't been to court. So that was some introduction on my first night in a foreign jail. Anyway, the next day the solicitor comes to see us. What a fucking waste of space he was. He cost us about £300. M says to me "Gerry, if you have any money, there will be no problem. You will make feonsa (Spanish for bail), and then you can just fuck off home". So we get a new lawyer. He wasn't cheap. £5,000. He says everything in Spain takes time so we must be patient. Patient? We've been here over four fucking months for a poxy bit of weed. He said "I've told you before. In Spain it is different to in England. Money talks. I need to grease the palms of about four or five people from a clerk to a screw". The first two months was really hard, but as a scouser I soon settled in and tried to make the best out of a bad situation. Out of just over five hundred prisoners there was about ten foreigners; Me, Billy, a kid from Ireland, two kids from London etc. The two kids from London were there for about four or five weeks. In for drunk and disorderly or something poxy. They had to pay about £500 each to get out. What a legal system! There was also a couple of kids from Denmark and a French fella. The only thing I found better in the Spanish jail compared with an English one was that you weren't locked up in your cell all day. There were jobs to do but with wages at the end of the week, but thankfully for us, you didn't have to work if you didn't want to. If you had money or someone to send you money you could have a bank account where you could spend £40 a week. A couple of good mates sorted that for me. I don't want to mention their names but you know who you are lads. Thanks for everything. The jail was unbelievable. Very similar to the one in that classic film, Midnight Express but not as violent.

Mind you, saying that, after being there for about four months all hell broke loose. There was a full scale riot in the jail. Three young lads in the young offenders' wing had died in their cell. Apparently the three lads were tripping on LSD when a fire broke out in their cell. All the other hundred or so kids could hear them screaming and shouting but the screws took no notice until it was too late. They all died. Then all the other kids just started rioting, breaking down the two big wooden gates and smashing their way into the main jail. It didn't take long for the rest of the jail to riot. They were blaming the screws for not being quick enough to rescue them. I really find it hard to put into words what happened in the next couple of hours. You remember a couple of pages ago I said I had never been so scared in my whole life? Well I was wrong. Fuck me, the jail just got trashed. The whole of the inmates barricaded themselves into the main dormitory which by that time was just bare, like an empty aeroplane hangar. All the bunk beds had been ripped up. It was like a big dome, all cells going in a circle, then on top the big dormitory. The next thing we know we hear a big loudspeaker coming from below saying something in Spanish. We can just about understand what he was saying. "Come out now, or we we'll come in and drag you out". Then we heard this noise. Probably the most frightening noise I've ever heard in my life. It was the riot police. Visors, batons, tear gas, guns, the lot – marching on the concrete floor. It was frightening. Then again the loud speaker "Ariba, Ariba, Ariba" meaning move now. No one moved. The two big gates had been barricaded with loads of bunk beds, but it didn't take them long to break it down. I have never seen anything like what was about to happen. The riot police just ran wild. Lashing out with their batons and squirting their tear gas. It was fucking mayhem, everyone just running up and down the dormitory. There was this black kid, a Nigerian lad. He was running around with a wet towel gesturing to everyone to wet their towels to stave off the tear gas. Anyway the riot police started herding everyone into the toilets. Five hundred people all in the toilet. I could barely breathe. We were like fucking sardines. Just before we got pushed in one of the riot police tried to smash his baton into Billy's head. I managed to push me arm forward and take the blow from the baton. How my arm broke I'll never know. Billy's legs actually went. He more or less fainted. I had to drag him into the toilet.

Eventually, after how long I'm not sure, about an hour or so I should imagine, they started marching everyone out of the toilet with their hands on their heads. We had to walk down a huge spiral staircase with a riot bizzie on every turn. They were just cracking people at random. My legs were like fucking jelly. Finally they marched us off to a cell. No beds, nothing. Just a fucking hole in the middle of the floor to go to the toilet in. Seven of us in a cell made for two. It fucking stunk. The paint was peeling off the walls. It was just unreal. Apart from me and Billy, there was a Dutch fella, three Spaniards, and a lad from Bolivia, South America. Me and Billy just looked at each other and said "All this for ten grams?" and just burst out laughing. Anyway all seven of us just picked a spot and sat down. I just couldn't believe what happened next. The three Spanish kids started banging on the wall and started shouting something into the next cell. Then one of them took this very small blade out of the sleeve of his coat. It was about the size of a Stanley knife but only half as wide. He just started picking at the plaster on the wall. Eventually he made a small hole, a little bit bigger than a cigarette in circumference. It took him about an hour or so, maybe more. Then next, one of the funniest things I have ever, ever seen in my whole life. Through this little hole, first came about six or seven single matches, then about six cigarettes, then a lovely little piece of hashish. Me and Billy were fucking amazed. They were good lads these three Spaniards. They threw me and Billy a joint or two. Fuck we needed that.

One of the Spaniards was a cracking lad, and spoke really good English. He was in for fraud, credit cards and so on. He was telling us what was going to happen in the next few days or so. He told us "A lot of people are going to have big problems. The authorities are not happy at all after the riots, especially with the three kids dying. For you English it should be no problem. It's just us Spaniards. We will probably all have to go to court and then sent to a really, really bad prison. You think it's bad here my friend? Wow. That is hell. You have to work ten hours a day picking vegetables out of the ground." And have a guess what you had to eat lads. Every day the same. Yes you've got it, Cabbage soup, with bread. No meat (or as we call it, blind scouse). Then the Spanish kid, his name was Louis by the way, says to me "You must say to the governor of the jail that you had no part in the riot. You just got swept along with hundreds of people running into the dormitory. You should be ok as you are foreigners. It's only us Spanish who they will make life hell for". Then he says to me "Gerry, listen very carefully for your own sake. Speak to the screw who's in charge of you and he will help you if you can. He is one of the few good ones in here". On the first night in the cell, eventually we fall asleep, resting our head in our knees, when all of a sudden a big fucking scream came from somewhere. "Take me, take me". This fucking Bolivian crank was on his knees looking up to the iron bars on the window. "Take me, take me" he was shouting. Then he just looked at me and said "Come with me English man, come with me". I just stood up, looked straight at him and said "Get your fucking head down you crank". Louis and his two Spanish mates were not as considerate as me. They gave him a bit of a kicking and told him to go to sleep. Madness. Anyway we ended up in this stinking hell hole for seven days, then it was back to the dormitory. Thank fuck for that.

We started working in the kitchens, preparing all the meals. It was really good. We could eat as much as we wanted. We could also buy one bottle of beer for 9 pesetas. We had money so we used to buy as many as we could off all the other cons for 50 pesetas a bottle. So by the time we had finished the dinners, me and Billy would be truly pissed. Unbelievable jail. One day the Governor came to see me and Billy as we were getting rid of all the slops after dinner, throwing it all down this big drain. He says to us "The jail is overrun with wild cats". There was fucking hundreds of them. He gave us a big lump of wood and said "kill all the cats and throw them down the drain". It was fucking crazy, me and Billy running round the drains, doing all the cats in. A couple of days later me and Billy are on the exercise yard, queuing up at the Econamato (little supermarket). It was just a little window where you could buy soap, toothpaste, cigarettes and all sorts of food stuff. As we were in the queue there was all sorts of pushing and shoving going on. Then I noticed this Italian guy who had come in the day before. I never forget a face me. He looked at me and said "Hello English, I know you. I've seen you at many Liverpool games all over Europe". He was a professional pickpocket. He was the one who was causing all the pushing and shoving in the queues. He was actually picking pockets. People were going nuts. It wasn't money he was taking, it was vouchers which you get off the prison for your work.

The nice screw was really good for us. He says "You must write a letter to King Juan Carlos of Spain explaining to him that you had no part in the riot in the jail. I will also add my opinion to your letter but don't worry, I will speak well for you". Then I had a bit of good news a few days later. The screw who was in charge of me and Billy came to see us and told us that King Juan Carlos of Spain believed we had no part in the riots. We were given an official pardon which meant we wouldn't be moved to another jail, believed to be a real horrible, horrible jail. What a relief. We'd been there now over four months and there was no sign of anything happening. Then Louis the Spaniard came over and said "Hey Gerry, who is your solicitor and how much does he cost you?" We told him and he just burst out laughing. He said "Gerry, fuck him off. He's no good". Then he says "Can you get good money from home in England?" I says "How much?" He says "I'm not sure but maybe £5,000, but believe me my friend it could be up to two or three years before you go to trial. If you can get money, I will get a message out to my friend who will go and see the lawyer for you". So I says "Nice one Louis" and gave him a number to ring back in Liverpool. My mate sorted it out. Now as I said before, the first lawyer cost £300. This one was costing £5,000. A couple of days later, he came to see us in the jail. He tried to explain the Spanish law. Everything takes time he was saying. "mañana, mañana" meaning tomorrow. Everything mañana. He tells us he will sort it but it will take about six weeks, maybe eight. Fuck me, I wasn't very happy about that. We'd been there already for about five months. The beginning of the new season is about to start. And here's me banged up again. What can I say?

Another seven or eight weeks dragged by, then right out of the blue, me and Billy are playing a bit of footy in the exercise yard, when over the tannoy came a message. "Will Gerald Blayney come to the centre, you have libertad" Fuck me I couldn't believe it. It means freedom. I rushed to the centre and the screw says to me "You see the judge now". He took me into a little room and sat me in front of a glass window. The judge was on the other side. He takes all sorts of papers and whatever out of his briefcase and then he starts to talk to me. My Spanish was still limited so he spoke to me in English. "You have been granted bail but you must report to the police station once a week". Then he asked me my address in Spain. I thought to myself "Fuck me, I've got no address in Spain." So I had to think on my feet. I remember about a mile or so before we had got to the jail, I noticed this big long street. It was called San Francisco Street, so I just said "Number 9, San Francisco Street". So he writes it down on one of his papers then pushed it under the glass and asked me to sign it. I did and passed it him back. Then he stood up and said "You are now free to go". I rushed back up to my cell and I was packed within minutes. Billy was a bit gutted but our lawyer said not to worry, this was the only way he could get us both out, one at a time. Then he said to Billy "You will have to wait about another three or four weeks maybe". True to his word, Billy was home about four weeks later. Thank fuck for that. Nightmare over. Back in Liverpool at last I couldn't wait to watch my beloved redmen. I probably missed about twenty games or so. I'm just so glad to be back from that nightmare. Seven and a half months of hell.

★

The Reds had a bad start to the season, drawing far too many games, eight out of the first fifteen or so. It was not looking very good. We went out of the FA Cup early doors against of all bastard teams, Everton at Goodison, losing 2-1. The only thing that was going ok for us was the European Cup. We are through to the quarter final against CSKA Sofia. The first leg was at Anfield. We absolutely destroyed them 5-1. I was just getting back on my feet so I couldn't get the money together to go to Bulgaria, but the main thing is that we went through to the Semi Final against the mighty Bayern Munich, the first leg at home at Anfield. It ended up a very, very nervy 0-0 draw at Anfield, then the next day the Germans were full of it, saying they would destroy us back in Germany, especially one great German player, Paul Brietner. Anyway we decided to drive to Germany, me and a few lads from Kirkby, but somehow we fucked the route up, thinking we had loads of time to get there when we realised it was still over two hundred and fifty miles to Munich. We only had just over two hours to get there and with the Autobahn (motorway) being chocka, there was no chance of us getting there. At best we could've made it for full time. I was fucking gutted, but what could we do? We met a few lads from Ipswich who were playing in Cologne in the UEFA Cup so we went to watch their game instead. The Ipswich fans were brilliant. Everyone knew Bayern had scored to make it 1-0 but when the news came through in the 83rd minute that Liverpool had scored to cancel out Bayern's lead, the Ipswich fans, to a man, started chanting "Liverpool, Liverpool, Liverpool". I was still gutted at not getting there but I was made up that I'd be going to see our beloved redmen in yet another European final. The Bayern game finished 1-1, with us going through on the away goals rule. So it's off to Paris. As far as I'm concerned it is one shithole Paris. But we didn't give a fuck as we were going to have a ball, and have a ball we did! We decided to drive. Me, Billy Swann, a couple of lads from Old Swan, Dave Parker and Gerard Cannon from Huyton. John Powell was with us as well. To be honest I don't remember much of the game. I was rather Stella Artwatted. Never drank it since. However I do remember Alan Kennedy smashing in the winner with only ten minutes to go against the mighty Real Madrid. Our beloved Liverpool Football Club were champions of Europe for the third time in five years. I was so proud of my beloved Liverpool Football Club. We are the talk of Europe again. We had a brilliant night when we got home. As I said, I was bladdered the night of the match but soon made up for that when I got home. The whole of Liverpool (apart from the Blue Shite) was still partying twenty-four hours later, so I just joined in as you do. Not long after this I finally, finally fall in love.

I'm in the Bow and Arrow pub in Huyton, it was a boss boozer with live music and loads of gorgeous birds. Then I noticed this young blonde bird walk past me. I just knew right away that she was for me but not in my usual way. Not just to take her to bed.

I just knew it. But it wasn't that easy. She was only nineteen and I'm nearly thirty-one. I tried to cop for her a couple of times. She just said "No thanks, I'm seeing someone". I just looked at her and said "Fuck him off coz I love you girl and one day I'll marry you". She just looked at me and started laughing. "That's the worst chat up line I've ever heard in my life. Look mate, I don't even like you. You're a womaniser". I just looked at her straight in the eye and said "I used to be a womaniser but from now on it's only you for me". She just got off laughing with her mates. A couple of days later I tried again. "No chance" she says, "Go away". I couldn't sleep thinking about her. It was driving me crazy. After about another three or four knockbacks from her she finally agreed to let me take her home.

We were in the Beachcomber Club on Seal St, just at the back of Duke St. She was in there with her mates, who actually liked me. So I had a word with a couple of them and they said "Annmarie does fancy you but she thinks you just want to take her to bed". I told them "Look girls, I love her and I don't even know her. I just know that I love her". At the end of the night in the Beachcomber, my blag finally worked and she let me drive her home. I'm in my new car, a Ford Capri. It was white. Nice and fast. I drive her home to Cantrell Farm. I got a kiss on the cheek and then that was it, she was gone into the house. I only lived about three or four minutes away. I was staying in my mum and dads for a while in my old room. I was seeing the other bird of my life, Annmarie, for nearly four months, probably four nights a week. I wanted seven but she wanted to go out with her mates. This will not sound like me lads but after four months, maybe I saw her forty or fifty times in that period, and we still hadn't slept together. The nearest I got was probably the tit over the top. I was happy to wait. It made a nice change to jumping straight into bed, wham bam, thank you mam, and then getting off. Anyway I says "Annmarie, when are you gonna stay in me mam's house one night?" She said "Ok, Saturday, but will your mum be alright about it?" I said "There will be no problem." I'm buzzing to fuck.

Before I go to pick Annmarie up on the Saturday night I say

to my ma "Annmarie is staying tonight, Ok?" My ma says "No it's not Ok. What do you think this is? A fucking knocking shop?" I'd never taken a bird back to my ma's before so I said to her "Ma, I love her and I haven't even slept with her yet". Me ma just looked at me and said "Gerry, you're talking to me now. I don't believe you" I said "Ma, I swear on your life, I really love this girl" and so on and eventually she said "Ok lad I believe you". So I says to my ma "She's made me wait four months with no sex so do me a favour; on Sunday morning I want you to make me a big breakfast with plenty of sausages on it and bring it up to my room. When you come in I want you to shout at Annmarie something like 'What are you doing in my house you little slut. Get out!'" It was so funny. Annmarie went white. Then my ma just burst out laughing and said "I'm sorry love, it was his idea. He said he wanted to pay you back for making him wait for four months." Fucking funny or what. Annmarie was even laughing about it after a while. "You bastard" she said to me. I got us a flat within a week, just at the back of the Bow and Arrow in Huyton. Before we moved in I said to Annmarie "I love you girl but before we start to live together, you must promise me that you will never ever try and stop me seeing the other bird in my life, The Liver Bird". She looked me in the eyes and said "I've been with you for over four months now. I think I realise how much you love Liverpool Football Club. You can see your Liver Bird every week, as long as you don't see any other birds

Me and Annmarie had just moved into the flat at the back of the Bow and Arrow pub in Huyton, getting it all nice and done up in a couple of days. She was well made up. Anyway on the Saturday night we went to a club in town, a new club that had just opened a week before. It was about 100 yards from the Beachcomber so we thought we would give it a try. It was called Emotions. Anyway we went in and had a drink. The next thing I noticed was two young lads in their early twenties dressed in nice suits. They were only standing about two yards away from where we were, when all of a sudden one of them reaches into the side of his trousers and pulls out a fucking big axe and lashes out at another lad who was only about two or three feet away from me and Annmarie. It was fucking mayhem. This lunatic chasing this other kid all around the club, birds screaming. Mental. I just looked at Annmarie and said "Let's fuck off". So we got off. Then funnily enough the next week we went back to the Beachcomber thinking "fuck that Emotions", we bumped into the same lad. We were at the bar getting a drink and this guy comes over and says "Ay lad, was you and your bird in Emotions last Saturday?" I just looked at him and thought to myself "what the fuck is going on here?" I says to him "Yeah, why lad?" He said "Let me buy you and your bird a drink coz I fucked your night up last week". He said the kid he tried to cut up was a wrong-un, a grass, so he deserved it. Anyway we got talking and he seemed to be a nice lad. We have become really good friends over the years, and we still are today. His name was Joe Morley, a blue nosed bastard, but he'd seen loads of our away games in Europe. Anyway Joe you asked me to mention you in my book (you lunatic) so here you go. Oh, I nearly forgot to tell you all that Joe is a handsome bastard. Now fuck off blue nose, it's my book not yours. Sorry about that redmen. You know what all these Evertonian twats are like. Back to our beloved redmen.

As usual, prior to the 1981-82 season every redman was so confident. We were that good. We just knew it was going to be a great year. Billy Swann had finished with the merchant navy. We became very close as the years passed by so Billy was with me every game now. We were both doing well, making a good living along the way. Happy Days. We both had younger brothers and would take them all over the country. My brother Alan and Billy's young brother Tony. There were also a few friends of our Alan and mine, John Kearnes, Fitzy (another blue nosed twat), and also Jimmy Allo, the hitch hiker, a boy out of the same mould as me, a really good lad and a great, great redman. Anyway Paisley had signed a young striker from Chester, a Third Division club, for £300,000 at the end of the last season. He only played nine games but never scored. A lot of people thought Paisley had made a mistake in signing him but this season he blew all doubters out of the water, scoring 30 goals in 48 games. His name was of course, Ian Rush. Wow. What a partnership. Rush and Dalglish. They were a joy to watch.

Title: Gerry Blayney

Title: Gerry Blayney

Title: Gerry Blayney

Anyway we got off to a terrible start to the season, winning only two of our first eleven games, and out of the FA Cup in the fifth round, it wasn't looking very good. We went out of Europe in the third round but we were still in the League Cup. We started to improve in the league and also made the final of the League Cup against Tottenham Hotspur. We won the final, but only after extra time, and that gave us the confidence to go on one hell of a run in the league. We won fourteen and drew two out of the last sixteen games, which meant that 87 points was more than enough to clinch the title. No really decent stories about this season as most trips were pretty much driving there and driving back. Nothing in Europe either as we went out early doors, but another double for our beloved redmen. The league and the league cup. That'll do us nicely. So it's onto the next season.

Bob Paisley made yet another great signing, Steve Nicol. Wow, what a player he turned out to be. He was very versatile. He could play anywhere across the back four, or even in midfield. He made the full-back his permanent position. He just loved to overlap from the flank and scored loads of goals. For me he would walk into my best ever Liverpool XI. Yes, he was that good. Better than one of my other all-time idols, Chris Lawler (Sorry Chris, but he was.) Anyway we got off to a great start this time around, winning five and drawing two out of the first seven games and playing nice football. We were really good to watch. Ronnie Whelan, who had signed in 1980 as an eighteen year-old from Home Farm FC in Ireland, was really catching the eye of everybody in midfield. He went on to be a brilliant player for Liverpool over the years, scoring loads and loads of goals for a midfielder. In my opinion, he was the most underrated player I've ever seen, but he certainly wasn't underrated by his teammates. He will always be one of my all-time favourite players. He combined perfectly with Graeme Souness, probably one of Liverpool's greatest ever midfield players, but one twat of a manager.

In the league we had a bit of a hiccup, losing two and drawing two of the next four games, but we soon put that right by going on an incredible run, winning nineteen, drawing five and losing only one out of the last twenty five games. With seven games left the title was almost won. But we couldn't win a single game out of last seven, and five of those seven were defeats. With eighty two points though, that was enough to secure another title. We went out of the FA Cup in the fifth round to Brighton and Hove Albion, with ex-red Jimmy Case scoring the winner. No joy in the European Cup, going out in the third round again, but much better things in the League Cup.

One memorable moment came when we were leaving Ipswich. The rain was so heavy the traffic was down to a crawl. I couldn't see a fucking thing. In the car with me were the usual suspects, Billy Swan, Our Alan, Tony Swann and it was either John Kearnes or Jimmy the hitch hiker. As I was saying, the rain was so heavy that when we were leaving the ground to go home, you couldn't see a thing. The rain was torrential. We came to a small roundabout. Fuck me we didn't even see it. We just drove straight over it. How the fuck we done no damage to the SAAB 900 I'll never know. Fuck your German technology, the Swedish SAAB is rated the safest car to have an accident in, and we proved it on that day. I'd only bought it three days before. It cost me a nice few bob, £4,800. It was only just over a year old, with only 9,000 miles on the clock. Anyway, when I picked it up from the garage where I bought it from in Aigburth, by the time we had signed the papers and whatever, it was about twenty past five. So I drove straight from the Old Swan to the Swinton insurance company where I was insured for my old SAAB. I needed to change the insurance over but it was closed when I got there. So I just drove it home to my house on Bowler Street in Kensington. I'd recently had a really, really nice bet on the horses and won £12,000. So I bought the SAAB plus my very first house. A two-bed terrace on Bowler Street. A mate of mine owned the house but couldn't keep up the payments on the mortgage. It was a funny old deal. I gave him my old SAAB, valued at around five to seven hundred pound, a grand in cash and I took over the mortgage. Anyway as I was saying, I drove to my new house and parked the new SAAB right outside. Then Annmarie said to me "C'mon I wanna take it for a spin and see what it's like". So I took it up to me brothers in Runcorn. He's got his own garage. He's a good mechanic so I wanted him to check it out for me. He said it was a beautiful motor but that I paid slightly too much for it. He said it was worth around £420, no more than that. He knows his stuff as well. But fuck it, I was doing really well. Anyway we drove back home to our new house in our new car, feeling great. Life was really good at the time. So we got home and were getting ready to go out for a nice meal. We had a really nice evening and then we drove home to Bowler Street. With us we had about five or six friends. We never all got in the SAAB of course. Me mate Billy Swan also drove in his new car, who he had bought from none other than... Bob Paisley. We had a nice little party in the house till about five in the morning. Everyone got off so it's off to bed. Woke up at about 12 the next day. As I woke up I says to Annmarie "I had a terrible dream last night love. I dreamt the car had been robbed". Fuck me, as I looked out of the window it was gone. I was going nuts. No Insurance. Oh no. So I reported it stolen to the police thinking that's the last I'd see of it, but around teatime I get a phone call from the bizzies saying that they had found a car on Breck Road, about two miles away from my house. Thank fuck for that.

Anyway sorry about all that bollocks redmen, back to the games. We are through to the final after beating Rotherham, Norwich, and West Ham, all at Anfield, then beating Burnley in a two legged semi-final, to face them horrible, horrible bastards from the end of the East Lancs Road. The Mancs. Really looking forward to this one. We owed them one for stopping us winning the treble in 1977. We drove down to Wembley. There were five of us, but we only had four tickets. No problem though as there was loads of touts as usual. We saw this Cockney cunt giving it the big 'un. We go over to him and say "We just need one ticket lad for the Liverpool end". He says "No problem. £150" I say to him "Ok mate I'll have that" and pull a wad out of me pocket. He pulls a ticket out of his pocket. He just passed me the ticket as I was passing him the money. I snatched it quickly out of his hand and pulled the money back too. I said to him "Now fuck off bollocks, you're getting fuck all". He started screaming and shouting but what could he do, there were five of us. We just walked off laughing our cocks off. I fucking hate them Cockney wide boys. They just never learn do they? In we go. The atmosphere was brilliant. Boss banners everywhere. The travelling redmen were really up for this one. But it didn't start very well and we ended up 1-0 down at half time. Things started getting a bit nervy now but the equaliser came from Alan Kennedy with a sweet left footed shot from about thirty yards into the bottom corner. Get in. Redmen going mental everywhere. It was magic. No more nerves now. We all knew we were on the verge of winning it for the third year on the run. Ninety minutes up. 1-1. Extra time looms. I really do believe that the greatest fans on this planet did their bit to make sure we won the game. I really am so proud to be a redman. We are known worldwide for our passion and our knowledge of the game. So many managers and players can't be wrong can they? Back to extra time. With the fans behind them, the reds were never going to let us down. Then it came with ten minutes to go - up popped the little Irish boy Ronnie Whelan. He just loves this competition, scoring twice in last year's final against Spurs. Anyway his goal was such a beauty – he was just outside the penalty box. He had a shot but it was blocked. It came back to him and in an instant, he curled it into the top corner giving the goalkeeper (Bailey) no chance. A goal fit to win any cup final. Absolute class. The United players' heads just dropped. They knew it just wasn't going to be their day.

At the final whistle red men were dancing, kissing, hugging, crying tears of joy and singing my second favourite song... "We love you Liverpool we do, We love you Liverpool we do, We love you Liverpool we do, Oh Liverpool we love you". We had a boss journey home driving down the M1. Taunting all the United fans. Redmen hanging out of the windows and sunroofs, it was magic. I think we got home to Liverpool at about half nine, ten o'clock. The other bird in my life Annmarie was so happy for me, especially as I had my usual nice bet on our beloved redmen. All told I think I won something like £2,500. In gambling talk it had been like buying money backing our beloved redmen over the last ten years or so. Anyway the new season is about to start. But not without a shock. Bob Paisley had decided that it was time for him to retire after nine years. He won an amazing six First Division titles, three consecutive League Cup finals, one UEFA Cup and the most prestigious of them all, three European Cups (smoke that Fergie). How on earth can anyone follow that? It was Joe Fagan's turn.

JOE FAGAN TAKES OVER

NOTHER OF THE BOOT ROOM STAFF was promoted. Paisley was so different to the Shanks in many ways but he was also a genius, just like the Shanks. Records are there to be broken and Joe did his bit for our beloved redmen. Joe made three new signings at the beginning of the 1983/84 season; John Wark from Ipswich, Michael Robinson from Brighton and Hove Albion and Paul Walsh from Luton. We got off to a nice start to the league, winning four and drawing two out of the first six games. You know what redmen, isn't it just heaven watching our beloved reds. Thanks to the Shanks.

I know I go on a bit about Mr. Shankly but all redmen of my age will understand me totally because they went through it all with me. You get that blue shit across the park giving it 'they are the people's club'. People's club my arse. The proper 'special one' is Bill Shankly (smoke it Mourinho). I'll prove it to you. When the great man Shanks went to the great Kop in the sky in September 1981, on all the phone-ins on Radio City and the local TV and radio, there were nearly as many blue noses as reds phoning in saying Shankly was a man of the people. He will be sadly missed. Anyway back to the games. We were doing really well in the league and also in the Milk Cup after beating Brentford, Fulham, Birmingham, and Sheffield Wednesday. We are through to the Semi-Final against Walsall. The first leg was at Anfield but it turned out to be a really, really hard game. They held us to a 2-2 draw with Ronnie Whelan grabbing both goals. He just loves this competition does this little Irish boy. So it's off to Walsall for the second leg. I actually bought forty tickets for the game hoping to make a few quid, but my heart wouldn't let me. There was so many redmen without tickets. I actually lost a few bob on the briefs. I just couldn't charge the young redmen. Anyway we made it through to the final.

So we're through to another final against of all teams, the blurts from across the park, Everton. Bring it on. Loads of blue nosed mates and me were having the banter for weeks on end. I couldn't wait for the final. It really was a special final coming up, without a doubt. There was no trouble whatsoever. Just loads and loads of scouse togetherness. The M1 and the M6 was just a mass of Red and Blue. Loads and loads of cars with a red scarf hanging out of one window, and a blue scarf hanging out of the other. Without a doubt, there is no other city in the whole wide world like Liverpool. Scousers rule. One special, special city. Anyway, so it's off to Wembley. As usual it was a boss trip down. We drove down. The atmosphere was unique, as it always is when we play each other, fans both mingling together, not a problem at all. And those idiot touts will never fucking learn. Tickets getting snatched left, right and centre. Anyway it's time to get in the ground. It was a very nervy game for both sets of fans. The game finished 0-0 so it's a replay at Maine Rd in Manchester. It was mayhem. There must've been about seventy thousand scousers, maybe more. I think there was about twenty thousand locked out without tickets. People bunking in and getting lashed back out. It was hilarious. The touts were finally getting the message. No way were we taking the tickets out of their pockets. They were just getting a punter and taking him for a walk. Anyway into the game. The atmosphere was amazing. It was a very, very tight game. Very nervy for the fans as usual. Then Graeme Souness grabbed the only goal of the game after about twenty minutes. Get in redmen. Yet another trophy, and the first one for Joe Fagan. But he wasn't finished there. Not by a long chalk. Back to the European Cup. First up it's BK Odense of Denmark. A nice 1-0 win thanks to King Kenny before we thrashed them back at Anfield. I'm gutted as we draw Athetic Bilbao in the next round and there's no way I can go back to Spain. The first leg was at Anfield. We just couldn't break them down and it finished a very disappointing 0-0 draw. But our beloved redmen went over there and thanks to a goal from the Welsh wonderboy Ian Rush, we got through to the Quarter Final against Benfica, the first leg at Anfield. We play really well but only manage to score once. Rushy yet again getting on the scoresheet. We made no mistake in Portugal though, destroying them 4-1. Rushy got one, Craig Johnson got one, and one of my favourite all time players, the much under-rated Ronnie Whelan, grabbing the other two. I can't remember much about the trip, think it was pretty much just in and out. So it's only Dinamo Bucuresti standing in the way of our beloved redmen reaching yet another European final. It was a very tight game at Anfield and we take a very slender 1-0 lead over there, thanks to a rare goal from Sammy Lee. We made no mistake in the second leg though, scoring early on and we end up winning 2-1. Rushy grabbed both goals. So it's off to Rome to play Roma on their own pitch. It was going to be very difficult but the team and all us redmen were well up for it. We actually felt invincible. But before the Roma game we have a small matter of clinching the league title.

With only four games to go, it's in our own hands. We only need five points from the last four games. The first of the four was away at Birmingham City. Fucking nuts them Zulu warriors (that was the name of their firm). So we knew we'd have to be on our toes for this one. If I remember rightly, two car loads of us went down together. There was me, Billy Swann, his brother Tony, our Alan, John Kearnes, Jimmy Allo (the hitch hiker) and Fitzy, the blue nose, but a good lad. We get there about half an hour before kick-off. It was getting very, very heavy outside. Loads of fighting. Me and Billy somehow got split up from the others, then the next thing our Alan and the rest of the lads came scorching towards us with about forty or fifty of them Zulu warriors right on their tail. But as luck had it, there was a load of bizzies coming towards them so the boys had an escape there. Me and Billy took the piss out of them all day long, fucking funny. So it's into the game and away from all this shit outside. It was a really poor game but we got the draw, 0-0. We were all happy with the point. Now we only need four points from the last three games. Next up Coventry at home. We absolutely destroy them, 5-0. The Welsh Wizard, Rushy, bagging four and also a very, very rare goal from the majestic Alan Hansen. He was simply a joy to watch - so cool, so calm.

He made defending look so easy. So it's off to Nottingham to play Notts County, needing only a draw to clinch the title. And that's exactly what we got. A 0-0 draw. As always the travelling redmen are buzzing, singing my favourite song (apart from 'You'll never walk alone' that is) "We love you Liverpool we do, We love you Liverpool we do, We love you Liverpool we do, Oh Liverpool we love you." We had a great trip down the motorway coming home. Everyone going mental as usual. We did some partying when we got home. If I remember righty, we all went on a two day bender. Not a minute's sleep in two days. How the fuck I did it I don't know. Wow. What a first season as manager Joe Fagan is having.

Finally it's off to Italy to play Roma in the final of the European Cup. Everyone was so confident. We didn't care that we were playing them on their own ground in front of their own supporters. The travelling redmen felt invincible. We just knew that with us behind them, we would bring old big ears back to Liverpool. Anyway there was me, Billy, Our Alan, Tony Swann and yet another blue nose, John Smith, from the Southend. He's in jail at the moment, doing twelve years I think. If you're reading this book John, GETSMASS-OLSEN. It means may your time pass quickly. It's what a Turkish judge said to William Hayes in the film Midnight Express. If for some reason anyone out there has not seen this film, do yourself a favour and watch it. It's a classic.

Also on the plane with me was one of the nicest people I have ever met in my life. A very, very good friend still to this day. He was a bookie form Bebington on the Wirral. His name is John Joe O'Neil. I would actually trust this man with my life. Very genuine, too genuine sometimes. I had one hell of a bet going with him at the time. I had a fifty pound yank on Liverpool to win the lot. The league, the FA Cup, the League Cup and the European Cup. For those of you who don't know what a yank is, its eleven bets. Six doubles, four trebles and one accumulator. So 11 x 50=£550. That was my bet. I think I got 2-1 for the title, 6-1 for the league cup, so that means I've already got one double up, getting me £875. If we won the final of the European Cup, I've got three doubles and one treble up. I think I had around 6-1 for the European Cup. So if we win the final I will get back just over £10,000.

Anyway back to the match. We got out of the airport and after the usual heavy handed welcome from the Italian Police, we made our way to the ground. There were two hours or so to go before kick-off. It seemed really relaxed, loads of redmen having a laugh as we always do. Flags and banners all over the place. Say what you like about us scousers but you can never say that we don't know how to enjoy ourselves. The atmosphere was building and we were really enjoying the occasion. But then it slowly started to change. The sound of motorbikes was getting louder and louder. Then it started to get heavy, little fights breaking out all over the place, and them horrible bastards on the motorbikes lashing out at the redmen with bike chains, belts and big lumps of wood. "Fuck this lads, let's get in" I said. As we get in, it's getting really nasty outside. I hate Italy. It's the same every time. Horrible nasty fans and the bizzies weren't much better. Anyway we are inside with an hour still to go before kickoff. The atmosphere was very hostile. You could feel it. Loads of stories were going around about stabbings outside, loads of young redmen taken to hospital. Anyway the kickoff approaches and the travelling redmen are in full voice as the teams come onto the pitch. It wasn't long before we were all in dreamland, Phil Neal scoring after fifteen minutes. Then we had a goal disallowed for offside, then Rush twice came close, only to be foiled by the great Italian keeper Tancredi. Roma had their moments too. They had some great players in Conti, Graziani, plus two Brazilian greats in Falcao and Cerezo. They made it 1-1 two minutes before half time. Conti crossed for Pruzzo to nod home, what a time to concede a goal, right on the stroke of half time!

After a very nervy second half the ninety minutes are up. Into extra time, no goals so it goes to penalties. The very first European Cup to be decided on penalties. What an experience. So many different emotions. First up it's Steve Nicol and he blasts it well over the bar. Oh no. Me arse has gone. The Roma captain stepped up, Di-Bartolomei, and scores to put them in front. The tension is everywhere. Everyone is feeling it, biting their nails. Up next Phil Neal, he scores no problem. Then up steps Conti. He misses. Yes!

Get in. We are right back in it. Rushy is up next. He strokes it in beautifully. Our beloved redmen are in front now as Graziani steps up and clips the bar, sending the ball over the bar. The redmen were going mental. With that miss it now means that if Alan Kennedy scores, the European Cup would be ours yet again. It was weird as he stepped up. It just went so quiet you could hear a pin drop. Then all hell let loose. He sends the keeper the wrong way. Get in. It was pure magic. An incredible performance by our beloved redmen. Our incredible fans as usual served as the twelfth man. It's an absolute honour to be one of them.

As usual we were kept in the ground for not far off an hour. But we didn't give a fuck. They could've kept us there all night if they wanted. 'We love you Liverpool' ringing out all over the place. I felt absolutely drained. I felt as if I had played in the game. But there was fuck all to laugh about when we got outside. It was mental. Hundreds, probably thousands of the Roma skins running riot. It was so frightening. We had to go under this big tunnel to get to the coach park. We got well ambushed. Bottles, bricks, anything they could get their hands on getting lashed down at us. How no one got killed I'll never know. It was a great relief to get back on the coach. Lucky enough all our lads were OK. Can't wait to get on that plane home. It's going to be some journey. And so it turned out to be. The journey just flew by. Everyone was buzzing, re-living the game. What an incredible season, especially for Joe Fagan, winning three major trophies. It had never been done before in the whole history of the game. Then there's my bonus – £10,000 plus! So I'll be off to the bookies the next morning, Ladbrokes I think it was. They are getting a bit sick of seeing my face at the end of each season thanks to our beloved redmen. We arrive back at Speke Airport at about three in the morning. Knackered, drained, can't wait to get to my bed. The other great bird in my life Annmarie was waiting up for me, her and the baby inside her. Yes she was due in September. We'd been trying for about two years now so we are both delighted. As I said earlier in the book I've got a boy to another girl. His name is Peter. He would be eleven years old at this time. I was looking forward to a nice holiday. A friend of

Annmarie's said she had just come back from Greece and it was beautiful. She also said that the people are really, really nice. Most people holidayed in Spain as it was very popular, but as we know I can't go to Spain so it's off to Greece, Corfu. We loved it. Two beautiful weeks to unwind after such an exciting season watching our beloved redmen.

By the beginning of the next season, me bird Annmarie was nearly bursting. Eight and a half months gone. I'm so excited. I'm hoping for a boy, but if it's a girl I'll still love her just as much. The season starts. First up it's Norwich away. A good five hour drive. It was some game, finishing 3-3. One cunt of a drive home. We got home at about half eleven. The first home game was against West Ham. Paul Walsh scored after a mere fifteen seconds. It finished 3-0. Not a bad start to the season. Then we draw with QPR and win at Luton. Next up its Arsenal away on the 8th September. Our baby is due and I'm really looking forward to seeing it being born. I got up early on the Saturday morning with Annmarie and she tells me "Gerry, the baby is definitely going to come today". I says to Ann "I'll phone Billy Swann and our Alan and tell them I can't go". But Annmarie says to me "What time do you think you'll get home from London?" I says "Probably about half eight with a clear run." She says "I know you don't want to miss the baby being born and I know how much you hate it when you have to miss a match so go the match and I'll hold it in till you get to the hospital. I haven't even gone into labour yet so even if it takes you an extra hour or so to get home, you won't miss it". And as always, she was right.

So it's off to Highbury. Billy picks me up at our house at about ten o'clock with our Alan and Tony. We go in Billy's car, a beautiful black Golf GTi. Our Alan loved nice fast cars so we let him drive. He's a good jockey. He was buzzing. We got to London at half past one. I phoned home to see how Annmarie was. I was told she had been taken into hospital about an hour ago but not to worry as it would be hours before the baby came. So it's into the game we go. As usual we are so confident but today just wasn't going to

1964-65 LIVERPOOL SUPPORTERS' CLUB
With me mam (first left, second row holding a fag)
and my dad (second from right, next to Ian St. John).

ROME 1984
(left) with my brother
Alan and John the bookie
(below) - before things
turned nasty - I'm with a
friendly Roma fan.

To Gerry, Best Wishes,
Roy Hodgson

I have welcomed all LFC managers to the club with a silver salver - as Brendan Rogers said, it has cost me a small fortune in the last years but hopefully Brendan will be here for years to come.

RED ALL OVER THE
WORLD
(*from top left*) Me and
Billy Swann in Austria;
Matty the pyjama man;
LFC on tour in Russia;
Me Dad with the cups
at Liverpool Supporters'
Club in 1984;
last but not least - me
kissing Old Big Ears on
the same night.

There's me holding up Aldo in the euphoria after the 1988 semi-final win over Nottingham Forest. One year later we'd be back at the same venue but with very different emotions.

Left: My son Peter, who died during the Hillsborough disaster in 1989.

Below: My Mam, Dad, daughter and I at the memorial service in 1989.

A GREAT DAY
Jerryann's appearance as
LFC mascot back in 1995
saw a 5-0 rout of Leeds.
This remains the only
game my wife Annmarie
has ever been to.

Here's me with some of
the Leros lads - there are
so many LFC fans there
it has been re-christened
Lerospool.

Here's me with various LFC legends (*from top left*) Phil Neal and Joey Jones; 'God' Robbie Fowler; Alan Kennedy and Roy Evans; big Sammi Hyppia; me and Carra; Michael Owen and I aboard the club plane on the way to Košice in 1998 and finally with Stevie G when I was voted Fan of the Year.

I was privileged to help Jan Molby during his testimonial year. (left) there's me with Jan and Mandy Molby; and (below) me and Jan well oiled sat up until the early hours.

Me bearing my Liver bird tattoo during an away trip.

(from left to right) Matt, John Kearns, Philip Olivier's (Tinhead off Brookside) dad, me and Franny who died recently, RIP

I seem to be conducting the homecoming party following our treble win of 2001.

Me and my all-time LFC idol Sir Roger Hunt.

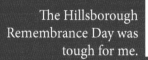

The Hillsborough Remembrance Day was tough for me.

be our day. Before we knew it we were 1-0 down and it could've been more. With ten minutes to go we end up 3-0 down. Fucking gutted. So we decide to get off so we can miss all the traffic. I'm starting to panic a bit over the baby coming. So we pulled up at a phone box (no mobiles back then boys) I was told she was in labour but she would be a good few hours. So we pull up at an off license and get a case of Budweiser, a bottle of Southern Comfort, plus a bottle of Champers to wet the baby's head. Off we got to the M1 at Kilburn. After a good run for about an hour, the traffic started to slow down to a crawl. There had been a bad accident. I think we only travelled eight miles in over an hour. I'm starting to panic. Billy is telling me "For fuck's sake calm down. Annmarie has told you she will wait" but by now I've downed about half a bottle of Southern Comfort and about six cans of Budweiser. Finally the road ahead is clear. We flew home, no more hold ups. We finally arrive at Mill Road Hospital just before ten o'clock. I'm like a cat on a hot tin roof. I get to the waiting room where the nurse says "It shouldn't be long now. She's been in labour for hours". I'm just like any expectant father – pacing up and down. There are another three fellas there just the same as me. When the nurse comes out and says "You have a lovely little boy, Mr Melia" to the guy sitting next to me, he didn't fancy watching it. Then the nurse said that it had been a really hectic day. That was the twelfth baby born there today, and all of them were boys. It's doing my head in all this waiting. Then it came...

The nurse called me into the ward and said "The baby is coming anytime now". So she took me to the bed where Annmarie was, pulled the curtain round us and told me to hold Annmarie's hand. I was shocked. It was just me and this midwife to deliver the baby. I always thought there would be nurses and doctors there. Typical man I suppose. Then within twenty minutes the midwife says to Annmarie "You need to push harder now". Annmarie's grip on me was like a vice. It was killing me but that was fuck all compared to what Annmarie was going through. The midwife says "One more push now. Come on. It's nearly there". I look down in between Annmarie's legs and just seen this big mass of Jet black hair coming out of Annmarie. Then in an instant the baby was in the midwife's arms. It was amazing. The midwife looked at me and said "You have a beautiful little girl Mr. Blayney". Me bird just looked at me and started to cry and said "I'm sorry Gerry. I know you really wanted a boy". I just bent down, crying my eyes out, kissed her forehead and said "Shut up you silly cow. She's gorgeous." It was so emotional. Crying tears of joy. I'm so glad I watched her being born. It was like watching our beloved redmen winning a trophy. It was all that, and much, much more. I was so proud. We named her after both of us. We called her Jerryann. Boy did she get spoilt.

Sadly at this point things start going from bad to worse on the pitch. The opening to the season looked good; winning two, drawing two, but the rot set in. We went seven league games without a win, losing four and drawing three. The league table is horrible to look at – not only are we third from bottom but after eleven league games it's the blue shite at the top. They beat us 1-0 at Anfield, they were just loving it the blue nose twats, taunting us with a chant of "going down, going down, going down". It was so, so hard to take but deep down we all knew it was only a blip. But in the middle of that blip, we also went out of the League Cup in the third round to Tottenham, losing 1-0. I just couldn't believe what was happening to our beloved redmen.

Things soon changed though. We cruised through the early rounds of the European Cup, setting up a Quarter Final date against Austria Vienna. Also we win six, draw two and lose only one of the next nine league games, pushing us right up the league to about sixth place. We were doing OK in the FA Cup, cruising through to the Semi Final to play them horrible bastards from down the East Lancs Rd, Man United. Everything looks back to normal now, thank fuck, so it's off to Austria. I wasn't really expecting much violence, but there was more than enough. There was kick off everywhere. We were outside the ground; Me, Billy Swann and yet again my very good blue nosed mate Ritchie Harrison who was with his mate Jay Daley and another great red Jocky who now runs Anfield FM. I tell you what redmen. Ritchie has seen more Liverpool European away games than most redmen I know. Mind you, he didn't get much chance of going to Europe with the blue shite! Anyway there is about an hour or so to go till kickoff. As we approach the ground there was running battles everywhere so we did an abouter and started making our way back towards our end when about eight of these Austrian skinheads came towards us. There was one big cunt with a bird on his arm and all his cronies giving it the big 'un. We just tried to walk past them but this big cunt was having none of it. He just bumped straight into me and looked at me and said "Do you vont trouble?" I said "Look lad, we are only here to watch the match. We don't want any trouble." They just circled around us with this big gobshite pushing his muscles out and pointing in my face. Then all of a sudden these three or four Austrian bizzies got on to what was happening. They came over and told the skinheads to move on. Thanks copper. Anyway about half an hour later we decide to get a nice beer and a burger or something.

So we're just standing there enjoying our pint and burger when Billy says to me "Is that that big gobshite from before standing over there, just him and his bird?" She looked more like a man. Big tattoos, ring through the lip, you know the type, fucking brain-dead. There's no way she would have got a kiss in a brothel. Anyway I says to Billy and Ritchie "C'mon lads, let's see how hard he is now without his cronies". He was just standing there with his big back to us, his arm round his slag. We moseyed over towards him. He didn't even see it coming. I just tapped him on the shoulder and as he turned around I just fucking butted him bang on the bridge of his nose. Fuck off. He just stood there and then all of a sudden his legs buckled. Delayed reaction I suppose. Then he fell in a heap to the ground. I leaned down to the floor and in to his face and said "YOU VONT TROUBLE? YOU GOT TROUBLE" Me, Ritchie and Billy were pissing ourselves laughing as we walked away, just looking at his slut trying to wake him up. Boy was that some fucking butt. That wasn't the end of the violence I'm sorry to say. Into the game we go. It was very, very hostile. The reds didn't start the game very well and ended up 1-0 down at half time. After a battling second half display, we manage to equalise with about five minutes left, with a goal from Steve Nicol, so we got a 1-1 draw and most importantly, we got the away goal. Happy days.

As usual, we get kept inside the ground for about thirty minutes so that the Austrian Police can clear the skinheads from outside the ground. We finally get out and start to make our way to the train station so we can get back to the airport. Fuck me, it was absolutely mental outside the train station. Running battles everywhere. Police on horses just wading through the crowds. Me and Billy got split up from Ritchie but we both got a few cracks from the Police with batons before we managed to get away from the crowds. Boy were we fucking lucky. This young Austrian guy, about thirty, maybe thirty-five, really helped us out. He saw what was going on and he knew we were only trying to get on the train to get to the airport. So he ushered us away. He was a really, really nice guy. He took me and Billy to his car and said "My father has a bar not far from here. Come with me to the bar, have a few drinks and I will drive you to the airport. I apologise for some of our fans the way they treated you. Some of them are real bastards" He was so apologetic. A really nice man. Anyway he gets us to his father's pub and tells his father what had happened. His father was absolutely disgusted. He said to us "I am so sorry. We have many, many nice people who support our team, but sadly we also have many hooligans". They were such nice people. I think we had about two hours before our flight was leaving when the guy's dad says to us "I am so sorry that these hooligans make your visit a problem. We have a really nice support but sadly this scum appears when a big European team like your world famous Liverpool Football Club comes to our city". I thanked him again, telling him that he and his son had really helped us so much. I says to him "I think we'll get a taxi and just go to the airport now". He said "No way. You will stay here in my pub, have a few nice drinks of Schnapps with me and my son, and then I will drive you to the airport". "Schnapps? What the fuck is that?" I says to Billy. He says "I think it's their local drink". Fuck me, it was one of those ones, down in one. I think I had about three or four. Fuck me my legs really went. I went the colour of boiled shite. I had to sit down. Billy was the same. One of the strongest drinks I've ever had in my life, not like that shite you get today. Anyway after about twenty minutes and a bite to eat it was time to leave and get to the airport to catch our flight home. I really can't thank those people enough. We're soon on the plane and we both slept like babies, all the way home.

The return leg at Anfield was no problem at all. We cruise through to the semi winning 4-1. Next up is the Semi Final of the FA Cup, to be played at that shithole, Goodison Park, home of the blue shite. It was against them horrible bastards from down the East Lancs Road. The atmosphere was absolutely electric before, during, and after the game. We got to the ground about half an hour before the game. Seen a load of the lads from the match and they told us that there had been running battles for about the last hour or so. I didn't want to get involved. I was a bit long in the tooth for all that malarkey. So in we go. I think it was Me, Billy, our Alan, and Tony Swann. It looked like it wasn't going to be our day. 1-0 down at half time and not looking good. The second half was frantic. We had a few really good chances to draw level but time was running out. I must've looked at my watch ten times in the last five minutes. There is now only three minutes left. We are throwing everything at them and then it finally came, in the 88th minute. The little Irish boy Ronnie Whelan popped up to make it 1-1, taking it into extra time. What a time to score. Only three minutes to go. Every Liverpool fan was so confident that United would wilt in extra time. But no, the Manc bastards came right back at us and scored to make it 2-1 to them. I'm fucking gutted, just like all the other redmen at the game. We were all frantically willing them on as the twelfth man was in full force. And just like the end of the first ninety minutes when Ronnie Whelan levelled it up at 1-1, Paul Walsh nudged one in with his knee to make it 2-2 in the 119th minute. The travelling redmen were going mental at the final whistle.

It's down to a replay at Maine Road, four days later. Bring it on.

Every redman was feeling so confident. It was absolute mayhem at Maine Road. Loads and loads of fights all over the place. You had to be on your toes there. So it's in we go. Frantic game with both teams well up for it. Then about five minutes before half time, the excellent Paul McGrath put into his own net. Get in. 1-0 just before half time, we felt really good at the break. Wembley is well within our sights. But sadly it wasn't to be. The Mancs fought back and scored twice to end our FA Cup dream. It took some time to get over that result, but we still had the European Cup Semi Final against Panathinaikos of Greece. And after a brilliant run, winning eight and drawing two out of the last ten games, there was only one game left, away to the blue shite. We lost 1-0, finishing 2nd in the league, who were crowned champions of England. They just kept on winning but we pushed them all the way. That horrible bad start to the season cost us big time. Anyway, back to the first leg of the Semi Final against Panathinaikos at Anfield. We destroyed them 4-0, making the second leg a mere formality, which we won 1-0 thanks to a rare goal from Mark Lawrenson. So it's off to Brussels to face the mighty Juventus of Italy. No one could've imagined the way the day would end.

Everything seemed so special on the way to the game. The day started brilliantly. That special atmosphere that only our beloved redmen can bring was in evidence everywhere. People dancing, singing and really getting into the occasion. There was loads of friendly banter with the Italian fans and the atmosphere was almost perfect. Time was getting near to kickoff so we left the big Square where all the redmen had gathered and made our way up to the ground. We couldn't believe what we could see when we arrived at the ground. It was a shambles. Not fit to host a game of this magnitude, it was more like a Third Division ground. We had decent seats though. We sat next to the Chairman of Burnley Football Club. Then just behind us was Debbie Greenwood, who was Miss Great Britain or something like that. Anyway our Alan was really drunk as he was not used to drinking a lot. He was only about twenty. The ground was filling up. Not long to go before kickoff now. Then it all just happened. The terraces to our right just went mental. Loads of fighting. We watched it all. Some Italian hooligans were kicking fuck out of about six young Liverpool fans, and when I say young I mean around fourteen, fifteen, no older than sixteen. Loads of other Liverpool fans saw what was going on so they all ran over to try and help. And just like the Italian shitbags did in the war, they all turned and run back into their own fans. We all know what happened next but as normal Liverpool fans got the blame. It was horrible. Then the news started spreading all over the ground that loads of Italians had been killed due to a main wall collapsing. People had been crushed to death in a panic. It was like a horrible nightmare, but it wasn't. It was reality. I can't really remember much else to be honest.

The players came out to start the match. I couldn't believe that the game was still going to go ahead. I just put my arms round our Alan and said "This is bad kid. Loads of people are dead. I'll tell you now kid, there is no way on earth that Liverpool will win this game. If we do manage to win, the Italians will riot and there will be many, many more deaths". The only goal of the game was a penalty for Juventus. I'm more or less certain it was Platini who scored it. It was never a penalty in a million years. He was at least four feet outside the box, yet not one Liverpool player contested the referee's decision. I can't remember another thing about the game or the journey home. This tragic event led to all English teams being banned from all European competition for five years. The whole of the country was blaming Liverpool fans.

Any redman who was there knew it wasn't our fault. But what can we do? Fuck all. The ground was unsafe. It was a disaster waiting to happen. And very sadly, on that day it did happen. It changed everything back home in Liverpool, especially the very special relationship between Liverpool and Everton fans. That had all finished now. The Everton fans were going crazy, blaming the Liverpool fans for them not being able to enter the European Cup as champions of England. The special bond which the whole of the world witnessed at Wembley the season before in the League

Cup Final with reds and blues in harmony, that has all gone now, thanks to all the bitter Evertonians. Even to this day they still chant "murderers" to us. The atmosphere at derby games is total hatred now. No more red and blue scarves in harmony. Just hatred. Joe Fagan, our manager, was in bits. It affected him so much that the next day he resigned as manager. He just couldn't carry on. What a horrible, horrible end to the season. So many people lost their lives over a game of football. It's just not right.

KING KENNY

OUR NEW MANAGER was none other than the great Kenny Dalglish. He signed a new contract as Player Manager. Many people in the game seemed to think that it was too demanding for a person of Kenny's age (he was only 34 at the time). Anyway he made one big summer signing in Steve McMahon from Aston Villa. Just like every other redman, I was going to miss travelling abroad for the next five years to watch my beloved redmen in Europe. The season starts and King Kenny got us off to a good start at home to Arsenal, beating them 2-0 thanks to the little Irishman, Ronnie Whelan, and the excellent Steve Nicol. What great players they both turned out to be for our beloved redmen. Both of them went on to play for over ten years for Liverpool, both getting a testimonial for their services. Nearly one thousand games between them. Ronnie Whelan was a very, very underrated player. I don't know why? For me he was an integral part of winning so many trophies for our beloved redmen. Right through the Eighties, scoring vital goals and especially in the League Cup, he scored twice against Tottenham Hotspur at Wembley, helping us to a 3-1 victory and lifting the trophy yet again. And also a much more pleasurable goal, the one he hit the year later against them horrible scum from down the East Lancs Rd, the Mancs. I close my eyes and I can still see it now. Curly Wurly. Whelan had a shot blocked on the edge of the penalty area but it came straight back to him and he just curled it into the top right hand corner. Yet another Wembley winner.

Early that season we went off to St James's Park to play Newcastle United. I like the Geordies. They are really fanatical supporters. Anyway there is me, Our Billy, Our Alan and Tony Swann. For the life of me I don't know how but we got lost. We were about five miles from the ground. It was funny as fuck. We were just pulling up at these traffic lights so I banged the leccy window down and shout to a guy on the inside lane "Ay mate, which way to St James's Park?" He puts his window down and fuck me it was only Terry McDermott, an ex-fabulous Kirkby lad who was absolutely brilliant for our beloved redmen. We all pissed ourselves laughing, Terry as well. I think he said something like "Fuckin' 'ell lads, how many times have you been here and you're getting' lost!" It was so funny but it wasn't as funny on the way home as we got beat 1-0. Anyway, after ten games or so we are doing OK, but them Manc bastards have got off to a flyer, winning most of their games. We drew three and lost two so we were a few points behind. Next up is the League Cup. Back then it was a two legged affair. We get Oldham, first leg at Anfield. We win at a canter, 3-0. Even though we are 3-0 up in the first leg, their home fans were there in their numbers. But thankfully for us it was all in vain. We cruised through the night, winning 5-2 on the night and 8-2 on aggregate. Next up it's Brighton & Hove Albion at Anfield in the third round. No problem whatsoever, winning 4-0.

We get Man United in the fourth round at Anfield. As always the atmosphere was amazing. We just taunted them from the first minute to the last. They were playing really, really well in the league, about seven or eight points clear, but our beloved redmen soon brought them back down to earth. We even let them score first. Half time we were losing 1-0. But then one of my all-time favourite players, Jan Molby, grabbed the game by the scruff of the neck in the second half, scoring twice in two minutes just before the hour mark. Big Jan picked the ball up inside his own half, pushed on to about thirty yards from The Kop goal before unleashing a tremendous shot which flew straight into The Kop net. Get in, 1-1. It was some goal. We didn't even have time to catch our breath when we got a penalty. Big Jan stepped up and made no mistake - 2-1, and that's how it finished. It's always so sweet beating that lot from down the Lancs.

I got to know Jan and his lovely wife Mandy really well. What a name. Mandy Molby! Much more about Jan in the next ten years of this book. What a fabulous player. But he was not only a fabulous player, he was also a fabulous person. I am really so proud to say that he is a really good friend of mine. Without a doubt, an honorary scouser. If you ever meet him you will understand why. Anyway much, much more about Jan later on. Anyway back to that season – every redman is thinking we can kick on in the league now. Fuck me we couldn't have been more wrong, winning only one of our next seven games, drawing four and losing two. Fucking gutted. It wasn't looking very good, with only twelve games to go, I think we were third or fourth, ten points or so off the top. King Kenny had only played around twelve games all season, mostly due to injury. He picked himself to play at Tottenham Hotspur away. What a scary day that was. There was me, our Alan, Billy Swann and yet another blue nose cunt John Smith from the Southend, and a kid named Cossa. Sadly Cossa is dead now following a car crash and John Smith is doing a big jail sentence. If you are reading this John 'Getshmas-Olsen' – May your time pass quickly.

That day stands out because me and Billy had a bit of business to do while we were in London buying a couple of cars so we had a lot of cash on us. We had about £6,000 between us. We get to the ground and park the car, about a five minute walk to White Hart Lane. I didn't really fancy leaving all that money in the car just in case it got robbed – yes, it's not only in Liverpool where cars get robbed! Anyway, off we go to the match with the six grand on us. We get about 500 yards from the ground when all these Tottenham skinheads get on us. We got on our toes, we were well outnumbered. Five of us and about thirty of them. Thank fuck they never got on us further away from the ground, but as it happens the bizzies were there in force for a change so we had a touch and in we go. We're in boss seats above the stand with the travelling redmen. It didn't start very well and we were getting beat at half-time. The second half we were much, much better. My mate Jan Molby made it 1-1 in the sixty sixth minute. Then in the last minute up popped the Welsh Wizard Ian Rush to get the winner. Fucking get in. Made up. There was no time for Tottenham to recover. We are just about to leave when about fifty, maybe more, skinheads just appeared from nowhere. Fuck me, it was mental.

They just charged at us. People running and jumping over seats, all sorts. Cossa jumped about seven rows of seats to get away from them. Somehow we managed to get to the exit. Fuck me imagine if they had of got hold of us. Kicking us all over the place with all the cash going everywhere. It doesn't bear thinking about. Wow I was really relieved to get back to the car. All safe again. Fuck me was that scary. Anyway we do our little bit of business and it's off home.

That win was the start of an unbelievable end to the season. With eleven games to go King Kenny had brought himself back into the team after being out injured for a couple of months. He then played all but one game out of the last twelve. Back to the League Cup. Were through to the Semi Final against Queens Park Rangers, with the away leg first up. So it's off down the motorway again! I've enjoyed going to QPR over the years, especially with the M1 being so close to the ground. We only had to drive up to Kilburn, about fifteen, twenty minutes or so and then straight onto the M1. The game itself wasn't up to much. We end up getting beat 1-0, but we are feeling really confident of turning that round at Anfield with The Kop behind us. But I was wrong. They held us to a 2-2 draw. Unbelievable. Two fucking own goals, both coming from Gary Gillespie (very good player though). Absolutely gutted as we were so near to yet another Wembley visit.

In between the two QPR games we played Southampton away in the league. Me, Billy Swann, Our Alan, Jimmy Allo (the hitch hiker, great redman still to this day) and Tony Swann. We drove down to the game. We won the game 2-1 thanks to goals from Rush and John Wark. Southampton is only about twenty miles away from Bognor Regis where I spent many good summers as I've talked about earlier in the book. So instead of driving home after the game we decided to have a night in Bognor. So after leaving the game we make our way towards Bognor but then I realised most of us had jeans and trainies on. So we decided to stop at this big ASDA and helped ourselves to five pairs of black trousers and about ten pairs of black socks. Anyway we get to Bognor, go and have a nice meal, a nice few bevvies, then about half ten we

decided try to get into a club. There was only really one club in
Bognor. It was the The Pier, right on the waterfront. Before we
went we got changed into our black kecks and two or three of the
lads put a couple of pairs of socks each over their trainees to make
them look like shoes. So as we're going into the club the doorman
stops us and says "Do you know what lads, I'm going to let you
in, just for your cheek. But you're going to have to leave me £50
in this envelope. Don't cause no trouble and you can have it back
on your way out". I think he was a bit wary of us, being scousers.
We had a boss night in the club. The bouncer gave us the envelope
back and we got off to the hotel we were staying in for the night.
Anyway, when we were getting off in the morning I opened the
envelope to get my £50 back. But there was only £30 in it. And
everyone calls scousers robbing bastards!

For a change we'd made a bit of progress in the FA Cup. After
thrashing Norwich City 5-0, we get that scum Chelsea at Stamford
Bridge. Horrible bastards them so called Headhunters. As I've said
earlier on in the book, you have to be very careful there. And you
didn't get much help off the bizzies either. They just didn't want to
know. We beat them 2-1, thanks to a goal from the Welsh Wizard,
Rushy, and a rare Mark Lawrenson goal. Next up is York City away.
They held us to a draw 1-1, and then held to us another draw, 1-1
at Anfield, but our class and fitness finally saw them off, scoring
twice in extra time thanks to John Wark. What a good buy he was.
I think he scored something like twenty-six goals that season. Me
old mate Jan Molby got one from the penalty spot. King Kenny
sealed the victory making it 3-1. Next round is Watford at Anfield.
Boy do we owe them one from 1970 when they knocked us out
of the same competition at the Quarter Final stage. It must've
inspired their players. They held us to a 0-0 draw. I wasn't very
happy, thinking 'Oh no, not history repeating itself again'. It's one
of those games that's imbedded in my brain. I can still see it now. I
was in shock as I was walking out of the game at nineteen years of
age, so as you might imagine, I was a little bit less confident than
normal. That feeling got worse when they held us again in the
replay, 1-1. Nervous a fuck I was going into extra time. But there

was no need to worry as the Welsh Wizard was at it again. We really enjoyed the journey home. I let our Alan drive so I could have a good bevvy on the way home. Happy days.

So it's yet another Semi Final coming up. We get Southampton at a neutral ground, White Hart Lane. We drove down as usual and after a very tense and nervy ninety minutes the game was level at 0-0, so it's into extra time. Then the Welsh Wizard was at it again, scoring twice to send us to Wembley to play the Blueshite from across the park. Wow. Really looking forward to that. Anyway so it's back to the league. There is only six games to go. After winning five and drawing one of the last six games, I think we are only three or four points off the top. Then we thrash Coventry 5-0, then it's down the motorway to that twat of a ground, Luton, with its plastic pitch. Plus they didn't allow away supporters in the ground. Do you think that would stop about sixty or eighty of us redmen getting in? No fucking way. It was hilarious. John Wark gave a few of the lads complimentary tickets. A few jumped the turnstiles but without a doubt the best was a few of the Scotty Road lads saw a couple of people in wheelchairs heading towards an entrance. I remember a Scotty Road kid, Jim Salts, got behind one of the wheelchairs and helped push the lady in. Then as soon as the door was open they were in. All of us! About fifteen or twenty of us dashed straight through before anyone knew what was happening. Absolute class. Where there's a will there's a way! And thanks to a Craig Johnstone goal it was another three points for the reds.

Next up it was West Brom away. Yet another win, 2-1, Rushy and Dalglish. No problems whatsoever in the next game at Anfield. We absolutely destroy Birmingham City 5-0. We've only got two games left to play, both away. First up it's Leicester City, so it's down to Filbert Street to play our bogey team. Everton were also playing away to Oxford. I think they were a point ahead of us at the top of the league. Man United had well blown their chance and fell away so it was just between us and Everton now to see who wins the league. We soon took control at Leicester with the Welsh Wizard Rushy and Ronnie Whelan putting us 2-0 up. Then all of a sudden it came through on the radios that the blue shite were getting beat at Oxford – there were redmen bouncing all over the place. Everton finally lost 2-0, and we win. So it's down to the last game of the season. We've got Chelsea away and if my memory serves me, Everton are playing Birmingham City at Goodison Park. If Liverpool win there is nothing Everton can do about it, so it's off to Chelsea, yet again. The motorways, as always, were just chocka with red and white. I'd just bought myself a beautiful Audi Sport in black. Fast as fuck, seated five, no problems. We get down there and as usual the atmosphere is amazing. You know the one, the one only our beloved LFC can provide. King Kenny grabs the only goal of the game. Me, our Alan, Billy and Tony are bouncing everywhere. What a feeling. As always, what an amazing journey home along the motorways – Champions of England for the sixteenth time. Boy that feels good.

Now just the small matter of another Wembley Cup final where we play the blue shite, who we have just pipped for the league. They wanted revenge. But they never got it. I'm afraid the atmosphere at the game, before, during, and after, was a total contrast to the last time we were at Wembley in 1984. The friendly final that was dubbed but this time all you could feel was hatred. There was loads and loads of fights everywhere. Loads of insults getting lashed about. It just wasn't nice at all. Fuck them, chanting 'murderers' to us. We'll just have to beat them yet again and rub it in more and more. We then let them score first through big ears, Gary Lineker, but as you know, the Welsh Wizard Rushy just loves scoring against the blue shite. He was a total nightmare for them, scoring goal after goal after goal against them. Just as the song goes 'Rush scored one, Rush scored two Rush scored three, and Rush scored four', then 'Nar Nar Nar Nar Nar Nar'. Anyway Rushy nets twice and Craig Johnston scored to make it 3-1. Game Over. King Kenny bags the double in his first year as Player/Manager and I'm looking forward to my usual winnings from the bookies. A nice few bob thanks to my beloved reds.

I was looking forward to a nice summer holiday so come July, we're off to Leros. Me, Annmarie, our daughter Jerryann who was only two then, my youngest brother Ian and his girlfriend. We had a boss two weeks' holiday but it just wasn't long enough. We came home and a week later we flew back again! This time with another of my brothers, our Alan with his girlfriend Joanne. What a fabulous holiday! Two weeks of bliss, thanks to our beloved redmen. My bets on the reds more than covered the holidays. Happy days! We got back to Liverpool on the Wednesday, three days before the season was about to start.

1986-87 did not start that well however. After eleven games, we had won six, lost three and drawn two, then next up is Luton Town away. Then disaster really struck. We drove down, the usual, Billy and Tony Swann, me, our Alan and our Ian. We got absolutely destroyed in the game, 4-1, so we got off with about ten or fifteen minutes to go. We had a nice run all the way home, until we got to Stoke, about fifty miles from Liverpool. All of a sudden I just heard a big bang. We had a blowout. The car just went into a horrible spin across three lanes of the motorway, from the outside lane straight across towards the hard shoulder. How the fuck no other cars got involved in the accident I'll never know. We ended up in a ditch just behind the hard shoulder. Me and our Alan were in the front seats and as the car finally came to a standstill, I turned around to see if the lads in the back were OK.

Fuck me there was no one there. The back window just blew out and Billy, Tony and our Ian had been sucked out. Fuck me, Billy was about sixteen, seventeen stone. Me and Alan scramble out of the car. Billy was about fifteen or twenty yards away sprawled across the hard shoulder, with one arm and leg in the first lane of the motorway. I rushed over to try and drag him back onto the hard shoulder but I knew he was dead straight away. Our Alan shouts over "Is he alright kid?" I shouts to Alan "He's dead lad". Then we see our Ian, he's only sixteen, he's about twenty-five yards away from Billy, also on the hard shoulder. He looked in a really bad way, blood everywhere. He just kept shouting "Help me kid, help me". Then all of a sudden the paramedics were there. Then we see Tony Swann, at least thirty-five yards away in a field. The ambulance rushed them off to Stoke Hospital and a Police car took me and our Alan. Then the Police officer gets a call on his radio, the guy on the other end says "There's two dead and one with multiple injuries". Me and our Alan went to pieces screaming "no, no, no, no, no", then a few seconds later the radio goes again and he says "Sorry about the last call, it's not two dead, it's just one, Billy Swann". Fuck me. Me and our Alan were thanking god that our Ian was still alive. He broke his collarbone and had to have about thirty or forty stitches in various places. Tony Swann's injuries were similar to our Ian's.

We got to the hospital. It's like I'm in a dream. I feel like a zombie. Then I feel our Alan grabbing my arms and saying "Gerry, you'll have to phone our mam and dad, and Billy's mam and dad". But first I phoned one of my other brothers, our Bimbo, who lives in Runcorn. I told him what happened and he left straight away to get to Stoke Hospital. It took him about forty five minutes. It felt like an eternity. Anyway our Bim took complete control when he got there (I love him to bits). I just couldn't think straight. There was no way I could phone my maa or Billy's maa. Our Bim says "Come on, we won't phone, we'll just get home first!" We gets home and me mam and dad just looked at us. We just broke down and I said "Billy's dead maa". She just collapsed in a heap but me dad caught her. She just kept saying "Oh Gerry, Oh Gerry". Then she says "Gerry, you will have to go and see Billy's mam and dad." I was still like a zombie, crying like a baby, saying "I can't maa. I can't". Then our Bim said "Come on kid, I'll come with you".

Billy's mam and dad only lived a couple of minutes away from our house. We got outside the house and I just froze. "I can't do it kid, I'm in bits". Our Bim says "Come on Gerry, it's got to be done. Try and be strong kid". It was without a doubt the worst moment of my life. I can't even remember what was said. The build up to the funeral was really hard. Billy's mam wanted to get Billy buried but me and Billy, as best mates, and also as he was godfather to my beautiful daughter Jerryann, we had a pact. If one of us happened to die, the other would get his ashes buried behind The Kop goal at Anfield. I just said to his mother "It's up to you Kitty". The she said "If that's what Billy wanted then so be it". It was a beautiful funeral, there were loads and loads of redmen paying their respects. And as I promised to Billy, I got his ashes buried behind The Kop goal. King Kenny dug the little hole for him. It was so emotional. I really did love Billy. We were really close. He was godfather to my daughter Jerryann.

It was a bad season all over really. We finished second in the league, behind Everton, and got beat in the League Cup final by Arsenal. For us redmen, not only did we lose the game, the brilliant Ian Rush lost his record of never losing a game that he had scored in. Rush does his job and scores but we end up getting beat 2-1. Boy have they been a thorn in our side over the last fifty odd years or so. Firstly, they beat us in the FA Cup final in 1950, again in 1971, and at Anfield in 1989, and so on. But I have a great respect for the Gunners. A very well run club. Thirteen or fourteen titles mean respect. So it's a very rare season for us. No trophy in the cabinet. Dalglish had pinpointed our problems however and made some magnificent signings in Ray Houghton and the brilliant Peter Beardsley in the summer of 1987 – what a player Beardo was, simply a joy to watch, he had great vision.

Then we come to one of the greatest ever signings for our beloved Liverpool. Wow. The magnificent Johnny Barnes. He simply was the player of the decade. He came to the reds from Watford. If my memory serve me well it was for £900,000, nearly a million. Big money at that time for a young starlet. With him being a Jamaican, that didn't really go for him at first, but he didn't let it affect his game. He just tormented full backs to death, he really was that good. He had absolutely everything; pace, power, vision, a great shot etc. He scored loads of goals and created loads of goals as well. I remember his first season. Them horrible bastards from across the park started throwing bananas at him while he was trying to take a corner. It just made him stronger and stronger. The Evertonians, they like to think of themselves as 'The Peoples Club'. Peoples' club my ass. More like the racist club. Fuck them. Also the great John Aldridge, another good mate of mine, had signed late on the season before. What a treat we had in store…

The new players gelled instantly. They were simply a joy to watch. Pass and move. We were just like Brazil. We just blew everyone away, winning twenty-two and drawing seven of the first twenty nine league games. Then it came to an end at, of all places, Goodison Park. Everton winning 1-0, but it made no odds. We won the league in style, losing only one more game, away to Nottingham Forest 2-1. Champions yet again. Get in there. We get to the FA Cup final to play Wimbledon. Yes, Wimbledon. They had risen from the Fourth Division to the First Division in three years. Every redman was convinced that there was no way that a long ball bullying team could beat us at Wembley. We were odds on favourites to win. The odds were 1/2. I had £5,000 on that. It was a losing bet. The referee had a lot to do with it mind you. He made a terrible decision in disallowing a goal from the brilliant Beardsley when it was still 0-0 but that's football. I did manage to pull me dough back in the Charity Shield. I had £7,000 on Liverpool at odds of 4/7. Still a grand down on the two games but that's OK. I had £5,000 for our beloved redmen to win the league at a beautiful price of 5/2. Happy days! Apart from missing my old mate Billy Swann. I made myself a promise that any great player Billy saw and who went on to get a testimonial game, playing ten years or more, would be presented with a silver salver from me and Billy: Molby, Nicol, Whelan, Rush, Dalglish and Hansen all got a salver from me. On Jan Molby's salver it read 'Thanks to our Great Dane for a glorious ten years, from Gerry Blayney and Billy Swann (deceased)'. What a player and what a man Molby is! I know he treasures my gift. I was still trying to take it all in that me old mate Billy had gone. What could I do? We all have things happening in our lives but it was just so hard to adjust to this situation.

★

After we got home from our annual holiday Ann-Marie found out she was pregnant, we were over the moon - good news at last! But sadly after seven months Ann-Marie was rushed into hospital. She had haemorrhaged and lost six pints of blood. The paramedic said "I'm trying to save her life and the baby's". I went numb I couldn't believe what was happening, she had to have an emergency Caesarean and a blood transfusion. Our beautiful little daughter had to go into an incubator, two months premature and only weighed 3 lb 2 oz. She was so tiny and see through, she looked like a baby chicken. They said the next 48 hours were crucial for her to survive. The surgeon said he needed to talk to me but needed to return to another emergency in the theatre, all kinds was going through my head. All I could think about was what will I do without them and whens my luck going to change. Finally after waiting nine hours for the surgeon to come back (felt more like nine days), he said "your wife and your baby are so lucky to be alive". I just broke down and cried, looking at our little girl in the incubator with and wires and tubes sticking out of her she looked so tiny and struggling to breathe. I felt so helpless. Then the nurse came up and said "have you decided on her name yet?" I said no, as Ann-Marie was still unconscious and didn't know what had happened. The last thing she remembered was going into the ambulance. The nurse told me "you should call her Lucky, she is so lucky to had made it through". The nurse took a polaroid photo of the baby and said I'll take it you to your wife.

Ann-Marie had just come to, we showed her the photo and the first thing she said was " she looks like a little bird that has just fell out of the nest, she's so tiny and you can see through her skin". We called her Toni-Marie after her granddad. Over the next couple of days I must have prayed every hour – God please let her survive and get stronger. All I wanted to do was give her a big cuddle and tell her everything was going to be ok but I couldn't, I could only put my hand through the hole in the side of the incubator and stroke her tiny fingers. Our prayers were answered, she got stronger and stronger. Ann-Marie got better and was allowed home but we had to leave Toni at the hospital. We went to see her everyday and finally after about three months we could finally bring her home as she now weighed 5 lb and she finally got to meet her big sister Jerryann. Happy days thank god.

By now I really thought I had accepted the nightmare of losing Billy, but I could never in a million years predict what would happen the next season. I told you earlier in the book that I had a son, Peter Andrew Harrison. I was only twenty-two when he was born and mother and I didn't really love each other so we had decided that we wouldn't see each other anymore, but Pat, Peter's mum said "I won't stop you seeing him", so every Sunday she would bring Peter to me maa's. Me maa loved him. I'd throw Pat a few bob whenever I could and me maa used to spoil him rotten. When he got to about seven, his mum fell in love with a really nice guy. So I sat Peter down and tried to explain to him that I wouldn't see him as much in the future as I did now. I just remember saying to him "You are a very lucky boy Peter. You have got two dads now. You won't see me so much now, but don't ever forget that I'm your dad and I'll be there if you ever need anything". So I didn't see him much over the next five or six years.

Then one nice summer's day I'm having a pint at the Bow and Arrow pub in Huyton, sitting outside. Then I notice this kid standing about twenty yards away from me just staring at me. I knew it was Peter. Boy had he grown. Nearly six foot. He'd be fourteen now so I shouts over to him "Ay kid, come here". He comes over and I says "Do you know who I am?" He says "Yes, you're Gerry Blayney" I said "Yes, but who am I?" He says "You're my dad" It was so weird. I said "Come on, I'll take you round to your mums and ask her if I can start taking you to see the reds with me". Pat says "You can take him to some of the away games as his step dad has been taking him to Anfield for the last three seasons or so?" I was made up. At the time I owned a joinery business in Liverpool town centre which my brother Alan managed for me. Plus my brother Ian worked there as well. Peter went to the same school as Ian and Alan so he was made up when I got him a part time job with his two uncles. He was the ringer of me: tall, dark and very handsome but he was very different in other ways. He was a bit shy. Not like his dad. Anyway, he was loving coming to the

away games with his dad and his uncles. I remember taking him to
Millwall. I don't think he spoke a word the whole journey, unlike
his dad "blah, blah, blah".

Anyway the season was looking very good. Top of the league
and in the Semi Final of the FA Cup against Nottingham Forest at
Hillsborough, Sheffield. So it's off to the game. Me, our Alan, our
Ian and Peter. He's fifteen now, nearly sixteen. We get down there
and it's buzzing outside. So Peter says to me "Dad, there's a couple
of my mates over there so I'll get in with them now." I had a seat
for him with us but he said he didn't really like sitting down and he
wanted to go with his mates. "You don't mind do you dad?" I said
"Of course not lad, if that's what you want." I sold the spare ticket
no problem. I said "You know where the car is so get back as soon
as you can after the final whistle." So in we go. Me, our Alan and
our Ian. Peter gets in the queue for the Leppings Lane end. We all
know what happened next. Me, Alan and Ian get back to the car
but Peter wasn't there. After ten or fifteen minutes we started to
fear the worst. The number of dead was just going up and up. Oh
my god what could I do! I knew he wasn't coming back. I could
feel it. I knew my mam and dad, plus Peter's mam and step dad
would be really worried as the news came in. We eventually find a
phone and phone home to me mam and dad. Without a doubt it
was the worst phone call I have ever had to make in my life.

I can't really remember much of what happened in the next
few months, I was in a daze. Peter's mother was in bits. At first she
blamed me saying I took him and never brought him back. It was
so hard to take. I couldn't sleep, I couldn't eat. All I did was cry,
drink and take loads of drugs, mostly cocaine. It nearly killed me.
I know I was having a breakdown but I didn't care. All my family
were very concerned and I think that without my brothers, Bimbo,
Billy, Alan and Ian, I would never have got through this nightmare.
I didn't think that I would ever go to another match after this
disaster. But I just thought to myself "Would Peter want me to stop
going to the games?" I just knew in my heart that Peter would
want me to carry on watching our beloved redmen. If I remember
rightly I went the next thirteen seasons, only missing a handful of

European away games – all the Spanish games mostly. I didn't miss a game in England – league, FA Cup, League Cup. I'm very, very proud of that.

★

The semi-final replay against Nottingham Forest was at Old Trafford. As always the atmosphere was amazing although there was a strange feeling which I can't really put into words. We made no mistake, winning our way through to a date at Wembley, once again against the blue shite from across the park, thanks to two goals from John Aldridge and an own goal by Laws of Forest. We won the game 3-1. So it's off to Wembley yet again. What a glorious day it turned out to be. Thanks to two goals from the Welsh Wizard Rushy and one from John Aldridge we win 3-2. It was a brilliant trip home down the M1 and the M6 with the usual mayhem – horns beeping, scarves out of windows, red men everywhere going mental. Nothing on earth compares to watching our beloved redmen! Once again I would like to thank each and every one of you for helping me get through Hillsborough. I can't thank my fellow redmen enough. Without a doubt, the greatest football fans in the world. Their passion, their wit, their appreciation for their football, their sportsmanship, are all known worldwide. There is nowhere in the whole world with an atmosphere like at Anfield in a big European Cup game.

Because of the disaster there were two games in the league left to play, both at Anfield. We destroy West Ham United 5-1 but they scored a late consolation goal which ended up costing us. Arsenal also won which meant that the title came down to the last game of the season. Liverpool vs Arsenal at Anfield. Our beloved redmen are three points clear with a two goal better goal average, meaning Arsenal needed to win by two clear goals. The games and the Hillsborough Disaster caught up with us. It was heartbreaking to see the team run themselves to the ground. If memory serves me right, we played five games in nine days. We ended up losing the game 2-0. The winning goal was scored with only seconds to go. The final kick of the game. I was devastated. Stood in shock. I remember saying to the lad next to me "This is it lad, there is only thirty seconds to go" and the ball is still in their half. One last big hoof up from their centre half. Nicol went into a challenge but the ball bounced off his thigh and so fucking lucky, it ran through for Michael Thomas to net the winner, it was basically the last kick of the season. We kicked off and the ref blew straight away. That result also cost me £12,500. I had a £1,000 double on Liverpool to win the League title at 6/4 and I had 4-1 for the FA Cup. But thankfully, I also had £1,000 single on the FA Cup at 4-1, so as usual it was a profitable year backing my beloved redmen. Season over.

As usual it was back to Leros that summer for a nice relaxing holiday with my family. Took a load of scarves over to the island to give out to all the young lads. Boy did they love me over there. Before you know it were back home and here we go again. The last season of the eighties is upon us. In 1989-90 we won the title again, just like we did ten years before, in 1980. Wow what a decade, winning seven League titles, three League Cups, two FA Cups and two glorious European Cups, as well as two European Super Cups and eight Charity Shields. So it's into the nineties we go. But sadly the times are starting to change for us. Nowhere near as glorious as the eighties. Our European ban is nearly over but sadly it makes no difference to us because we are having a really bad time and did not even qualify for the UEFA Cup. I was just not used to this lark. I don't like it at all. But what could we do? As our anthem says "Through the wind, and through the rain". We will make sure that the team will never ever walk alone.

Nevertheless in 1989-90 our beloved redmen were simply a joy to watch. Dalglish had created one of Liverpool's greatest ever sides. It was a shame he never got to test himself against the European teams but the ban ruled that out. The magnificent Johnny Barnes, Peter Beardsley, Ray Houghton, the big Dane Jan Molby, Rush and Aldridge, and in my opinion, the most underrated Liverpool player ever, Ronnie Whelan. He was such an integral part of the brilliant side of the eighties. Ten years plus he done, and boy did he love scoring goals. So it's into the nineties we go. The summer break was so different to all the other summer breaks in the past. Everyone was still in a state of shock. But as the saying goes, life goes on. We got off to a decent start, winning four and drawing four out of the first eight games. A couple of games stood out. A 3-1 win away at Everton. The brilliant Johnny Barnes bagged one and, as usual, the Welsh Dragon Ian Rush bags two more against the blueshite. Another game was Crystal Palace at home. We absolutely destroyed them., 9-0. Yes, nine-nil! Eight different players scored and believe me it could've been 15. We really were that good. What a team Dalglish had put together. Then came our first defeat of the season with a shock 4-1 result at Southampton. Then we beat Tottenham 1-0 at Anfield. Two defeats on the run after that, one at Anfield, 1-0 to Coventry, and the other was 3-2 away at Queens Park Rangers, but we soon put that right. We lost only two of the next sixteen games which pushed us right back into the title race with only seven games to go. Dalglish decided to play a new signing, Ronny Rosenthal, from Israel. He was a sensation. He scored seven goals in the last seven games including a hat-trick in a 4-0 away victory at Charlton Athletic. In the end it was more than enough to win us our eighteenth league title. The team was truly a joy to watch. I never missed a game all season. To be totally honest, I can't remember most of the games. Most of them are all a blur. All I know is that the support I got from our massive family helped me to survive the aftermath of Hillsborough. So I would like to thank each and every one of you from the bottom of my heart. You'll never walk alone.

That pre-season everything with the side seemed perfect and what a start we got off to as well in 1990-91 - winning twelve and drawing two of the first fourteen league games. Then came our first defeat - we got absolutely destroyed away to Arsenal, 3-0. Then it was up and down in the league after that, but with nine games left of the season we were still in touch, I think only two or three points off the top. Then it was the fifth round of the FA Cup against Everton. We had beaten them the week before in the league 3-1. Big Jan Molby scored one and two goals from what turned out to be Kenny's last signing, David Speedie. They held us to a 0-0 draw taking us back to Goodison Park for a replay.

That night I witnessed the most incredible derby game in my life, and boy have I seen some. It finished 4-4, after we'd led on four occasions. Everton just kept pulling it back. So it meant the referee had to toss a coin to decide where the second replay would be, Anfield or Goodison. Everton won the toss so it's back to that shithole Goodison Park. It was not a good night at all. We lost 1-0. But that was nothing compared to what was going to happen in the next day or two. King Kenny had had enough and resigned. The aftermath of Hillsborough, going to all 96 funerals, had finally taken its toll on Kenny. I totally understood his actions. I felt so much for Kenny and his beautiful family. Kenny was quite similar to the Shanks in many ways. But what could we do?

SOUNESS - WHAT A MISTAKE!

OOT ROOM STALWART RONNIE MORAN took over as caretaker manager for just over two months. Then the Liverpool board announced that Graeme Souness had been named as the new manager with five or six league games to go. The appointment of Souness was greeted with universal approval from every red fan. As a player he was a living legend with Liverpool supporters. Simply world class as a player, awesome power with skill and a very, very clever player, he was an absolute joy to watch. He went on to play over three hundred and fifty games for the reds before a move to Serie A, Sampdoria, where he was a big success. Then he went to Rangers and he transformed them to nearly a decade of dominance, as a player and a manager, over their deadly rivals Celtic, who were ruling the roost at the time. So every single redman, just like myself, was made up. He breezed into Anfield with his usual arrogance, the same arrogance he took to the pitch for our beloved redmen.

He was so committed and so confident but in the end it became his downfall. He told everyone he was going to get Liverpool back to where they belong, but insisted he would do it his way. Firstly, he insisted that Liverpool appoint his Rangers colleague Phil Boersma (ex-redman) as his assistant. Despite the unbelievable knowledge of the boot room at hand he refused. He wanted to do it his way. Big, big mistake. Then he changed the players' diets. Spaghetti this, spaghetti that, plus training techniques. But the treatment of some of the older players caused unrest in the dressing room and also on the Kop. For some unknown reason he put the brilliant Peter Beardsley, Steve McMahon, Ray Houghton and Steve Staunton on the transfer list. It made no sense. These players had plenty of years left in the locker, but no, he had made his mind up and he was doing it his way. Where the fuck was his head selling Beardsley?

I'll never understand that one. (Maybe Beardsley was shagging his bird, 'cause Beardsley is so handsome.) Anyway, his first full season in charge was a disaster. After selling quality he signed the likes of Dean Saunders, Mark Walters (who thought he was Ronaldo), Isvan Kozmar (who the fuck was he?), and Michael Thomas from Arsenal. Yes, the same player who snatched the title away from us two seasons before. The injuries we were getting were unbelievable. The likes of Barnes, Rush, Molby, all out through the change in training.

'If it ain't broke, don't try and fix it' had always been a Liverpool motto. Souness made far too many changes early on. No wonder we only finished sixth in his first full season, our worst finish for twenty-seven years. We won only sixteen out of the forty two league games scoring a measly forty-seven goals. It just wasn't good enough. For the first time in a long time I was not looking forward to the new season, especially after hearing of the new signing, Paul fuckin Stewart for £2.5million. He was a joke. A laughing stock. But at least Souness won us the FA Cup at Wembley against Sunderland. But there were big, big problems ahead for Souness. Just after the semi-final win against Portsmouth, it went to a replay and Liverpool won on penalties. The next day Souness announced that he needed an emergency by-pass operation. Happily the operation was a complete success and Souness, flanked by his doctors, even managed to walk on to the Wembley pitch as Ronnie Moran led the players out. It was less than a month after his operation and thanks to the Welsh Wizard Rushy, and of all people Michael Thomas, we comfortably won 2-0. We drove down to Wembley, me, our Alan, Tony Swann and I'm not sure but it could've been Jimmy Allo (the hitch hiker). If I remember rightly we were about thirty or forty miles away from London, doing about seventy miles an hour in the middle lane in my lovely red Audi Quattro, registration number LFC 932, when all of a sudden there was a big bang from underneath the car. The steering just went tight. Fuck me, the back axel hand gone. We were so, so lucky getting it across to the hard shoulder. I was fucking gutted. I had bought it about eight months ago for £8,500 and it'd had been nothing but trouble ever since, it was never out of the garage. Anyway we got it onto the hard shoulder and luckily enough a couple of cars pulled over, friends of ours. For the life of me I can't remember who it was now. So me and our Alan went in one car and the other two in the other. I just put a note in the window of the Audi. 'Gone to Wembley to watch our beloved redmen'.

It was fucking funny thinking back to it, but it wasn't funny when it happened. It was fucking horrible. It brought back so many bad memories. The season was our first season back in Europe. Boy it took a long time coming, but sadly it didn't take long for us to get knocked out. We played Auxerre of France. I had a couple of young lads, about nineteen, twenty, from Leros with me. Takis and Lefteris (Terry in English). They were staying with me and my family for a month or so. I took them to Auxerre and I also took them to Norwich away in the league. We went on the train and it was an absolutely brilliant trip down there. Lefteris was a really good looking young boy, spoke absolutely perfect English, whereas Takis was a decent looking guy and spoke about as much English as I do Greek. Not a lot, but enough to get by. Anyway we were on the train. It was fucking chocka. All the usual suspects on the train. Loads of me mates. So I introduced them to all the lads. Then I says to them all "Look, the boys want to become Liverpool fans, is that Ok lads?" They all shout "Yeah, of course. But they will have to do the initiation". So I looks at Lefteris and Takis and says "Do you understand?" Takis didn't have a clue what had just been said so I looks at Teri and says "Do you understand the word initiation?" He says "Of course. What do we need to do?" I looked at him and smiled and I'm sure he already knew what I was going to say. "Drop your trousers and show the lads your cock." He just looked at me and said "Do I have to Gerry?" I says "Yes, if you want to be a redman". He says "Ok" and drops his kecks. Fuck me you should have heard the gasps coming from the lads' mouths. I'm sure you could stand about nine budgies on it! The last budgie might only be on one leg. As for Takis, who could follow that? So we didn't embarrass him.

They didn't want to go back to Greece. They had fallen in love with Liverpool. Me and the other bird in my life, Annmarie, took them to a big all night rave in Blackburn. It was the height of the ecstasy boom. Everyone just seemed to be on them. Anyway we get to just outside Blackburn, the bizzies were everywhere, blocking all the roads off as there was convoys of cars coming in from all directions. The bizzies were going fucking nuts. Three police cars pushed us into a side street, jumping out of the cars waving batons everywhere. They just surrounded the car, smashing at it with the batons. It was frightening. We just managed to speed away from them. Takis actually pissed himself with fright as the bizzies were smashing against the window. Anyway back to the redmen. I took Lefteris and Takis down to watch them horrible bastards from down the East Lancs, Man United. They were amazed. They just couldn't believe the passion of our travelling redmen. Both of the boys own a little bar in Leros, my little Island. And still to this day there is a Liverpool scarf proudly on display above the bar, along with photos of past great players. I took them to a big reunion dinner for the 1981 European Cup winning team. I got them photos with all the players. Then they flew home the next day, back to Greece. They were the talk of the island for many months after that. They had the time of their lives with all the past legends of our beloved Liverpool Football Club.

Anyway, back to Auxerre. What a miserable night, losing 2-0, so it left us a lot to do back at Anfield, but it was another of those magnificent European nights at Anfield. We won 3-0 on the night, enough to take us through to the next round. In the next round we get knocked out by Genoa of Italy, losing 2-0 away, then 2-1 at Anfield, making them only the fourth team to beat us at Anfield in Europe in twenty-five years. By then I couldn't wait for the season to end, I wasn't happy at all. Everyone was stunned with what had gone on, but it got no better. Worse in fact.

The next season 1992-93, was worse than Souness's first. Every redman I knew felt exactly the same as me, we were devastated. We all knew it was only a matter of time before he got sacked, but we were all concerned with the long term damage he may have caused. But Liverpool Football Club are not a club that sacks the manager after a couple of bad years so he was given another season to prove himself. Souness was even more out of favour after he sold a story to that horrible, horrible newspaper The Sun. All our redmen supporters never forgave him for that. Even though he donated the fee to Alder Hey hospital, it wasn't enough for me, or any other proper redman. But David Moores gave him his last chance. He didn't take it. He just had to do it as he put it, 'his way'. Things just got worse and worse with Souness. The board brought in Roy Evans to be his assistant manager but Souness still did it his way and brought in more bad signings. Torben Piechnik, fucking joke, Neil Ruddock, not bad, and Julian Dicks. What the fuck was he doing? But for me the signing of calamity James from Watford was the worst of all. I think he cost us at least one title with all his errors. But Souness' sacking was only just around the corner. We go out of the Coca-Cola Cup against Wimbledon on penalties, then the final straw came when after holding Bristol 1-1 away, the replay at Anfield was a shocker. We lost 1-0. It was such a horrible feeling walking out of Anfield that night but at least it had to be over for Souness now. And thankfully it was. Five days later he was sacked. Probably the worst three seasons of my life watching our beloved redmen.

ROY EVANS - CLOSE BUT NO CIGAR

ROY EVANS WAS SOUNESS' SUCCESSOR - he had so many players out injured it was untrue, due to the new training methods. Roy had about nine league games to go. We finally finish eighth. Yes, eighth. Fuck me. Roy has got one hell of a job to do after the mess Souness had left us in but he got the reds back playing some beautiful football with McManaman, Fowler, Redknapp and my mate Jan Molby. Jan had lost a lot of weight and got us flowing again with his sublime passing ability. Then there was the slimline Johnny Barnes - what a player! He dropped back into midfield. It was just a delight to watch these redmen playing the Liverpool way. Us redmen are not soft. We knew it would take time to address the mess that Souness left. Roy Evans was delighted to get the manager's job. He said "The pride I feel is almost indescribable. As a Liverpool lad I stood on The Kop so I understand the expectations of our supporters".

That said, The Kop was no more after the all-seater stadiums rule came into force following the Hillsborough disaster. Roy assembled the back room team and steeped it in Liverpool tradition. Bringing in Doug Livermore, who had played under the great Shanks, Ronnie Moran with his unrivalled experience and Sammy Lee from Fagan's treble winners. Steve Heighway was grooming a succession of youngsters for the first team. His kids were really looking good. McManaman was a very similar player to Heighway. Then there was God - Robbie Fowler. The whole of the league's teams were happy to see the back of Ian Rush but fuck me, in my opinion, and many others, this kid was as good, if not better than the brilliant Rushy. He just scored goals for fun. He also had that scouse swagger that I love. Rushy was getting older and coming to the end of his career. Every redman was gutted but as always Liverpool Football Club had replaced one legend for another.

For some reason or another Rushy just couldn't score against the shite from down the East Lancs, but thankfully Robbie Fowler just loved scoring against them. In his first three seasons against them he scored five times. Yessssss. We won it five times. Robbie was an instant hit with The Kop and the rest of the Liverpool fans, scoring seventeen goals in just under half a season. He scored all five goals in a 5-0 win against Fulham at Anfield. The Toxteth Terror had made his mark. Fowler was the new kid on the block now and with him being one of us, it made it all that sweeter.

Roy Evans did a brilliant job with the mess he had been left. We finished a respectable fourth in the league, getting to the quarter-final of the FA Cup and winning the Coca Cola Cup against Bolton Wanderers. Another trophy in that famous cabinet. McManaman was awesome that day at Wembley, putting in a master class of wing play. He grabbed both goals in a 2-1 victory. Things were looking up after three years of hell. Every redman was really looking forward to the new season. Not like the last two. Evans made a big signing, smashing the British transfer record bringing in Stan Collymore for £8.5million from Nottingham Forest, after he scored over forty goals in sixty games for Forest. He made his debut for us against Sheffield United at Anfield. He was an instant hit with the Kop, scoring the only goal of the game with an absolutely beautiful shot into the top corner. Then he hits a screamer at Blackburn Rovers in a 3-0 win. But not to be outdone, Robbie Fowler went out and scored four against Bolton Wanderers in a 5-2 win at Anfield. Things are looking really good. Such a change from them horrible few seasons.

I'd been going to the away games on the train the last couple of seasons. That's when I met Matt, Gary and all the boys - some great redmen. But it was through a massive friend of mine, H (Harold Hughes) fuck me what a handsome bastard, better looking than Joe Morley. H was the ringer of Paul Newman, the movie star. I first met H in a casino, Soames, at the side of the famous Grafton ballrooms. We just clicked instantly. Two jack the lads started a beautiful relationship. I can honestly say I love H and I know he loves me. If I was queer I would fucking bang him everywhere, but I'm not so tough H! Anyway H's dad was a legend in amateur football. Canada Dock was his team. He was a no-nonsense centre forward. Hard as nails but a fucking lovely man. A proper scouser. You're really going to enjoy this true story redmen. We've all heard of the Kray twins, Ronnie and Reggie. Well back in the early sixties, these pair of fruits and their cronies arrived at Lime Street Station on the train. H's dad was well known in town. He worked some of the night clubs. The Krays sorted a meet out with Big H but they weren't very happy with the outcome. Who the fuck do this pair of queers think they were, coming to our city and demanding a piece of the pie? As you can imagine, they were told in a certain manner "Fuck off". They got a good beating and they were dropped off at Lime Street for the next train to London. They never came back. That's a true story that. Who the fuck did they think they were? The morale of the story is... do not fuck with scousers or we will fuck with you.

As I was saying, I had been going on the train for a couple of seasons. It was as if I hadn't been away as the card schools were very, very fruitful. I can't really remember which game it was but I won nearly £3,000. Most of that was off one fella, Eddie London. He's dead now. He was absolutely gutted. I just fucking loved it. But it didn't last long as my reputation had gone before me. It was hard getting a decent game on – it was all very low key, with £1 maximum bets so it was difficult to win any major dough. But the journeys were boss. All me new mates, H, Matt, Gary, Jersy (John Calvert), Ted, Robbie, Mick, the list goes on and on. A lot of them were bringing their kids with them. All from the age of about five or six I would say. Fuck me there was some fun on the train with the kids. There was about eight or ten of them. Typical scouse kids. Throwing nuts, sweets, all sorts. You know the stuff. Loads of little play fights with each other. Mayhem basically. Then you would hear something like "dad, dad, he's just hit me". Then it's threats everywhere from the dads. "You're not going to the next away game". Then the silence from the kids. Then one of the kids said "If I'm good for the rest of the journey dad can I come to the next away game?" It was so funny. Most of them young lads are working now, still going all the games. I even have a bevvy with them now. The next twenty years or so, most of them will have travelled all over Europe. When I was a kid, the furthest I got was probably Villa Park or somewhere like that. I didn't even have a passport.

Anyway, every redman was looking forward to the season starting. The arrival of Stan Collymore was mouth-watering. Him and Fowler had everyone buzzing. Roy Evans had got the team playing like teams of old. Mean at the back and lethal up front. After about eight games it was down the East Lancs to play that shite Manure. Fowler had dyed his hair bright blonde. Boy did he get some stick. There had been building work going on at Old Trafford to make it bigger. It was also the return of that overrated French twat Eric Cantona, after his big ban had finished for kung-fu kicking a fan for giving him stick. Cantona literally flew into the crowd feet first. Fucking lunatic. He was a good player but he was no Dalglish, Pele, Maradona or Messi but he really thought he was the bollocks with that French swagger. Liverpool Football Club had absolutely no allocation for the game, but there were about fifty of us who managed to get tickets. We had to pay £100 a ticket. At the time the face value was about £15. It was more than worth it. We get into Old Trafford, me and all the lads, the usual crowd. There is about fifteen or twenty of us standing, chatting, and waiting for the players to come out. Out of nowhere came this beaut Manure fan, he had a black eye, obviously he had been fighting earlier. He just came up to us and got right in my face and stated giving it the 'Ooh Aah Cantona'. I just shoved him away and said "Fuck off Manc". He just looked at me and said "Me and you now you scouse twat". All the other lads were shouting "Do one Manc" but he wouldn't have it. So I just looked at him and said "Do one divvy, there's bizzies everywhere you idiot". He just looked at me and said "There's none in the toilet". I had had enough. "Let's go" I said. "I'll follow you down". So about thirty seconds later I follows him down. There was just one steward about thirty yards away from us. I just got to the bottom of the steps when the Manc come flying out of the toilet, digs flying everywhere. He missed me by a mile. I got one good dig in, then the next thing I know my arms are right up my back - two bizzies. And also two bizzies grabbed the Manc. "Fuck me, I'm in trouble here" I'm thinking, but as they marched us away. This Manc steward came running over and said to the bizzies "Ay lads, it's nothing to do with the Liverpool fan. I saw what happened. As the scouser walked into the toilet, the Man United fan just attacked him". They lashed the Manc out and let me go back to my seat. Fuck me what a touch, thanks to the very nice steward. Back to the game. Robbie Fowler was on fucking fire, with two absolutely stunning goals. I'm just re-running it in my head now like a video. A long ball through to Fowler, running alongside that thing Gary Neville, Robbie just brushed him off with a shoulder barge, sending him to the floor. Schmeichel came out and Robbie chips the world class goalkeeper making him look like a rookie. The second goal was simply a missile. Fuck me, I've seen some great strikes of a football but that will take some beating. He got the ball wide left and just let rip. It just flew in. I don't think Schmeichel even saw it. But there's always a fucking 'but' with Man United and referees. We outplayed them all afternoon, but a dubious penalty robs us of all three points. We had to settle for a 2-2 draw. That ref, I can't really remember who it was now, but it could've been any one of about ten refs. Fact. It just had to be Cantona grabbing the headlines. Fowler was magnificent that day, just like he was in the return at Anfield a week before Christmas. It was a brilliant Christmas present, especially for me as I'd had a nice bet on Fowler to score the first goal at 4/1. He duly obliged. 1-0. Half time. So I see my bookie at half time. I said "Do you want to do me a bet on Fowler next goal?" "How much do you want on it Gerry?" he says. I says "A grand". He said "I won't be able to lay it all off. I'll do you another £500 at 4/1". Robbie does the business again. £4,000 up on the day and the game finishes 2-0. That'll do me. Mind you, Matt has got more than his own back over the years, he's a very, very shrewd man.

The highlight of the season for me was without a doubt Jan Molby's testimonial game against PSV Eindhoven. I was really privileged to be named as assistant manager for the celebrity match which took place before the main game. I got to know Jan and his beautiful wife Mandy. It was amazing. I don't think I had ever been more excited in my whole life, even when watching any of the big European Cup final wins. It was just unbelievable. As I said the main game of the night was against PSV, with the celebrity game about an hour before it. It was an Everton XI against a Liverpool XI. I was so excited but also so nervous. Here's me sat in the Liverpool dugout, just where the great man Shanks sat, but about ten minutes before kickoff I am in the Liverpool changing room when in walked Derek Hatton, the so called politician. He just looked straight at me and said "Gerry, the blues are a man short for the game. Do you fancy playing centre half?" My answer was something like "Get to fuck you blue nosed cunt!"

Elton Welsby was doing the commentary on the touchline. Quite a few Liverpool fans paid handsomely to have the honour of playing for a few minutes on the legendary Anfield pitch. One kid paid £4,000. So as the team goes on the pitch, I say "Look lads, it's only fifteen minutes each way. So when your name gets shouted out by Elton, just come straight off so everyone can get a game, OK". So they kick-off. After about six or seven minutes we had to make at least two subs as there are seven subs, me one of them, who have got to get a few minutes on the hallowed turf. So me as assistant manager calls Elton Welsby over. I says to Elton "Get on the microphone and call off the number 7". He wasn't having a good day. Actually, he was shite. But it was so funny when Elton Welsby got on the microphone and called the number 7 to be substituted, the kid took no notice and the ball was played to him wide and fuck me he just went past about three defenders and unleashed a cracking shot at The Kop goal. The keeper was well and truly beaten, but it hit the crossbar. The kid was on his knees. He was fucking gutted. And straight after he walked off to be substituted. Everyone needed a few minutes on the pitch. That was the deal. It was fucking hilarious. All the other subs were getting impatient but I sorted it all out. If memory serves I put myself on with about ten minutes left. It felt unbelievable for me to actually play on the hallowed turf. But then I was clean through, went round the goalkeeper and hit the post. It was a sitter. I didn't even hear the whistle but I was offside. I just shouted to the lads "I knew it was offside. That's why I missed" (Big Fat Liar). The game finished Liverpool Celebrity XI 3 Everton Celebrity XI 0. One of the greatest Liverpool Football Club moments of my life (and boy have I seen some).

After the game big Jan Molby had sorted out a big party at the Shangri-La Chinese Restaurant in the town centre. There was live music, a couple of really good bands, it was chocka. Jan had all his family over from Denmark for the event. The restaurant made a big top table for all Jan's family. So as we get there after the game, me and Mandy Molby were having a chat waiting for Jan to turn up. I showed Mandy my present which I had bought for big Jan. It was a silver salver inscribed 'To our Great Dane, Thanks for ten glorious years, from Gerry Blayney & Billy Swann (deceased)'. I gave it to Mandy to have a look. She just read the inscription, then looked me straight in the eye and said "Oh Jan is just going to love this Gerry". So me and Mandy are just having a drink at the bar when Mandy says to me "Gerry, here he is now." I turns and sees him with about six or seven other fellas, so Mandy says "C'mon let's go and see him." I just said "Let him finish with the people he is with now first." Mandy just said "No way, you are much more important to Jan than those other people so come on now." So we walks over and Jan was still talking to people and Mandy says "Jan, here's Gerry here. Wait and see what he's got for you." We gave each other the usual big scouse hug, then I passed him his silver salver in its box. He looked at me and said "What is it?" I says "Take it out and have a look." He took it out and read the inscription. He looked at me and said "Gerry, that is beautiful lad" and gave me another big scouse hug. Typical scouser. "Thanks lad. I love it!" Then he said "That salver Gerry, believe me, is going straight in the trophy cabinet, right at the front. It will take pride of place. Thank you very, very much. I really appreciate it." He continued "You will have to come over one night and I will show you my trophy cabinet with your silver salver taking pride of place". I went over a couple of weeks later and true to his word, my silver salver was sitting proudly in the middle of his trophy cabinet. I was absolutely delighted. Anyway back to the party at the Shangri-La. The meal was just about to be served. Jan was talking to a few people so I turns to Mandy and says "Where shall I sit girl?" She turns to me and says "Don't be daft. You're on the top table with me and Jan and all his family". It was awesome. Me, the only scouser on the top table with Jan and all his family. I sat between Jan and his mother and father. I just can't tell you how proud I felt that night. But that's only the beginning.

As the party finished at about 2.30am, it was everyone down to the Moat House Hotel to finish the party. I think Jan had about ten or twelve rooms booked for his family and friends. After an hour or two, every one of Jan's family and friends were ready for bed. But me, Jan and my brother in law Ian, who would be nineteen or twenty at the time, were nowhere near ready to go home. Me and Jan were having a ball. Everyone else went to bed, then young Ian, me wife's brother, had had enough. I put him in a taxi and sends him on his way home. It's about 5 o'clock now. The bar is well and truly shut. But me and Jan are still having a laugh. I put one of them paper crowns on his head, you know the ones, the ones you get in them Christmas cracker. So I pulls over the night porter and says "Do us a favour lad, get us a few beers." He says "The bar is well shut lad." But I was having none of that. I says "Look mate, Here's £50 mate. Go and get me and Jan a crate of Budweiser" Twelve bottles I think we got. Me and Jan downed them all in about an hour and a half. Mind you, you get about two mouthfuls in them. Finally at around 7 o'clock, half 7, we'd both had enough. Jan phoned me a cab to get me back to Crosby and he went to bed. Wow. What an amazing night for me, one that I will never ever forget.

We were also back in Europe that season. But sadly it didn't take long for us to go out. In the first round of the UEFA Cup we got Spartak Vladikavkaz (fuck me try saying that one). For some reason or another, in fact, for the life of me I can't remember why, me and Matt's usual crew couldn't get a flight. Only a couple of dozen managed to get on the players' plane. Fucking really expensive though. Anyway, I'm living in Boaler St, L7, so we all decides to meet at the pub next to my house, the Sir Walter Raleigh, and watch the match on the big screen. There were ten or twelve of us I think. But as happens, it was a blessing in disguise for me. There was no way I would've had the mad bets that I had in the pub with Matt if we had managed to get to the match. That night there was an awful lot of games on, League Cup games, European games and so on. So all the lads are having bets with Matt. He got hammered that night with Liverpool winning 2-1, and me having my mad bet. I'd been losing fortunes the last eighteen months or so. I owed an awful lot of money out. I really, really needed a good win. And that night my TWO mad bets came in. I had a £200 accumulator on four games all to finish a draw, and also I had a £100 accumulator on the same four games to finish a draw along with another game to finish a draw, making it five draws.

It was time to leave the pub so I says to all the lads "E r, I only live next door. Let's all go back to ours and have a few beers". They were well up for that, but one of the lads insisted on bringing his mate Charlie. Funny cunt but keeps you up all night. So it's off to ours. I totally forgot about me bet as on the big screen only three were drawing. One was actually losing 2-0, the other one 1-0 with only injury time to play. So it's back to the house. We had a boss night as our beloved redmen had won. That Charlie was well on form. Had us up all night. I love him and I hate him sometimes. You know the score lads. So all the lads leave about four in the morning. That fucking Charlie. Cunt he is. So when they all go I'm just finishing the last of my Southern Comfort, I decided to put the telly back on and see all the results. Fuck me, it comes on the teletext, Burnley 2 and for life of me I can't remember who they were playing, 2. Own goal 89th minute and a penalty 90th minute. The other game a penalty in injury time makes it 1-1. Fuck me you couldn't make that up could you. £32,000. Get in you fucking beaut! Mind you, as I was saying, I've been getting murdered with me gambling, but that has really eased the pressure now. Not a good game for the faint hearted this gambling lark.

In the next round it was Brondby, away leg first. It was a boss trip. About twenty of us stayed for two nights I think. We got there the day before the game. Loving it being back in Europe. We got to the ground early, about an hour before kickoff. So we are walking around the ground when all of a sudden bricks and bottles were getting launched at us from a load of Brondby fans who were leaning over from the inside of the ground. Welcome back to Europe. We ended up having a boss night there though. Most of us ended up in bed by 2 or 3 o'clock. Yes, me an all. I'm usually the last up singing me head off. About six of the lads stayed up. I'm well asleep, then there's a big knock on my door. So I'm up to open the door in my birthday suit and there's this gorgeous bird, about twenty-five. She says to me "I'm so sorry to disturb your sleep but your friends downstairs are causing a lot of problems". I just looked at her, put my cock around my wrist and said "What time do you call this love?" She looked at me and said "Please, please come down and tell your friends to go to bed." So I goes down and they were all in stitches at what had just happened. So I get them all to bed. End of the night. The game itself finished 0-0 which was a good result we thought. But no, they beat us 1-0 at Anfield. So that's us out of Europe this season.

We finish third in the league. A slight improvement. The reds were getting closer. But without a doubt, the worst moment of the season, maybe the decade, was losing the FA Cup Final at Wembley against that shite from down the East Lancs and that arrogant French twat Eric Cantona. It was a horrible game. I just hate talking about it so season over, with one more heartache. That was the last time the Welsh Wizard Ian Rush wore the red shirt. He scored an amazing 346 goals. Most young redmen think Rushy is the all-time top scorer in league games for our beloved redmen but he's not. That honour belongs to my all-time favourite idol, Sir Roger Hunt. He scored 245 league goals. You learn something new every day redmen. I think Rushy scored about 238 in the league. It was close anyway. I got to know Roger quite well and believe me he's so proud of that record. I bumped into him on the train coming back from a London game once, Roger was sitting with three ex Scottish internationals. I can't really remember their names but I think they all started with Mc. Anyway it was fucking boss. "Hello Gerry" he said as I was walking past to get a drink. So I joins Roger and his mates. We had a really good chat. Roger was in London doing the Pools Panel results. There was a lot of games abandoned that day so the panel had to give their forecast of what the score line would've been. Anyway after about half an hour, a good bevy and a good chat with Roger I says to him "It's been a pleasure as always Roger. I'll get back down with my mates now. Before I go could you sign this programme for me?" I'm ninety percent certain we were playing Arsenal that day. I asked him to sign it 'To Jerryann (my daughter) from Sir Roger Hunt'. He looked at me and said "Gerry, there's no way I'm signing it Sir". Then the three Jocks started giving him loads of stick. Fucking funny. Anyway he eventually signed it for me. I found Roger to be one of the most modest people I've ever met – a joy to watch on the field and a joy to be around.

There was one more stand out game that season. It was Newcastle United at Anfield. An unbelievable game. Newcastle were pushing for the title with that other shite from down the East Lancs. It was one of those games you would never ever forget. It finally finished 4-3 to our beloved redmen. It broke Kevin Keegan's heart who was Newcastle manager at the time. He had Newcastle playing beautiful football but it just wasn't enough and those twats won the league again. We finished third after a disastrous November. We didn't win a single game. We did qualify for the Cup Winners' Cup though as United did the league and cup double. So we get to go to Europe as beaten FA Cup finalists. All in all it was an improvement again. So it's off on holiday for me and my family on the usual little island of Leros. I end up bringing another Greek lad home with us. I swear, loads and loads of the young lads on the island used to beg me "Please Gerry, take me with you this time. I want to go to Anfield". Fucking funny. Every year I take Liverpool scarves and shirts which I get very cheap. We call our beautiful little island Leropool. Every bar on the island, probably about a dozen, has a Liverpool shirt or scarf hanging behind the bar. As always it didn't take long for the new season to be upon us again.

Stan Collymore, after scoring seventeen goals in his first season, was starting to cause problems. He refused to move house to Liverpool. He was travelling from Cannock every day to training, about eighty miles or so. Roy Evans wasn't pleased with all the hours that he was driving. Probably three or four hours a day. So it wasn't perfect. But everyone knew that there would only be one winner in this situation and it wouldn't be Collymore. The man was a fool. A brilliant footballer but far too in love with himself. So it was no surprise when he got sold at the end of the season. Fucking idiot. He could've gone on to be a Liverpool great. He scored fourteen goals that season but that was nowhere near enough for a player of his quality. One of the games which stuck out this season was yet another classic against Newcastle United. Unbelievably, it finished the same score-line as last season. Yes 4-3 again. A fabulous game. McManaman and Fowler (2) with Patrick Berger getting the other. After an up and down season we finish fourth again. Out early doors in the FA Cup and out of the Coca Cola Cup after beating Burnley in the third round where Collymore scored the only goal. We then came unstuck at Chelsea in the next round. I still can't believe how we lost that game.

At half time we were cruising, dead easy - 2-0 up. Then in the last minute of the first half McManaman missed a sitter to make it 3-0. At the beginning of the second half Chelsea bring on ex Man United legend Mark Hughes. Fuck me. He ran the show. And unbelievably Chelsea score four in the second half to win the game 4-2. We had a really good run in the European Cup Winners' Cup. First up was MYPA of Finland. We win both legs, 1-0 away. It was a good trip but can't really remember much about it. The home leg finished 3-1 with Berger, Collymore and Barnes getting the goals. Next up it is FC Sion of Switzerland. It was a really good trip. We had a boss night out after the game but it nearly turned out to be a bad night for me. There was about six of us making our way back to the hotel. We were well tanked up. There were some sort of roadworks getting done outside our hotel. A favourite redman of mine, Ted Edwards, was on the books for our beloved LFC, cleaning the likes of Dalglish and Rushy's boots, he was a decent player but sadly just not good enough for Liverpool Football Club. So he does the next best thing. Instead of trying in the lower divisions, he decided to become a top Liverpool fan. Still to this day, he very rarely misses any game. Anyway as I was saying, as we gets outside the hotel one of the lads who was already back in the hotel, decided to give me a bit of a fright. He lashed a bottle out of the hotel window. It missed me by about eighteen inches, smashing everywhere. I was going fucking nuts.

"What the fuck's going on?" I was shouting up to the rooms. One of the lads shouts down

"Sorry Gerry I was just having a laugh".

I shout back up, "You fucking divvy. You nearly smashed a bottle on my head"!

A kid named Chinney shouts down "Sorry again lad, I was just having a laugh".

I shouted back "A laugh? Well I'm not fucking laughing, lad".

I suppose it was funny but not at the time. It could've tuned out nasty. The game finished 2-1 to the reds and the return leg at Anfield finished 6-3. In the next round we get SK Bran Bergen of Norway, away leg first. We had a brilliant night after the game. We met up with a load of old mates of mine from Huyton. There must've been at least seventy of us in the bar so you can imagine what it was like. I don't think I got back to the hotel until about six o'clock in the morning. The game finished 1-1 with Fowler netting for the reds. So it's back to Anfield for the second leg. We cruise to victory, winning 3-0, with Fowler getting two and Collymore the other. But sadly, we go out in the next round. We get Paris St Germain of France. We got well and truly twatted at their place, mostly down to that calamity James - 3-0 it finished. I couldn't wait to get home and out of that fucking France. It was fucking horrible. The bizzies were really up for it. They just went nuts, lashing batons everywhere. But what could we do? Fuck all that's what. Loads of redmen ended up in hospital for getting chased and battered for no reason at all. It was scary believe me. In the return leg at Anfield we gave it a really good go but the damage had been done in France. We won 2-0 with goals from Fowler and Mark Wright.

Oh, I forgot to mention a game from last season that I'll never forget (but I nearly did). It was against Leeds United at Anfield. Barnsey was captain. I had just paid £2,200 for my eldest daughter Jerryann to be the mascot for the day. I think she was eleven years old. We hadn't had a penalty for about eighteen months at Anfield but on this day we got two. We totally destroyed Leeds 5-0. As we were having a drink in the player's lounge after the game, Roy Evans came over and said to me "You can bring Jerryann again. That was our first penalty in nearly a year and a half" (see photo). It was also the one and only game that the other bird in my life, my wife Annmarie, had ever been to. Annmarie has been absolutely brilliant with me over going to the games especially Europe where I can be away for two or three days at a time. Thanks darling. Wow, did I have a touch with her.

So, no silverware this season but we don't look far away. Especially with the emergence of a seventeen year old striker, Michael Owen. He had pace to burn. He was so easy to spot as a future Liverpool legend. He had made his debut in the 1996-97 season, scoring in a 1-1 draw at Wimbledon. I think he scored seventeen or eighteen goals that season. Apart from that there was no real improvement and we finished third again in the league. No joy in the domestic cups and also out of Europe at the second hurdle. We had a great tussle with Celtic, drawing 2-2 away with Mcmanaman scoring the goal of his life. An amazing goal. He picked it up roughly on the half way line out wide. He went on a mazy run past four or five players before curling it into the bottom corner. The return leg at Anfield finishes 0-0 meaning we were through on away goals. Next up was Strasbourg of France. Fuck me, the day of the first leg away in Strasbourg the shit hit the fan. The company we had booked to fly with went bust. What a fucking downer. Cost us brewsters. No fucker ever got any compensation. Dirty bastards. The front page of the Echo read 'FANS FLEECED' or something like that, so another disappointing season. Not good this redmen is it but as our anthem says 'Through the wind and through the rain, they will never walk alone'. The new season is about to start.

In 1998-99 Roy Evans signs ex-Man Utd star Paul Ince from Inter Milan plus Patrick Berger was coming on a treat. Then the boy wonder Michael Owen was electric. He was just leaving defenders for dead. They just couldn't handle his pace. For parts of this season we were just brilliant. A joy to watch. Then the other side of the coin came. That calamity James has got a lot to answer for in my book. Just like Phil Babb. Wow. What a blurt. We bought him on the back of a brilliant World Cup for Ireland. He looked excellent but sadly it was Paul McGrath, ex-Man United, who made him look good. In pre-season Liverpool brought in Gerard Houllier to be joint manager with Roy Evans. It was a strange decision, most redmen not knowing if it was a good thing or a bad thing. We didn't have long to wait. It came in November after a disastrous run. Black November again. We lost four league games. In Europe, Paul Ince and Steve McManaman were sent off over in Valencia. I couldn't go to that game for obvious reasons. Even with nine men we managed to hold on for a 2-2 draw which was enough to send us through as we drew the first leg at Anfield 0-0. Next Tottenham knocked us out of the League Cup at Anfield - all this in one month. The day after the Tottenham defeat Roy Evans decided that he had had enough. "I went into the partnership hoping it would work. But sadly it never did. I feel I have done a good job. Some people may disagree but I think fourth, third, fourth and third again in four seasons is not bad at all". At any other club it would be success but not at Liverpool Football Club. There was a lot of sympathy from the reds fans for Roy but it was time for a change.

HOULLIER AND THE TREBLE

I WENT TO MELWOOD AND introduced myself to Gerard Houllier, presenting him with a silver salver, as I do with all new managers who come to Liverpool Football Club. Roy Evans got his at Southampton on a Wednesday night four years earlier. Football was changing and Gerard knew this. UEFA were about to change the rules in the next season or two for qualification into the Champions League, making it the top four to go through into a new group stage format. This brought in a major influx of foreign players due to the TV rights involved. Big players on big wages and big, big transfer fees. I feel so sorry for players who played just before these idiot wages came into play. The likes of Jan Molby, Johnny Barnes and players of that ilk earned a fraction of the wages players get today. If I remember rightly, Jan was telling me that his top wage at Anfield was £1,200 a week. Fuck me, Yaya Toure of Manchester City is reputed to be on £220,000 a week – that's nearly a quarter of a million pounds every week. Let's forget about wages. It makes me sick, especially when the average redman may take home £250 a week after taxes. Players get that for about one minutes play nowadays. Joke.

Anyway back to the games – it was a really disappointing season finishing seventh and no joy in the cup competitions. In the UEFA Cup, before beating Valencia, we played FC Kosice of Slovakia. One of the best and funniest trips abroad ever. And it was a first for me and a whole load of other redmen because, as it was impossible to get a flight about thirty of us managed to book on the players' plane. The only thing that separated us from the players was a curtain half-way down the plane. There was one fella standing by the curtain acting as a steward. It was all the usual lads on the plane – Matt, Marty, Robbie, Ted, Gary, Mick McNally and a good few more. Anyway I decide to go through the curtain to have a chat with Carra, Michael Owen and Stevie G. The guy standing by the curtain puts his arm across and says "You can't come through here mate, it's players only". I says "Do me a favour mate, just go and tell Steven, Michael or Carra that Gerry Blayney is here" but he said "No, no one gets past me". I just looked at him and said "Eh lad, you're on a freebie here but it's cost us Brewsters so just ask for me would you?" Within a minute I was sitting with Carra, Michael and Stevie. It was a boss journey going. When we arrived at the airport there was a coach waiting to take us to the ground where we were greeted by about a dozen bizzies. They were all carrying guns in their holsters. We were having a buzz with them. Then while I was messing around I grabbed at one of the guards guns. Fuck me bad move. I just started saying "Sorry, sorry, sorry, only a joke". Thank fuck he took it that way. They were really nice actually the bizzies. They weren't bad at all. Makes a nice change that. So it's into the ground we go. Marty (the pyjama man) was at it again, dressed in his usual pyjamas. He climbed up the wire mesh fencing and started conducting the redmen to sing. It was fucking funny. Even all the bizzies were pissing themselves laughing. It's probably the least redmen ever at a European game. Probably about seventy or eighty. We cruised the game 3-0 – Berger, Reidler and Owen. It was a formality at Anfield, winning 5-0, with Ince scoring and two apiece from Fowler and Redknapp. We lost both legs in the last sixteen against Celta Vigo, 3-1 away and 1-0 at home.

We needed to improve an awful lot for the next season. Gerard decided he needed someone else to be his assistant and he brought in another Liverpool legend of the past, Phil Thompson - a proper scouser. Tommo said "It was probably the best day of my whole life". Gerard instilled a new professionalism into the squad. He banned mobile phones from the training ground and discouraged the drinking culture that was very much in evidence in football. He even went as far as saying to Steven Gerrard "Forget all about nightclubs for now and then when you are in your thirties you can go and buy your own nightclub". He was a really nice guy Gerard Houllier. I got to know him quite well over the years. Believe it or not he is a funny cunt. Very dry. He's definitely got that scouse humour. He really did love Liverpool Football Club. In his first full season we only conceded thirty goals in the league with some brilliant buys, especially Sammi Hyppia, some player and a really lovely guy to meet, a true gentleman. Then Houllier signed Dutch international goalkeeper Sander Westerveld. Bye, bye calamity James. Then Vladimir Smicer from Czechoslovakia and the magnificent Dietmar Hamann from Newcastle United. The German, as we all know, went on to become a bit of a Liverpool legend. He also signed Stephane Henchoz from Blackburn. Put that lot together with the quality that was coming out of the reserve team – Carragher, Gerrard, Owen, Murphy, and things are looking up. We finish fourth in the league, booking us a place in the UEFA Cup. Gerard strengthened his squad again by signing three more players. He broke the club's transfer record by signing Emile Heskey from Leicester City for £11m. Then Houllier caused murder across the park by signing Nick Barmby from Everton before he found a bit of class in his next signing with Marcus Babbell coming on a free transfer from Bayern Munich thanks to the new Bosman ruling. Then he surprised everyone by offering a new lease of life to Gary McCallister. What a buy. A great player. Done a brilliant job for our brilliant redman. Every redman was so looking forward to the new season 2000–2001.

And what a fabulous season this turned out to be. We went on to win a treble – the FA Cup, The Worthington Cup and the UEFA Cup, and finish third in the league. But it wasn't just a treble, it was actually five trophies in that calendar year. We also won the Charity Shield at the Millennium Stadium (we always win in Wales) and the Super Cup in Monaco. What made the Charity Shield so special was that it was against the shite from down the East Lancs Road. Shall we say it wasn't the friendliest of finals ever. Both fans were taunting each other. Loads of fights. The hotel we were staying at was only about six or seven miles from the ground. Loads of scousers but sadly loads of Mancs as well. So as you could imagine, something had to give. And it did. Firstly, one of my favourite redmen John 'Dudek' Calvert (ringer of Jerzy) was having a drink at the bar with us when two Mancs came walking in and started giving him a bit of mouth. John says to them "Leave it out lads, we've got our kids with us here", the kids would've been about seven or eight. Great lads and John brought them up well. He lost his wife a few years before, but made a great job of bringing up his two little boys, John-Paul and Ben. Anyway, the Mancs wouldn't stop, giving John loads of verbals. Fuck me John is only little and very slim but he just let this right hander go and BANG, fuck off! The Manc didn't even see it coming. He went down like a bag of shite. His mate just shit one and that was that. Then one of the lads, thinking on his feet as us scousers do (chips n gravy), Terry Daley realised that this would be on CCTV in the reception so he decided to go behind the counter and take the tape out. Well in Tex. See you soon. Then, about half an hour later, me and Tony Swann went outside for a ciggy. All of a sudden two more Mancs came walking up to the hotel. One shouts to us "Eh lads, you've got shit on your shirts there". We just looked at them and said "Fuck off Manc or you're getting' it". It was fucking funny. One Manc shouts "Let's go then". One of them didn't want to know, but the other beaut came at us. Tony chinned him and I booted him in the balls. It was funny really.

Back to the three cups. Firstly, it was the Worthington Cup at the Millennium Stadium against Birmingham City. Great atmosphere, great stadium. We ended up winning on pens. The atmosphere was totally different to what we had against the Mancs. The Birmingham fans were delighted that they took it to pens so everyone was happy. We went on the coach. There was hundreds of coaches travelling from Liverpool and Birmingham, all travelling the same route there and home. Absolute mayhem on the way back. Total gridlock. I swear no coach moved an inch for maybe two and a half hours. We finally get moving very, very slowly. Eventually we see a services so in we go. There must've been thirty coaches stopped there, Birmingham and Liverpool fans. It was absolutely chocka. The shelves just got emptied with probably about £20 going in the till. As I'm walking out to get back on the coach I hear these three brummies say "Fuck this waiting in this big queue, let's just do what the scousers are doing and walk out without paying".

It was classic.

A couple of months later it's back down to the Millennium to play Arsenal in the FA Cup final. They battered us. They were absolutely brilliant. They were by far the better team on the day. But thanks to two brilliant goals from the boy wonder Michael Owen, we won the game 2-1. I've waited thirty years for this day. Yes, thirty years. Back in 1971 we battered Arsenal at Wembley but they beat us 2-1. So revenge felt very, very sweet for me. So that leaves the UEFA Cup final. What a brilliant journey to the final. First up it was Rapid Bucharest. Can't really remember much about the trip, I think it was just in and out. We won 1-0 anyway and after a 0-0 draw at Anfield we are through to the next round. We get FC Slovan Liberec. What a brilliant trip. We stayed for two nights. The locals were boss. Everything was so cheap so the bar tills were ringing all night. Loads of locals were selling their tickets for three times the face value, but I still think it worked out at about £15. Anyway it's about half an hour before kickoff so we decided to get into the ground, but it was fuckin chocka. I think there were only two turnstiles, people were all pushing trying to get in. Then me and Marty Mullen noticed these big security guards with leather gloves on, big fuckin meatheads. They were giving out loads of slaps to young redmen in the queue. Marty said "Gerry, just watch this lad". We go down the side of the queue right at the front of the turnstiles where the security guards were giving it loads. Then Marty just tapped him on the shoulder and as he turned round, Marty gave him the Liverpool kiss. A sweet butt. But fuck me. He went down and bounced back up in a flash. His mates got on what was going on so it was time for Marty to do his Linford Christie impersonation. It was fucking hilarious. These four or five meatheads chasing Marty, but they had no chance. He was well gone, whereas they were getting tripped up everywhere. Anyway into the game we go. A great game. We end up winning 3-2 thanks to goals from Barmby, Heskey and Owen. We had an absolutely brilliant night on the town. As usual, all sorts of fun and games going on. I ended up with a massive hangover, as normal.

Next up it was off to Greece to play Olympiakos and their

fanatical fans. I was made up that we were going there as I speak a little Greek myself. The town was bouncing with redmen dancing and having a ball with all the locals. We are sitting outside this bar when a few of the lads come over and say "Eh lads, there's a boss lap dancing bar round the corner. The beer is dead cheap and the dancers are boss". So off we go to see what it was all about. It was packed with scousers and quite a few local lads as well. There were two girls dancing on the stage around a pole. Me and all the lads are watching them and having a good laugh. Then I shouts over to them "A. C. E. Say Oraya Polly Oreya" which translates in English to 'You are beautiful. Very beautiful'. Then the two of them left the dance pole and starting crawling on the floor towards me and all the lads gesturing to me to come over on the stage. All the lads were going fucking nuts. "Go on Gerry you lucky bastard, they want you. Get on there" I just stood up and looked at the lads, took me shirt off and said "Watch me go". I just crawled along the stage like a panther. All the Greek lads were going nuts shouting "Bravo, bravo, bravo Inglaise". It was fucking boss. Then they got me to sit on a seat which they had pushed up against the pole and started gyrating all over me. Then they stood either side of me and one of them poured a bottle of beer all over the other, letting it drip down into my mouth. The lads were going wild. It was a night that I'll never forget. Anyway, after I got off the stage I noticed a really good friend of mine, who I thought had just come in. The two girls were having a drink at the bar which I bought for them. So just before I go over to see my friend John Powell who I've known for about thirty-five years. He's probably got the best job in the whole world as he is the official Liverpool FC photographer. He takes photos of our beloved redmen all over the world, and gets paid for it. Wow - what a job. Love you John you jammy bastard. Anyway I says to the little Italian girl "I'm going to see my friend now. Thanks for the dance, but give me one minute then when I'm talking to my friend shout over to me 'Gerald, Come kiss me now'." So I look at John, walk over gives her a little peck on the cheek then casually walked over to John Powell. We just looked at each other and burst out laughing. Then John just looked at me and said "I 'aven't just come in Gerry. I've seen the whole show. The way you crawled on that stage was unbelievable". We just couldn't stop laughing, but that wasn't the end of the fun. Not by a long chalk. A Rolling Stones number came on so I was in my element. I was right up there on the stage doing me Jagger impression. All the lads were loving it, and the Greeks, "Bravo, bravo" everywhere. I was strutting my stuff then all of a sudden I literally backed up and fell off the stage. But in true Blayney fashion, I was up again and finished the number. All the lads talked about that night for years. Definitely one for the scrap book.

Next up we get them horrible, horrible bastards Roma. Fucking sick of going there. As I have said before their fans are mental. Animals. And the Policia are just as bad. It really is frightening there. Probably the most violent fans I have ever encountered. And believe me I seen some, I've seen them all, but these bastards are worse than animals actually. Well organised and very, very dangerous. We arrive at the airport. All the usual suspects. Matt, Gary, Ted, Terry, Nicky, Nicky, Robbie and so on. We all make our way to the passport control, there are probably two or three hundred redmen. All of a sudden the lads noticed that they had sniffer dogs all over the place looking for drugs. It was fucking hilarious. There must've been about eight dogs. Everyone who had a bit of weed or a bit of beak started flapping and trying to get rid of it. There was a couple of kids just in front of us in the queue. One of the dogs got on them so they were dragged out of the queue and took into the toilets to get searched. Fuck me the two kids had a real touch. They told us as they come back into the queue that one of the bizzies had found a piece of hash, about ten grams probably. The kid said that he just looked at them and said "Is this hash good?" The kid said he didn't know what to say so he just nodded his head and said "Yeah". But what happened next was unbelievable. The bizzy snapped it in half and said "Half for you, and half for me, OK?" The kid said he thought he was dreaming or something, but the bizzie just let him go. Funny or what? So we're all on the coach on the way to the hotel. As usual it was a boss hotel (thanks Matt). So it's into the hotel. A quick shit, shower, shave and then it's out on the ale, but as usual the nightlife in Italy is shit, there are very few clubs. So we ended up about 200 yards away from the hotel. For a change I had had enough. I was one of the first to make a move back to the hotel to get me head down. It was probably about 2 o'clock in the morning when I got in. I'm well away in bed when I hear a bit of commotion coming from downstairs. It must've been about half four in the morning when five of the lads had come back to the hotel rotten drunk. So I go and lets myself out of the room naked, walks to the stairs and shouts "Come on lads, there is people trying to sleep here". Then one of the lads (Tommy the drum banger) shouts up "Get back to bed lad. You look like a three legged Biafran standing there". A backhanded compliment or what.

Anyway, it was a twat of a day going to the game. A beer ban all around the streets outside the ground, all the lads are well clued up - stick together and keep your mincers wide open. In we go. The usual hostile welcome. Fuck them. Who the fuck are they? The hostility didn't affect our beloved reds as the boy wonder, Michael Owen, bagged both goals as we won 2-0. As you can imagine the natives weren't very happy. They were going fucking nuts, lashing all sorts of objects at us redmen. We got kept back after the game for the usual forty five minutes, an hour. But we didn't care. Thousands of redmen dancing and bouncing everywhere to the chant of "Olay, Olay, Gerard Houllier, Olay, Olay, Olay". We taunted those Itie bastards to death. Eventually they let us out of the game. So it was a Police escort to the airport to fly home. Before we got on the plane Marty Mullen was at it again, setting off a fire extinguisher and causing mayhem with the bizzies. Fucking funny. Marty just hated the foreign bizzies and wanted to get them back for the way they treated us, like herds of cattle. Even to this day, I still can't believe that nothing ever happens to these mobs at the games in Italy. They always blame it on the English fans, especially Liverpool, but what can we do? We've had it since the 60's so it's nothing new. So it's back to Anfield for the second leg. The Kop absolutely destroyed them before kickoff. It was one of those famous European nights at Anfield, but it didn't seem to affect the Ities . The taunts of "Go back to Italy, go back to Italy" just seemed to inspire them. They took control of the game and went 1-0 up. The alarm bells started to ring. It was getting very, very nervy. Then there's mayhem. The ref gives a penalty to Roma, but notices the linesman has got his flag up. So he goes over to consult the linesman. Thank you very much linesman. The ref then overturned his penalty decision. Lucky one. Roma kept coming at us but somehow we managed to hold on and it finished 1-0, sending us through to the quarter-final to play Porto.

What a horrible, horrible journey it turned out to be for me and a load of my redmen. It was mobbed walking through the town, all having a laugh. But one redman went too far and gave a drink seller, selling trinkets, a smack for fuck all. The prick caused absolute murder. I didn't even see it happen. A couple of lads came over to us and said "Be careful lads, the bizzies are just grabbing anyone with red and white on". The next thing we knew there were bizzies flying everywhere. Sirens going, the lot. Bizzies just grabbing anyone and lashing them into the vans. So I just walked into a shop doorway to keep out of it. Then two bizzies just grabbed hold of me, manhandled me, and dragged me along the cobbles. Literally dragged me to one of the Police cars. They handcuffed me with my hands behind my back, but they were so, so tight. They were cutting my skin causing it to bleed. There were two other redmen in the car with me and about six or seven other cars with two or three redmen in each, all parked up alongside each other. The cuffs were really cutting into me. Blood all over them. So I shouted out of the window to one of the bizzies "Please can you loosen these cuffs. They are far too tight" Fuck me, this angry, angry bizzie just came up to the window of the car glaring at me and said "Oh, you want to get out?" Then just standing behind him was a plain clothes policeman. He just looked at me and gestured to me 'Don't get out'. So I just looked at the bizzie and said "No, I'm ok now, they have loosened". I just knew I was going to get one hell of a beating so I bit the bullet as any good scouser would. After about half an hour we ended up getting took to an old bus depot. There were about fifty of us. The bizzies were so violent it was untrue, but then again there is no surprise there.

Quite a few of the lads ended up having to go to hospital. One fella must've been in his 60's. The twats battered him everywhere with the batons. All he'd done was ask how long we would be there for. That was it. They just kicked off on him. They kept us there for about two hours, then started taking us all to different police stations. The only good thing to happen was one of my favourite all time redmen Joe O'Donnell, one funny man, ended up in the same police station as me. The plain clothes police officer from earlier stayed with us, taking down all our details, name, name of father, the usual. Anyway he came up to Joe and asked him the same questions. Joe just looked at him very casually and said "I don't know, I am a bastard. I was brought up in an orphanage". It was so fucking funny. How Joe kept a straight face I'll never know. Then the policeman said "I can let you all make one phone call to your families to let them know you will be home tonight after the match. No charges will be made, but you must remain here in the police station until after the match". The match had already started by now, so the bizzie says to me "I won't put you in the cells. You can watch it on a 12 inch television in reception." Another old mate of mine, the one and only Anthony Hogan (The Colonel) is another funny guy but in a much different way. The Colonel says it all. He was one of the leaders of the Urchins, our skinhead crew, a great redman. Anyway, when we were back in the bus depot they put us in one area and taped it off saying "You must stay behind this tape", but the Colonel was having none of it. He was going nuts. He was shouting at one particular bizzie. The bizzie pushes forward over the tape with his rifle in his hands but as he was pushing at the Colonel, the Colonel grabbed at the middle of his rifle to stop himself falling over. It was fucking funny. The bizzie had lost his grip on the gun and ended up on the floor on top of the Colonel. So the rifle was in between the bizzie and the Colonel, they raised their rifles and guns. "No one move, no one move". I really thought someone was going to get killed. It was frightening.

After the match finishes, the bizzie says "You can go now. We will escort you back to your coach to take you to the airport". He apologised to us all and said "I know it had nothing to do with you boys. I did my best for you but it is the people above. I have to follow orders". I was getting on well with this particular bizzie. He was a really nice man. Saved our lives really. There was a little supermarket on the way back to the coach. The bizzie says "If you want to get some food and drink on your way back we can stop here". So we go in. All the lads are buying things but I just waited until the bizzie looked at me and let him see me put a sandwich in my pocket. As we go to walk out he says "You didn't pay for sandwich". I said "I have no money, someone stole my wallet in all the commotion". He says "Give me the sandwich". Then he took it to the till, paid for it and gave it me back. I told you he was a nice bizzie. Funny or what. So after a horrible night there it's back home to Liverpool. Then comes the semi-final.

We draw Barcelona. I was fucking gutted. Not because we draw the mighty Barca, but because I will not be able to go to the away leg for reasons I explained earlier. I just can't go to Spain. If memory serves me well, it was the only game I missed all season. We played 65 games in total that season. I decided to watch the match on my own, in my own house. I couldn't bring myself to watch it in the pub because all I would've got all night was "How come you're not in Barcelona Gerry?" Not everyone knows I'm banned from Spain. So it was just me in the house. It was horrible watching it, especially when the cameras went onto our beloved travelling redmen. We get a fabulous 0-0 draw so it's back to Anfield. We just need to win and we're in the final. And our redmen didn't let us down, they duly obliged, but boy was it close. It took a penalty from the brilliant Gary McCallister to settle it. As usual The Kop and the rest of the Anfield crowd more than did their part in getting us through to yet another European final to play Deportivo Alaves of Spain. A couple of weeks before that I had probably had the greatest honour I could ever imagine. I was voted the very first Liverpool FC Fan of the Year by the Liverpool Echo. Loads of redmen were in with a shout, I can name plenty, but all my mates were saying "Don't you worry Gerry, you're gonna piss it lad". So I must've had a good chance. I personally voted for the great Lenny Woods. He's one of the few fans older than me that still goes the game. He's a legend. Not this kids' stuff 'legend' what you get on your Twitter and all that crap, but a proper Legend. There from the fifties all the way through, just like me. Anyway, we were playing Aston Villa at Villa Park. We win 3-0 no problems. There was about three or four cars of us. We normally go to the Setter & Vine on Queens Drive after we get home from the game but I'd had a late night the night before so I just decided to drive home. I was only home about ten minutes when me phone goes. It was a great redman, Ted Edwards. He says "Have you bought the Pink Echo yet lad?" I said "Not yet lad, I'm just on me way to do the lottery and get the Pink". He said "You've only gone and won it lad. You've won the very first fan of the year". Wow. I was buzzing. I just shouted down the phone something like "Get the Champagne in lads. I'm on me way". I just loved it. I was so proud to read my name in the Pink. I was presented with my trophy by big Sammi Hyypia and Phil Thompson. Stevie G, Carra, and maybe a few more players were there. I'm not sure what hotel it was now, but one of the nicer ones, The Crown Plaza or somewhere like that. When I got called up to the stage I felt so proud. It was chocka with redmen and players past and present. I think it was Phil Thompson who put the microphone to my mouth and asked me "How do you feel Gerry?" I just looked at him and emotionally said "I feel like I have won the lottery or something". Tears of joy were dripping down my face. It was such a magical moment for me and is probably the greatest personal moment watching my beloved redmen. A night I will take to my grave.

So it's back to the final against Alaves. My prize for winning the fan of the year award was a trip for two, all expenses paid, to the 2001 UEFA Cup Final, plus a signed shirt of a team player of my choice. I obviously went for Stevie G. What a player! It's only about a week or so to go before the final in Dortmund, Germany, and there is still no sign of my match ticket, hotel reservations, flight booking or whatever, fuck all. So I phone the Pink Echo. What a cock up! Good job I phoned up. I finally got the tickets two days before the game. I wasn't happy at all. I obviously assumed I would be flying from Liverpool or, at worst, Manchester. But no. We had to get a train from Lime Street to London Stansted Airport. We flew from there. Anyway it went from bad to worse. The prize read 'Red Carpet Treatment, Five Star Hotel' and so on. I swear, we ended up on an industrial estate in a very small hotel, if you want to call it a hotel. There was fifteen, twenty rooms maximum. The bar was so small, six to eight people and it would've been chocka. Me and me brother Alan, who I took with me, just looked at each other and said "Fuck this, let's fuck off into the town centre". As we were walking out of the hotel to get a taxi, two young redmen, friends of our Alan's, came over and said "Is there any rooms in there Alan? We can't get a room anywhere". Me and our Alan just looked at each other and said "E R lads you've had a touch. Rooms all paid for but you'll have to pay for your ale at the bar". Cheeky bastards. What happened to All Expenses Paid? Red Carpet? My arse.

Anyway, so we're off into the town centre. Didn't take us long to bump into all the usual suspects. It was an amazing day. We just ended up bunking in one of their rooms for the night, as you do. Anyway as I was saying, it was an amazing day. We all congregated in this massive square. Loads of shops and places to get food. Loads of little bars. Allsorts. It was like a little carnival. It was magical. Especially with our scouse humour. As for the weather, it was just pissing down. And I mean really pissing down, but no one gave a fuck. The atmosphere was electric. Girls dancing out of the windows in the offices above the square. They had never seen anything like it. You know what lads, I am so, so proud to be a Liverpool fan. We are just one massive, massive family. After a beautiful day it was time to get up to the match. And what a lovely change. The atmosphere was so relaxed. I think every redman knew we were going to complete the treble. So me and our Alan decide to go in and fuck me, you wouldn't believe it, our tickets were in with the Alaves fans. Absolutely unbelievable or what. That fucking Liverpool Echo had totally made a fuck up with my prize, but in the end that didn't matter. It was an unbelievable final. The greatest and most exciting UEFA Cup Final of all time. It didn't take long for the goals to start flowing. Markus Babbel, the German international, opened the scoring for us. What a good player he was. Then the magnificent Stevie G scored to make it 2-0. They pulled one back making it 2-1 before McCallister scored a penalty. 3-1. Then they pull another one back and its 3-2. Then God struck - Robbie Fowler made it 4-2. Then all of a sudden, fuck me, its 4-4, thanks to Jordi Cruyff, son of the legendary Johan Cruyff. End of ninety minutes. Onto Extra Time and Golden Goal, which means it's back to me old schoolboy days, next goal the winner. It was a free kick which led to the goal. The box was packed. They had everyone back and we pushed nearly everyone forward. McCallister, as usual, done a little dummy run first, then back up and crossed towards the penalty spot. He floated a lovely ball in, about four or five players went for it and it took a little flick off an Alaves defender's head to make it 5-4. Trophy to Liverpool.

The scenes were amazing inside the ground. After we finally got out of the game, I don't know how long we were in there for but it was ages, what a night we had, there were these massive function rooms at the side of the stadium. I've seen some spreads in my life but it was a feast fit for a king. Everything you could think of - full Chinese, Italian, Lobster, anything. It was amazing. What made it that much sweeter, it was a real posh do. Special invites only. Matt sorted out about ten tickets to get in from a good friend of ours, his name is Miles, from London. A good Arsenal fan. Well they weren't tickets, they were wristbands. So it was then in, no problems. After about ten minutes one of the lads, Fitzy (blue nose twat) from Huyton comes out with all the bands and passes them to the next ten. That went on for about an hour and a half or so. There was a minimum of sixty or seventy of us in there, but I was say closer to a hundred. The classic scouse ingenuity strikes again. Champagne, lobster, Salmon, you name it. What an unbelievable night and a glorious end to a magnificent season. The only thing missing is the illusive nineteenth title. Won a nice few bob on the treble, but to be honest I've had a terrible year overall with the gambling. It's my own fault. Backing them stupid horses. So I'm fucking them nags off and staying with the footy. Anyway the usual dance after the season ends. I'm off to me little Island Leros. We stayed for three or four weeks and really re-charged the batteries. Now I'm getting ready for the new season.

That August it was off to Monaco to watch our beloved redmen win another trophy, the UEFA Super Cup 3-2 against the European champions, the mighty Bayern Munich, with goals from Heskey, Owen and Riise. It was fucking brilliant. Boy, Monaco just stunk of money. The harbour was full of yachts and beautiful boats. The weather was brilliant. Sunshine and redmen everywhere. I can't really remember who it was but a couple of lads got onto one of the yachts and started singing "Popeye the sailor man". Everyone was well pissed, dancing around, really enjoying it. Then up pops none other than Marty Mullen. Lunatic. He's up for all sorts. Anything for a laugh. We are standing by the yachts and just chatting when Marty says "Watch this Gerry". This young lad, about eighteen, nineteen, with his dad I think, was walking past along the harbour when Marty just runs up and tries to throw him into the sea. The kid or the dad didn't find it funny at all. We did though. That's what he's like. The game itself was a cracking final. We finally won 3-2.

The season started so well and Redmen everywhere were buzzing, could this be the season we get to number nineteen? Sadly no one could have foreseen what was going to happen seven games into the season when Leeds United visit Anfield. At half-time there was all sorts of commotion on the bench, there was a big problem with Gerard Houllier. He was rushed away to Broadgreen Hospital, where he was taken straight to surgery with heart problems. Without surgery straight away it was certain he would die from internal bleeding so he had a ten hour operation and thanks to the surgeon, Dr Rashid, he made a complete recovery. Sadly for me, I met Dr Rashid five years later, more about this later. Houllier was laid up for months. Many redmen were worried the team would lose its way without him, but no one wanted him rushed back too soon so the reigns were passed on to Phil Thompson, the Assistant Manager.

Tommo got us off to a brilliant start. His first game was a 2-1 win away against Dynamo Kyiv in the Champions League, thanks to goals from Danny Murphy and the brilliant Stevie G. As usual it was a really good trip. I think we had a two day stay. Fuck me it's cold over there. I think every Liverpool fan bought one of those Russian hats. Anyway, if memory serves me well the two Marty's were at it again one way or another. The pyjama man was conducting the Liverpool fans from a small fountain in the middle of a little square with bars either side. Everywhere was chocka. Singing in the rain or what? He was soaking wet. He must've stayed there for about fifteen minutes. Even the Russian bizzies were pissing themselves laughing at the mad scouser in the fountain. It was a classic.

Then we have the other Marty, Mr. Mullen, wow, what can I say? He must've thought he was a member of The Who. He threw a television out of the window of the hotel. Fucking good job it was at the back of the hotel as it was just gardens. No public walking about. He got arrested obviously. Apparently the bizzies were banging on his door and when he opened it Marty said "Some lunatic has just threw a telly out of the window over there". One of the bizzies said "You are the lunatic" and arrested him. Apparently Marty said he was trying to get Sky on the TV. I'll let you think about that one. It wasn't really a nice trip with the Russian skinheads. Loads of fighting. Loads of good redmen got banned from Europe. They were only defending themselves. What do they want them to do? Pretend to be Italians and run away. It's all about money in Russia when a problem happens. Loads of the lads had a whip around. It wasn't cheap believe me. We had to sort one of the bars out where there had been some damage and also we had to pay for the television. It was a few grand believe me. Everyone put a few hundred quid in each just to save people getting locked up. Then there was the lap dancing bars. Not very nice at all. Very aggressive and very expensive. I was having none of it myself. I just had a nice drink. But I got a shock when one of my best redmen mates, he's only about five foot five, five foot six, I can't say his name because his bird would go mad. In all the trips that I've been on with this certain fella, and it's all over Europe for many, many years, he used to say "fuck that paying for a bird to dance for ya". But on this trip he was having loads of dances and all off the same girl. Funny thing was she was six foot three.

In his first six games Tommo won five and drew one. After the good win in Russia, he followed it up with a good 0-0 draw away in Boavista. I think we just flew in and out. Then a 2-0 home win against Borussia Dortmund, plus four wins in the league taking us top at that point, but sadly, the results didn't last. We got totally destroyed at Anfield against Barcelona, 3-1. Boy did they play really well. By mid-January, our bad run had dropped us down to fifth in the league. Things started going badly wrong. Then came the bombshell. The unbelievable was about to happen. Robbie Fowler (God) was leaving to sign for Leeds United for £11m. Every redman was gutted. What a loss. He'd played three hundred and thirty games for our beloved redmen, scoring one hundred and seventy one goals. But life goes on. We still had young Michael Owen, who was crowned European Footballer of the Year. We also signed Nicolas Anelka. Then after a 1-0 win at Old Trafford, Danny Murphy scoring, that moved us back up to third place, the title race was really hotting up, it was the most exciting title race for years - Arsenal, Man United and Liverpool were all in with shout with only seven games to go. There could not have been a better time for Houllier to come back after his operation. He came back to Anfield for yet another one of them European nights that only Anfield can produce. It was against Roma. The crowd, with The Kop leading them, was magnificent from start to finish. We needed to win by two clear goals to go through to the quarter-final. The noise was deafening as the players took to the field. Houllier emerged from the tunnel to view the magnificent 'Allez' mosaic and accept their rapturous and emotional welcome return. We got off to a great start, Jari Litmanen scoring from the penalty spot, but we still need another goal to go through. And it came just after the hour. Emile Heskey rose to head a Danny Murphy free kick bang into the back of the net. The whole ground went mental, but it was a very, very nervy last twenty-five minutes or so. The crowd were unbelievable, willing the team to hold on. And they did. At the final whistle Houllier and Thompson were visibly moved as thousands and thousands stayed back to chant their names. A magical night.

We got drawn against Bayer Leverkusen and win the first leg 1-0 at Anfield thanks to a rare goal from the magnificent Sammi Hyypia. But sadly it wasn't enough as we get well beaten, 4-2 over there. So we are out. Bastard. So near but yet so far. Gutted. Didn't have much of a night out there. I just couldn't wait to fly home in the morning. Back to the league. With only seven games to go, it's so tight between us, the Mancs and Arsenal. We'd been on a great run. Phil Thompson had had us on a late great run, winning seven and drawing three, no losses. We were top of the league but Arsenal had a couple of games in hand. United had dropped away so it was a two horse race. Houllier's first game back was a home game against Chelsea and thanks to a Vladimir Smicer goal, we win 1-0. Arsenal, however, also kept winning. It was so tight. We win five of the last six games but the one that cost us the title was the one at home to Tottenham Hotspur, losing 1-0. With Arsenal winning both games in hand we end up finishing runners up. Yet again so close, but no cigar. Taking everything into account, it was a good season, and thankfully Gerard had made a full recovery. So as usual it's off on holiday before the start of the new season, 2002-03. I really enjoyed our family holiday. Everywhere I look on the beach, all I see are Liverpool shirts, courtesy of me. Leros, or as I like to call it Leropool, is well and truly hooked on our beloved redmen. I just love spreading the gospel of Liverpool Football Club.

On to the next season and up first it's down the M6 to play Aston Villa. A great 1-0 win thanks to a John Arne Riise goal. We got off to an absolute flyer in the first twelve games, winning nine, drawing three. Then it all just went horribly, horribly wrong. We go an unbelievable eleven games without a win - losing six, drawing five. Everyone was just stunned. We couldn't believe it. So that looks like the end of our dreams of becoming champions of England for another year. We also go out of the FA Cup in the fourth round, beaten by Crystal Palace. After drawing 0-0 away, everyone was confident we would have no problems at Anfield, boy were we wrong. They deservedly beat us 2-0, but we do a lot better in the League Cup, going all the way to the Millennium Stadium in Cardiff for the final. After seeing off Southampton, Ipswich, and Aston Villa in a thriller at Anfield, we win 4-3 thanks to goals from Stevie G, Milan Baros, and two from Danny Murphy. Murphy scored the winner in the 90th minute. The semi-final was a two legged affair with Sheffield United. They beat us 2-1 in Sheffield. After ninety minutes at Anfield we were leading 1-0 so it was extra time. Michael Owen (Manc twat) found the net to send us through to the final to play Manure.

Oh what a beautiful day! More so for me as Stevie G gave me his shirt as he promised me the next final we won, the shirt was mine. It was a present from Steven for me winning the very first fan of the year award in 2001. And to put the icing on the cake, Stevie G scores as we beat the Mancs 2-0. Owen got the other one. What a lovely journey home. Taunting them Manc bastards on the motorways. Then it was straight into town where we had a ball. I think I finally got home about half four in the morning. Slept for more or less a full day. The Champions League was very disappointing but we had a couple of decent trips. As usual Matt had us a beautiful hotel sorted out for the Spartak Moscow game, but it turned out to be a very expensive trip for one of the lads. A kid named Mouse from Breck Road caused a few problems by taking the head off a beautiful statue in one of the rooms. It cost him Brewsters. Back to the game. We destroyed them 3-0 thanks to a hat-trick from Michael Owen (Manc twat). Can't remember much more but it had to be a good trip if we won 3-0 and the main striker grabbed a hat-trick. Next up it was FC Basel. We needed to win to go through to the next stage but sadly it finished 3-3. So it was a drop down into the UEFA Cup. What a disaster, but that's football. We didn't have a very good night on the town, couldn't wait to get home really. After beating Vitesse Arnhem and Auxerre we get Celtic in the quarter final, away leg first. And thanks to an Emile Heskey goal we come away with a 1-1 draw. So it's back to Anfield. The atmosphere was unique. Probably the two best sets of supporters in the world - Liverpool and Celtic but sadly we get well beaten, 2-0. It hadn't been a great season but at least we had a trophy and to make it that bit more special it was them Mancs we beat in the final. So it's another season and yet another trophy. But sadly, it wasn't the trophy we were looking for. We badly want that elusive 19th league title. There was no holiday this year as business had been really bad. I just about managed to get to the games this season but no matter how bad business is, I will always manage to get to the game, by hook or by crook. As the title of this book says it's 'In My blood' and will be until the day I die (and beyond).

By the following season I heard there was a coach going from Kirkby, The Fantail. How ironic is that. I went from there in the early sixties. Wow. I heard there was a very good card school going on every away game. I smelt money and I wasn't wrong. Firstly, I'll tell you about all the redmen on the coach. What a mixture of people there is on our coach. Where the fuck do I start? I tell you what, let's start with a typical scouser, the lad himself, Paul Cooke. What a lovely guy. He ran the coach with another great Liverpool fan Peter Jones. Paul is a proper scouser. Liverpool mad. And he brought his family up in the right way (love you Paul). We became really good friends. Paul was an ex-professional footballer himself, played for many clubs including Wolves (I think), Burnley, Coventry and a good few more. He's now a football manager in Ireland with Sligo Rovers and I'm happy to say that he has done well there. He's won a couple of cups with them. Made up for him. Then there's the rest of the lads who play cards. They weren't very good, especially Peter. He got too pissed. So easy to read. Then there's John the shirt. Another great redman, typical scouser, a little finger in lots of little pies. Then there's John the shirts mate, Black Joe, from Kirkby, another great redman. Then there was my very good mate Billy (Rasta) Nolan. Never stops smiling this one. He even wears a Rastafarian wig at some of the away games. A good guy and a good red. Then there's Wiggy, the motorway service station's worst nightmare, a funny lad. Then there is the one and only James Miller. A fucking lunatic. Funny as fuck. Another of my favourite redmen and a big handsome cunt. He didn't give a fuck. If he got his claws into you that was it. He would just keep slagging you to death, but in such a funny way. You just have to laugh along. Everyone gets a bit off James at some stage of the journey. So many good redmen, Ged, Frank, Stan, Craig, Graham, Colin, George, and Fletch, who runs the coach. We have become really good friends over the last few years. Another boss redman. Then there's Jay Harrison, another handsome twat. Should've been a male model. Then there is Lee O'Conner. Thanks for the music Lee. You're a good redman and good company. Then there is Neil the statman and Zack, always good company. Terry Tick, he's banned now. Then there's the Huyton crew. The list goes on and on. It's a coach and a half. You couldn't wait for the next away game. It goes from The Village Inn in Aintree, formally The Valentine. You may have seen the flag travelling all over Europe. It says Rockin' All Over the World. And boy did that coach rock down the motorways.

It was like a house party on wheels. Boss music, booze and whatever else. People singing and dancing down the aisles, and on the seats. We even had our own disco. Brian Davis, mad as a fucking hatter but really funny, I think he's a year older than me. He would start off on the mic with his rendition of Sitting on the Dock of the Bay by Otis Redding. He couldn't sing to save his life, but he was hilarious. Good entertainment. He even used to bring his wife with him to the London games, Margie. Boy you should've seen the state of the two of them by the time we got to London. Rotten. Then there's Custer Currie. He'd get up and do his bit. He could sing a bit, much better than Brian. So that tells you about some of the lads. Back to the season. We got off to a bad start, losing to Chelsea, then two 0-0 draws on the trot, but we had a nice big party the next game away to the blue shite at Goodison Park. We just blew them away 3-0 – two from Owen and one from Harry Kewell. But the inconsistency over the next few months put an end to any chance we had of lifting the league title. Not much better in the FA Cup but a couple of really, really rewarding trips for me. Firstly, the third round of the FA Cup away to Yeovil Town. That was some journey. We won very comfortably 2-0. I won about £600 on the cards going down there and about £1000 coming back. Wow, did that come in handy! Peter would get so pissed and he would be so easy to read. Paul Cooke was a bit better, and John the shirt was very cautious. So it was happy days for me again. Then next up, another long hike, Portsmouth. We get beat 1-0. Everyone gutted that we're out of the FA Cup. But it was a similar story for me going home on the coach. I won about another £600. In the League Cup we got out early, losing 3-2 to Bolton at Anfield. We didn't do much in Europe either but I got a few new stamps on my passport. Marseille. Fucking horrible violent bastards. Levski-Sofia, Steaua Bucuresti and Olympia Ljubljana. Nothing really happened on any of those trips. It was just in and out. Twat of a season really, but we just managed to creep into the Champions League. The club decided Gerard Houllier's time was up. It was a sad day for Liverpool fans as Gerard had done us proud over the years, especially in 2001 by winning the treble, but a change was needed.

RAFA AND ISTANBUL

S O THE CLUB CAME TO THE DECISION to hire Rafa Benitez. As I do with all the new managers, I took a silver salver to Melwood to wish him the best of luck. Jamie (Carra) took me in and introduced me to Rafa. He was brilliant. He thanked me profusely and told me how sorry he was to hear about my friend Billy Swann, in broken English of course. I told him about my son, Peter Andrew Harrison. He was so sincere. A lovely guy. As I'm leaving I turned to him and said "I'll see you in G.A.K Rafa". Rafa smiles and says "Que?" I don't think he understood me, but he understood when I said "the match in Austria". He smiled and said "Si, Si". So it's the beginning of the new era. And what a debut season it turned out to be for Rafa. It ended with what was probably the greatest game I have ever witnessed. Anyway we will start at the beginning, Rafa's debut was a qualifier against G.A.K Austria. We win comfortably 2-0 thanks to the magnificent Stevie G grabbing both goals, but we got a bit of a scare back at Anfield, losing 1-0. There was a big golf shop in Austria. I think about a quarter of it ended up on the plane on the way home. Talk about giving it what for. Rafa didn't waste much time bringing in some new players. His first two where from Spain – Luis Garcia, a brilliant little player, and the fabulous Xabi Alonso. Wow, what a player. He was simply a joy to watch. As the chant goes "Everyone wants to know, Alonso, Alonso, Alonso". Then he signed two more Spaniards, Morientes and Nunez. Morientes looked good but sadly the English game was too fast for him.

Anyway next up we get drawn in the group stage with AS Monaco, Olympiakos and Juventus. First up was Monaco at Anfield. A comfortable win 2-0. As usual the crowd played its part, but that's only for starters. The Kop soon pump up the volume in the up and coming games. The first away trip was to Olympiakos of Greece. But we came unstuck, losing 1-0. As usual Matt had booked us in a nice hotel, one of the nicest we'd stayed in. We had a laugh.

There was a massive swimming pool. All the usual suspects were there around the pool, Ted, Marty, Gary, Paul, Tommy, Terry, Robbie, Micky, Mac and so on. Anyway, me and Tommy (the drum banger) are always at it, always trying to wind each other up. So I says to Tommy "What are you like at swimming lad?" He says "I swim like a fish" (more like a crab!). I says come on then I'll race you. Do you fancy a bet?" He said "Naa I don't wanna take your money". Anyway all the lads are involved now, Matt shouting the odds, 4-6 Gerry, Evens Tommy. It was hilarious. So it's under orders and we're off. Fuck off I was gone. Head down like a torpedo. Roughly half way I take a look back to see where the drum banger is. He was about twenty five yards behind me. It was a big pool. Tommy was doing the breaststroke. All the lads were in bulk. So I complete the race and starts to walk back towards the end where the lads were. As I got to Tommy I says "What are you like at boxing Tom?" He didn't find it funny at all. Anyway, after a really good night everyone is off to bed. Just about able to walk. Rotten drunk.

We pack our bags the next day and it's off to the airport. It was fucking mayhem. Those Greek bizzies are hard work. Violent bastards. It's been the same every time I've been there. Anyway, they're at it again, pushing and shoving people and so on. So Marty Mullen shouts out "fuck off Hitler" to this big mountain of a man. He had to be at least six foot six. He was the top bizzie. He turned to where we were and started to march towards us. Then he shouted, looking straight at Matt "You call me Hitler" he screams into Matt's face. Matt went the colour of boiled shite. "Not me mate, not me mate". It was hilarious. So we finally get on the flight home. I think I slept all the way home. Then after a very disappointing draw at home with Deportivo La Coruna, it was off to Spain for all the lads. As you know I'm not really welcome there. Sick as a pig but what can I do? Anyway, the reds get a great result thanks to an own goal. We get the win we so badly needed but we slip up again away at Monaco. We lost 1-0. I think we just flew straight in and straight back after the game. So it was the last chance saloon back at Anfield for the last game of the group stages against Olympiakos. We need to win by two clear goals to see us through. It was one of the most amazing nights ever at Anfield. The whole ground was rocking. I really believe the crowd, especially our world renowned Kop, helped us more than just a little. I really do believe that. At half time it was looking really grim. 1-0 down. The crowd were doing their very best to get the team going and it worked. Sinama Pongolle scores after only two minutes of the second half to make it 1-1. Then with only ten minutes left to go, Mellor scores to make it 2-1 to the reds, but we still need another goal to go through to the next round. The crowd was amazing. They just never stopped. Then with only four minutes left on the clock, it just had to be, Stevie G. He got onto a knockdown by Mellor outside the box and hit a beauty. The keeper never even saw it. And that was it. The crowd went mental. We really believed we could go all the way.

Next up we get Bayer Leverkusen, home leg first. As always the crowd are well up for it. A great 3-1 win with a goal from little Luis Garcia, what a great little player to watch. He scored many vital goals for the reds, John Arne Riise made it 2-0. They pulled one back before Didi Hamann wrapped it up scoring a rare goal in the last minute to make it 3-1. We had some night in town afterwards as you can imagine. I think I ended up home at about five in the morning. Happy days. So it's off to Germany for the second leg. We cruise though 3-1 thanks to goals from little Louis (2) and Milan Baros. We just flew straight back after the game. So it's the quarter final up next against Juventus. As you know, I hate going to that Italy, it's shit. Anyway we are at home for the first leg and it turned out to be another glorious night. As always, the crowd was magnificent. Thanks to goals from Sammi Hyypia and yet another from the little Spanish wizard Louis Garcia we win 2-1. So it's back over to Italy. Not looking forward to Juventus at all. Not after the Heysel thing. They had a big banner which read something like 'There is a God After All' referring to the Hillsborough tragedy. The game ends 0-0 and we are through. It was one of the most horrible nights I've spent in a football ground. The hatred was unbelievable. They just pelted us with coins and those small AAA batteries. I actually got caught above my right eye. Only a little gash, no need for stiches or anything like that. Most people were just standing there with their hands over their faces trying to protect themselves from these batteries. But fuck them, we are through to the Semi-Final to play Chelsea.

This time It's the away leg first so it off to that fucking London. They want to grow up them. People in their forties and fifties looking for fights. So it's down the motorways again on the coach. Not the Kirkby one this time. It was a luxury coach, only a twenty-seater. Matt sorted it out and as I travel to all the European games with the same crew, I decided to go with them. We get to London early, about midday I reckon. We had a few hours to kill so we went to Trafalgar Square to feed the pigeons. Then it was off to Henry J Bean's, a boss boozer. It was about a fifteen minute walk to Stamford Bridge from there. It was a massive bar with a lovely big garden out the back where you can have a smoke, a sit down and have some nice food. So after a few hours there it's time to make our way to the ground. There was about forty-five minutes to go until kick off. And as always it was absolute mayhem outside, the bizzies haven't got a clue. We finally get in after about fifty minutes, missing the first five minutes of the game. Unbelievable. Same every year. The atmosphere was horrible. Those cockney bastards haven't got a clue about football. The game was very tight, very nervy, but a great performance got us a 0-0 draw. As we were walking out at the end of the game it was the same as always. Them horrible bastards spitting at us and everything. One cunt tried to trip me up but I saw him coming. The bizzies did fuck all about it. It was such a relief to get back on the coach. We had a boss journey home though, everyone got rotten drunk singing and dancing. Then before you know it the return leg is upon us.

You just knew it was going to be another special night and so it turned out to be. Inside the ground the noise was absolutely deafening. As I walked into the Centenary Stand the noise was that deafening I had to put my hands over my ears. It was unbelievable. In mine and a lot of other people's opinions, it scared Chelsea to death. And it didn't take long for our beloved redmen to respond. Four minutes to be precise. Get in you little beauty. Little Luis Garcia is at it again to make it 1-0. It was a very controversial decision. Milan Baros was clean through. Petr Cech brings him down but the ball fell to Garcia from only a yard or so out. He hits it and the defender tried to clear off line. The ref gives the goal. Mourinho, Chelsea's manager, was going fucking nuts, calling it the ghost goal afterwards. They were very lucky Chelsea as the referee should've given a penalty and sent off the goalkeeper, but The Kop didn't care, singing the Garcia song, you know the one lads. 'Luis Garcia, he drinks Sangria, He's five foot seven, he's football heaven, please don't take my Luis away'. What a song. Half times comes. 1-0 to the reds. Come on redmen. Only forty five minutes away from another European final. The second half was so tight and so nervy. My nerves were shot. Every minute seems like five. Then with only two minutes to go we get the fright of our lives. Chelsea were attacking, the ball came out of the box and fell nicely for Eidur Gudjohnsen. I can still see it now. He caught it perfect. I thought it was going into the back of the net. Fuck me, it just squeezed past the post. Wow. I nearly fainted. Fuck me ref please blow the whistle. It was agony. And then it came. The final whistle. I swear I don't know how the roof never came off the Kop. Everybody was hugging, kissing, dancing. Without a doubt, one of the most amazing nights I've ever seen at Anfield, if not the most. I was drained. I felt like I had played the full ninety minutes myself.

★

I'm so looking forward to the final because AC Milan are my second favourite team. They have had some great sides over the years and they have won six European Cups, two more than us. They have to be classed as a great club. Just about every redman I know was going to Istanbul. Some of them didn't know how they were going to get there but they made sure that they did – by hook or by crook. It was without a doubt the most amazing journey I have ever been on and I'll tell you what, I've been on a few, but this has to be the ultimate. It was just a mass of redmen all over Istanbul. The Turks were loving it. Their tills were ringing and ringing. They just loved us. Anyway, we arrived on the Tuesday, a three night trip altogether. I probably had about four hours sleep in them three days. As I said before, about every Liverpool fan I knew was there, selling cars, jewellery, anything to get over there. Now that's what I call class. Boy have we got the best supporters in the world. And I seriously believe that. You can argue as much as you like about who is the greatest team in the world but please do not even consider arguing who has the greatest fans. That accolade can only go to one set of fans, and that's us. Fact. Without The Kop and the rest of the ground, Liverpool Football Club would never have won as much as it has. And that's not just my opinion. Our famous atmosphere is world recognised.

AC Milan - what a club. They have had some unbelievable players over the years. Just like our beloved redmen. Players like Marco Van Basten, Ruud Gullit, the fabulous Baresi, then in my eyes the best of them all, Paulo Maldini. The greatest defender ever. The list just goes on and on. As I say we arrive on the Tuesday afternoon. We took in the sights and showed all the young redmen where all the best lap-dancing bars were. And boy they weren't disappointed. I tell you what though lads, I never believed for a second that I would witness such scenes as I did in Rome in '77, but this definitely took the biscuit. Unbelievable. The day of the match was just a mass of red. Not an Italian in sight. It was like a two week holiday wrapped up into three days. The Turks looked after us well. Had us off but nicely if you know what I mean. So before you know it the match is upon us so everyone piles on the coaches to make our way to the Ataturk Olympic Stadium. Fuck me I knew the stadium was off the beaten track but it was in the middle of nowhere, like a desert with loads of mountains around it. The traffic on the mountain roads was at a crawl at best. We finally arrive, getting dropped off by the coach about five hundred yards from the ground. We had to walk up and over hills and then down to the stadium. When we got to the ground I just remember looking back around to where we had just come from and it was just like a scene from the classic film Zulu. The redmen just kept coming and coming over the hill towards the ground. Hence the chants 'The reds are coming up the hill boys'. Amazing scenes. Never ever seen nothing like it and probably never will again. Mind you I'm sixty-one now. Fifty-five years watching my beloved redmen.

Inside the ground it was exactly the same as any big final I've seen. The greatest fans in the world were well up for this one. Come on redmen lets go. They kickoff then fuck me within a minute AC Milan score from the first attack of the game and of all people, it came from the incomparable Paulo Maldini. What the fuck was he doing in our box in the first minute? We were all in shock. Then before you know it Crespo makes it 2-0. Then before we knew what was happening, Crespo again – 3-0. I have never seen our beloved redmen torn apart like AC Milan did in that first half. To be honest we did well getting to the break at 3-0. It could've been five or six believe me, they were that good. I just remember at the half time whistle I sank to my knees with my head in my hands and thinking "This in untrue." Our beloved redmen were on the brink of being involved in one of the most one sided finals ever. I was dreading the second half. Milan were just incredible in the first half. Kaka ran the show with Maldini and Crespo was on fire. About five minutes before the players came out for the second half I gets off my arse, goes to the toilet, got a drink and then got back in. As I got back in I could hear a faint defiant chant of "You'll Never Walk Alone" coming from the redmen. Then the chant became stronger by the second. Come on redmen it's not over yet. Even to this day as I'm writing this book, I still can't believe what happened in this game, the second half. The second half started with Benitez making a massive decision to bring on Didi Hamann to stop the play from the magnificent Kaka. Hamann did it superbly, kept him in check and we finally got a foothold in the game. We pulled a goal back in the fifty-fourth minute from the brilliant Steven Gerrard. It got the crowd going mental. Come on redmen we can do it. Then before we had time to take a breath its Vladimir Smicer, a low drive from just outside the box into the bottom corner. Get in. Wow come on. Game on.

Unbelievable, three minutes later its 3-3. Stevie G bursts into the box with Gattuso closely on his heels. Down goes Gerrard. Blatant penalty. Alonso steps up... Bang. But the goalkeeper guesses right and pushes the ball away. But Alonso reacted first and thumped home the rebound. Absolutely unbelievable scenes. 3-0 down and in a six minute spell we pull it back to 3-3 with nearly half an hour to go. The tension was unbearable. Dudek was making save after save. Even Jimmy Traore cleared one off the line. But the double save by Jerzy Dudek from Shevchenko was unbelievable. Dudek, a good friend of the Pope, said afterwards that there was definitely divine intervention. Thank God.

The ninety minutes are up and it's into extra time. Jamie Carragher was incredible. Some of the blocks he made were a delight to watch. He was full of cramp but it never stopped him making tackle after tackle, block after block. It has got to be, without a doubt, one of the greatest defensive displays I have ever witnessed. The whole team ran themselves into the ground and they got their reward, winning by a penalty shootout. It was so tense to watch. A lot of the red fans just couldn't bear to watch. Then up steps Shevchenko. If he doesn't score it's all over. You could see the way he stepped up that he wasn't confident and so it turned out to be. He hit a weak shot which Jerzy Dudek saved. What amazing scenes followed! Some people were in a trance. They couldn't believe we'd won it. Even to this day I still have to pinch myself to believe it actually happened. The mountain road was chocka. People hanging out of taxis, coaches, allsorts going on. It took about an hour and a half to get back to the town to a big square called Taxim Square. Banners everywhere, people dancing and singing, hugging and kissing, people crying tears of joy. It was so emotional. Then after meeting up with all our friends we decided to go and have a party in our hotels. There were two dead nice big hotels right next to each other with just a narrow street separating them. Both hotels were bouncing. We basically drank the whole night singing and dancing. A great night.

It was in one of the hotels that I met a lad from Huyton called Rick Parry (no, not that prick). It was so funny, at the top of the hotel there was a big swimming pool. The party was in full swing so I made my way up there. The music was good and loud and there was this kid, my new bezzie mate, Rick Parry. He was as fit as a butcher's dog. He was doing summersaults, one armed press ups, all sorts. He was fucking boss. So me, big skinny cunt, starts doing my Mick Jagger impersonation. I've done my Mick Jagger thing all over Europe for the last thirty-five years. So after we entertained all the redmen at the rooftop pool I says to him "Where are you from kid?" He says "Huyton lad." I says to him "I was brought up in Huyton from the age of fifteen, I might know your dad. What's his name?" He says "Ritchie Parry" I just looked at him and said "Did you live in Bakers Green, Bluebell Estate." He says "Yeah, why? Do you know my dad?" I said "Yes. We were good mates. We used to go to The Plaza nightclub together in St Helens." We had a few fights with some of the lads in St Helens as they just didn't like us charming the knickers off all their birds. Then I said to Ricky "I remember pulling your chubby little cheeks when you were about a year old, and you used to cry like a little girl." I tell you what lads, I wouldn't try and pull his chubby cheeks now because I know what the outcome would be. Me put to sleep on the floor. Anyway, as I said before me and Ricky have gone on to become really good mates over the last six years or so. We just buzz off each other. Love you Ricky.

Back to the hotel, it was getting late, or should I say early. It was about half six in the morning and there was still about thirty or so of us up, still boozing and buzzing. I think there must've been a quarter of the famous Huyton pub, The Huyton Park, in this bar. It was hilarious. There was me old mate, Big Fergo (banned now, I'll tell you later). A hard lad, took no shit whatsoever off anyone. Then there was Beno, another great red. So just to have a laugh, me and Ricky start a bit of a spoof argument in front of all the lads. I says to Ricky something like "Sit down Ricky you knobhead or I'll put you down." Fergo was sitting down behind me and Ricky and he gestured to me "Don't Gerry. He's a fucking lunatic." Then me and Ricky just burst out laughing. We just love each other's company. Always looking for a laugh. We even go fishing for carp at the end of the season at a friend of mine's lake in Burscough. It's great to relax when the football season is over. Ricky is a good friend of ex-Liverpool player Steve Harkness. I've known Harky for years as well. We always have a nice relaxing day at the lake. A few sherbets in the sunshine. You can't beat that. That's apart from watching our beloved redmen of course. Right, back to Istanbul.

It's time for us to leave now after a glorious three days. It was time to get back home so it's bags packed and off to the airport. It was bouncing with redmen everywhere still pissed up. No problems though, just good boss banter. We had a good few hours to wait so I decided to dress up in loads of jaag gear. A pair of white trousers and one of the snidest leather jackets you have ever seen. I had everyone in bulk. But I left myself wide open to scouse humour. It didn't take long for someone to shout "Gerry, that's better than the gear you normally wear". Fucking typical scouse humour. It was a boss flight all the way back to Manchester, but that all changed. Those Manc bizzies and the baggage handlers were well out of order. Everyone was waiting at the conveyor belts for their bags and nothing came for ages. One of the lads went to the beginning on the conveyor belt, pulls back the black strips where the bags come through, only to see the bag handlers booting and throwing our bags all over the place. Fucking Man U fans no doubt. We complained to the bizzies but they just took no notice. I was standing there with Ted Edwards, a great Liverpool fan. Ted's mam and dad were also with us. So I decided to start doing my Mick Jagger on the conveyor belt, just to pass the time. Then this prick bizzie comes over and says "Get down now." I says "Or wa?" He says "If you don't get down I'll nick you." I says "I don't think so copper. See all of us here. We are sick to death of being treated like animals. If you arrest me you'll have to arrest us all. Now fuck off and sort our bags out. You are all way out of order." I really enjoyed that. The bizzie didn't know what to do. So he swallowed it and walked away. Finally the bags started coming through the conveyor belt. Some of them were wide open. All sorts of clothes hanging out. But fuck them 'cause we won it for the fifth time in Istanbul, we won it five times. I get back to my house and I think

I slept for the whole day, reliving the game in my head. We had finished a measly fifth behind Everton in fourth in the league and in the FA Cup Rafa got it all wrong as we got knocked out away to Burnley. Rafa picked a very weak team and he paid the price. We lost 1-0. I don't think Rafa knew how important the FA Cup was, but he soon learned as you will see. In the League Cup we went all the way to the Millennium in Cardiff, only to lose 3-0 to Chelsea, so that's yet another season over. What a debut season for Rafa Benitez! An instant legend. It was nice to relax in the summer, just lying on the beach. Sometimes I just lay there in the sun and asked myself 'Gerry, did that really happen lad?'

There was controversy before the season even started as we took a qualifiers spot in the Champions League. Rafa signed a new goalkeeper, Pepe Reina from Spain. What a buy, what a keeper. But the season started badly, winning only two, drawing four and losing two. One of the losses was a thumping 4-1 to Chelsea at Anfield. Then we went on a tremendous run, winning ten on the trot. One of them was against the blue shite. No problems with a 3-1 win at Goodison. We shut them pricks up yet again. Then the fucking wheels came right off again. In the next eleven games, we only win four, drawing three and losing four. What made it worse was that we lost to Chelsea again, then to Arsenal, then those pricks from down the East Lancs Rd. The damage had been done but we went on another brilliant run, winning all of our remaining nine games. Sadly it wasn't enough, eventually finishing third with 82 points, United finished second with 83 points. Chelsea were worthy winners in the end finishing with 91 points but it was a definite improvement from us. So it's the cup competitions now. Fell at the first hurdle away to Crystal Palace 2-1 in the League Cup, but it was a different story in the FA Cup. We get drawn away at Luton Town in the third round, it was an incredible game which we went on to win 5-3 with goals from Stevie G, two from Sinama Pongolle and two from the magnificent Xabi Alonso. One of them was a wonder goal from inside his own half. Just so nice to watch that one. Next up we get another away fixture down at Portsmouth. It's got to be the worst ground in the Premier League.

More like a Second Division ground. We win 2-1 thanks to goals
from Stevie G and John Arne Riise. What a boss journey home!
The coach rocked all the way. As usual I won a few bob. Not loads.
A few hundred, but that will do. Next up we get Man United at
home. The atmosphere was brilliant as always. Big Peter Crouch
scores the only goal of the game after twenty minutes. I'll tell you
what lads, I had a few sherbets that night. Next was Birmingham
City in the quarter finals, away yet again.

Another unbelievable game, or should I say a massacre. I was
made up we got Birmingham away because me and the other bird
in my life, Annmarie, were doing an antique fair in the famous
Birmingham rag market, where we have a stall. It's only on once
a month. We have to leave Liverpool at about half past two in the
morning to get there for four o'clock when it starts. We decided
to stay in Birmingham for the night after doing a really hard day's
work in the rag market. We finished selling about midday. So we
booked into a hotel round the corner and it was straight to bed. We
were both shattered from an early start to the day. The Birmingham
ground was literally a three minute walk away from the hotel. We
slept until about six o'clock in the evening, then it was up for a
shower and getting myself ready for the match, leaving my bird to
get herself ready as we were going for a meal after the game. So I
walk up to the ground, get there about forty five minutes before
kickoff, get in the queue but it was mayhem. Loads of problems.
Same old same old. Some of these people who police the games
just haven't got a clue. The queue just didn't seem to be getting any
shorter with only ten minutes to go until kickoff. They kicked off
and there was still about thirty or forty people in front of me. Then
we hears a big roar. Goal. "Who scored?" someone shouts. Yes, get
in! Sammi Hyppia scores to make it 1-0 in the very first minute.
Finally I'm at the front of the queue, just going into the turnstile
when I hear another big roar. Get in, 2-0. Big Peter Crouch in the
fifth minute. Fucking sick I missed the goals but we are two up so I
can't complain. But that was only the beginning. It finally finished
7-0. Yes, 7-0. Wow. Crouch scores another, Morientes with one,
Riise, Cisse and an own goal. Absolutely brilliant. I'm buzzing so

it's back to the hotel within five minutes of the game finishing. Me bird looked beautiful, all ready to go for our nice night out. She looked that nice we nearly never went out. What a lovely day. The till never stopped ringing in the market and our beloved redmen have booked their place in the semi-final of the FA Cup against that Chelsea. We beat them 2-1 thanks to John Arne Riise and yet another from the brilliant Louis Garcia. So it's back to The Millennium Stadium, our second home, to play West Ham United. After the game it was named one of the friendliest finals ever. The fans reacted to each other in a lovely way. It was such a refreshing change to back in the old hooligan era days. No more ICF (Inter City Firm) of West Ham skinhead days. Believe me it was scary back then. The cheeky bastards, even leaving their calling cards that read 'You have been had by the ICF'. I think back to them dark days and it still amazes me how many, many more people didn't die at football matches because these thugs just didn't know when to stop. The atmosphere in the game was really relaxed. Then they kickoff, but before we know it we are 2-0 down. One of them was a fluke but a lot of Liverpool fans put it down to Pepe Reina's misjudgment. Cisse pulls one back on the half hour, then enter the irresistible Stevie G. Cometh the hour, cometh the man. Just on sixty minutes it's 2-2. But the buzz of pulling it back was soon gone as West Ham score again to make it 3-2. I'm drained. It was agonising to watch. We were pushing and pushing but time was running out. Then with time nearly up, up pops the sublime Stevie G yet again, who hit a screamer from about thirty yards. Fucking get in. Final whistle goes. 3-3. Extra Time. No score so it goes down to penalties. No problem. We love penalties. We've won twelve out of thirteen. Anyway Pepe Reina saves from Anton Ferdinand, Rio the lip's brother. Get in. Wow, these finals always deliver the buzz. So it's yet another trophy in the cabinet.

In the Champions League we had a decent run, but sadly not good enough. After cruising through the qualifiers against the mighty TNS of Wales, we get FBK Kaunas. No problems again, winning comfortably 3-1 away. But sadly we came unstuck in both legs against Benfica. We lost 1-0 away and even worse at Anfield, losing 2-0. Nothing excited on our trips abroad to Anderlecht, CSKA Sofia, or at Chelsea. All just in and out. We stayed one night in Sofia. As always we're looking for a nice holiday to unwind. But the summer didn't go as well as usual for me. I hadn't been feeling too good for months but I'm not one for going to the doctors. I usually let things sort themselves out. I was getting breathless and everything so in the end me bird Annmarie said "Gerry, you are obviously not right. I have booked you into the doctors in the morning." It was about two weeks to go before the new season was about to start. I went to see my doctor and after a load of tests, he confirmed I had Emphysema, mostly due to forty years of smoking cigarettes. I walked out of the doctors in shock. He said I would be needing a heart operation in the very near future. I was devastated. I knew there was something wrong with me but I didn't think it would be this serious. I was really scared. A major operation on my heart? The season was now only a couple of days away when I get a phone call from Broadgreen hospital to say a slot had opened up for me to have my operation. The only problem was it was only two days away! I had no time to prepare for it. But I had to say yes. Let's do it. I have never ever been so afraid in my life. I had to sign a form that if the operation was not a success that the hospital had done the best they could possibly do. As I said it was so, so scary. All I can remember is my bird driving me to Broadgreen hospital, then going into a cubicle. The nurse came in and gave me a good shave all over if you know what I mean. Then the Surgeon comes in, a certain Dr Rashid. Yes the same surgeon who operated on our man Gerard Houllier a couple of years ago. All I remember is Dr Rashid looking at me and saying "Mr. Blayney, I do probably two of these operations a day so do not worry. You will be OK." Then he put the needle in my arm and that was it. Off to the operating theatre.

The next thing I know I am lying in my bed after an eight or nine hour operation. I don't know how long it took for me to come around but I felt like I was dead. I was so weak I couldn't move. The operation I had usually means five to seven days in hospital but as usual with me it wasn't so simple. I ended up in hospital for fifteen days. My family were really worried but there was no need. Being a redman helped me battle through the wind and the rain. It was roughly two or three months before I could even walk twenty yards. I needed a stick for help or my daughter would walk me through the park. I missed the first thirteen games of the season. Then I thought I was well enough to go to the next game but me bird was going fucking nuts. "Gerry you can barely walk. Give it a few more weeks." But no, I decided I'm well enough to go to the Reading game at home. It was much too soon for me to go back. I actually left the game at half time. There is no way I can go next week so I'll have to wait a few more weeks. It was killing me having to watch Sky Sports to see the scores. Then finally I'm up and running, well, not quite running, but just about fit enough to travel to see our beloved redmen.

The season hadn't started as well as we had hoped, winning only five of the first thirteen league games, but that soon changed, winning ten out of the next twelve games, drawing one, losing one. Sadly that run came to an end, winning only four of the last ten games of the season, finishing third, a massive 21 points behind champions Man United. Fucking gutted. In the cup competitions it wasn't much better, going out in the third round at Anfield against Arsenal. Arsenal done us again in the quarter final of the League Cup, beating us 6-3, yes 6-3 – an incredible game. But in the Champions League we had a great run, getting all the way to the final in Athens, Greece, against of all teams, AC Milan again. On doctor's orders I couldn't fly for a couple of months so I missed a few trips to PSV Eindhoven, Galatasaray and Barcelona. But it was Chelsea in the semi-final. I really do not like going to that Chelsea. The first leg was away. A boss journey all the way down on the coach. Everyone was dreaming of another European final. In a very, very tight game we lose 1-0 but everyone was dead confident that the return leg would take us to the final. And boy they weren't wrong. The crowd was magnificent. The Kop in full voice. Then in the twenty-second minute the roof nearly came off the Kop. Get in there. And of all goal-scorers it was Daniel Agger. It was a really tense game after that, finally finishing 1-1 after extra time. So it's down to penalties. We love them. Dirk Kuyt scored the decisive goal so we're off to Greece for the final. I am alright to fly now. It's been a really horrible year for me personally. I just hate being out injured, just like Carra and Stevie G. Anyway it's off to Greece for yet another European Cup Final.

It was a nightmare for us from the minute we started. It was really hard to get a flight. I went with my brother Alan and his two sons, Todd and Elliot. We finally got a flight. We booked it in Prescott. A Pakistani guy was running it. He made a fucking fortune. Me and our Alan worked it out. He made about a quarter of a million quid. Anyway we get to the airport and as we are about to board the plane me and our Alan looked at each other and said "What the fuck's this?" The plane was a joke. It was so old. Without a doubt the worst plane I've ever been on. But that's only the start. We arrived in Greece and get to the hotel. Hotel my ass. It was a disgrace. Just loads of camp beds in rooms. Paint falling off the walls and the ceiling. I wouldn't even have a shit in the toilet it was that bad. I think we paid around £1,000 each for the trip. There was no way we were staying in this poxy hotel, sharing with about six or seven people. We didn't even unpack our bags. We just got straight off. What a joke. As to the match itself, I can't really remember much about the game, just that horrible feeling at the final whistle. I just got rotten drunk and ended up in bed early. I couldn't wait to fly home in the morning.

Oh, there was one thing about the game I remember. It was fucking hilarious. Gattuso had the ball and I just screamed at the top of my voice "What's new pussycat, Whoa whoa whoa whoa whoa" and all as one the travelling redmen joined into it and sang the whole song. Todd and Elliot were pissing themselves laughing. A couple of weeks before the final Steven Gerrard called Gattuso a Pussycat in the paper, hence the Tom Jones song 'Pussycat, Pussycat I love you'. You had to be there really to appreciate it. A couple of months before the final we finally found a buyer for our beloved club, on the 6th February. Hicks and Gillette, from America. They promised us everything we craved. A new stadium with 60,000 plus capacity. They promised to make us great again, saying the funds were there for Rafa to buy the quality players that we needed but what a load of bollocks. They just saw us as a money machine. To me, and I'm not talking in hindsight, it stunk from the very beginning. I was watching Liverpool FC on the TV, just like every other fan, to see what they had to say. For me it was comical. Hicks and Gillette standing there with their sons, all wearing nice brand new scarves round their necks and drinking coffee from a Liverpool mug. They looked so nervous. It just didn't sit right with me and many, many other redmen. And sadly, at the end of the day we were right. So the next three and a half years we had a really, really horrendous time. I felt so sorry for Rafa. But what could he do without a massive injection of cash to buy proper quality players. Nonetheless, we are heading in the right direction, finishing third to qualify for the Champions League yet again and also another trophy for the cabinet. Sadly, it was only the Charity Shield. We beat Chelsea 2-1, which is always nice, thanks to goals from John Arne Riise and Peter Crouch. As always when we win the coach bounced all the way down the motorways, everyone singing and dancing and me doing me Jagger impersonation.

Rafa signed a few players in the summer, the main player being Fernando Torres from Atletico Madrid. In my opinion, Rafa took a gamble paying £24m on a centre forward with a goal average of just less than one in three games, but he actually played as a lone striker at Atletico with no support really. But boy did that change when he came to our beloved club. He was an instant hit with the world famous Kop and the rest of Anfield, especially when we found out that he used to wear an armband for Atletico that read "You'll never walk alone". It was a marriage made in heaven, especially watching him with the magnificent Stevie G just behind him. It was an amazing partnership. Just a joy to watch. Torres's home debut was against, of all teams, Chelsea. And it didn't take him long to make his mark. Fifteen minutes to be precise. A magnificent goal. His pace was frightening. If he turned you, you were left for dead. We had a brilliant start to the season, going unbeaten in the first fourteen league games, winning eight, drawing six, but there were too many draws which cost us dearly at the end of the season. But the next two games is what really hurt our chances of becoming champions. The first game was away to Reading where we got well and truly fucked 3-1, but that was fuck all compared to the next game against them horrible bastards from down the East Lancashire Road. Manure at Anfield. The crowd was brilliant, willing the team on, but we end up losing 1-0. Then another six match unbeaten run, winning two, drawing four. Far too many draws. Then we really pushed on the last fifteen games, losing only one which really, really hurt. It was against....Yes, you guessed it, Manure again. We got well and truly spanked 3-0. We ended up finishing fourth in the league, a good eleven points behind United. But believe me it was much closer than that overall.

Torres and Gerrard were magnificent all season. Torres scored a fabulous 34 goals in all competitions, 24 in the league. Plus the magnificent Stevie G scored 20 goals. It was so nice to watch the two of them play together. In the domestic cups, Barnsley knocked us out 2-1 at Anfield in the FA Cup, in the League Cup we got to the quarter finals, only to go out to Chelsea at Stamford Bridge. Then we had another brilliant run in the Champions League beating Toulouse, FC Porto, and Marseille. Then it was away to Inter Milan. The first leg was at Anfield, and as always the redmen were well and truly up for this one. The atmosphere was electric. The Italians, as usual, just came to spoil the game, trying to hang onto a 0-0 draw. To be honest, they defended brilliantly. Wave after wave of attack from Liverpool but we just couldn't break through. Then with only five minutes left the goal finally came. Dirk Kuyt makes it 1-0. The crowd went mental. There was still a few minutes to go. The Italians had no option but to try and attack us. But we caught them beautifully on the counter attack. The magnificent Stevie G scores to make it 2-0 it the last minute. At the final whistle the Inter Milan players just sank to the turf. Then The Kop gave it them in no uncertain terms, "Go back to Italy, Go back to Italy". It was pure magic. I'm really buzzing now. As I said earlier in the book, my favourite other team apart from Liverpool is AC Milan. Wow, some history, very similar to ours. I've always wanted to go to the San Siro Stadium but sadly we have never been paired with them in Europe apart from the finals. So when the draw for the last sixteen came and it gave us Inter Milan I was made up because they share the San Siro with AC Milan. I was delighted. And when we got to the stadium I wasn't disappointed. It was magnificent, an 80,000 capacity. The atmosphere inside was brilliant. Nearly, and I say nearly, as good as Anfield, but not quite. The reds played brilliantly and then it happened. Cometh the hour, cometh the man. The ball got played to Torres just outside the penalty area with his back to goal. He controlled it and turned the defender like a kipper, smashing it into the bottom corner of the net. That was enough to see us through to the quarter final against Arsenal. It was a really, really special night for me at the San Siro as me old mate Carra gave me his shirt from the game which just happened to be his 100th European appearance for our beloved redmen, becoming the first ever player to play 100 games in Europe for Liverpool. Wow, I was in heaven. Thank you so, so much Jamie. It looks beautiful in my shrine with all the other past great redmen shirts.

Right, so it's off to Arsenal for the first leg of quarter finals of the Champions League. The coach was bouncing all the way down the motorway. The travelling redmen were well and truly up for this one. So it's into the game we go. After a very nervy fifteen minutes or so, Arsenal score. 1-0. Oh no, come on redmen. But it didn't take too long. Get in. Dirk Kuyt makes it 1-1 on the half hour mark. Fuck me here's that feeling again. It's so, so nice. Much better than sex. And it lasts a lot longer. It was a really good game. Both us and Arsenal creating chances. It finished 1-1. A fabulous result for the redmen. So it's back to Anfield for the second leg for yet another glorious night. And I've seen them all. The atmosphere was really electric. Too hard to put it into words, the feelings on these European nights at Anfield. No other football club in the world can match the passion of the world famous Kop and the rest of the Anfield crowd. It was just magical as usual, but it didn't start very well. We went 1-0 down. Then on the half hour mark big Sammi Hyppia makes it 1-1. The crowd had willed that one in. Boy are we the best 12th man in the world. It was another brilliant game, both teams playing really well, then it happened, get in. Fernando Torres scores to make it 2-1 in the sixty ninth minute. But soon after Arsenal made it 2-2. The Kop and the rest of the crowd were stunned for a couple of minutes. It was silent. But at the Anfield Rd end where a few thousand Arsenal fans were it was bouncing with chants of "Where's your famous atmosphere?" Boy did they find out where the famous atmosphere was in the last ten minutes. As it stood Arsenal would go through on away goals but our magnificent crowd just as one, got right behind our beloved redmen and we roared them on. Then it finally came in the eighty-fifth minute. A penalty. There was never any doubt. Up stepped Stevie G, get in, 3-2. Only five minutes to go. But we have to be so, so careful because if Arsenal equalise we would be out. They threw everything at us. They had no option but to. Then our beloved redmen hit them on the break in the very last minute of the game, with that blurt Ryan Babbel. One bad player he was. He made it 4-2 on the night, 5-3 on aggregate to take us through to the semi-final against Chelsea. I was fucking drained coming out of the match. I felt as if I had played in it. It was a beautiful drive home to Crosby for me, only about six miles. I just beeped my car horn all the way out of Anfield, then along County Road. It was amazing, people dancing, punching the air. So it's a quick stop off at the off license, a case of Budweiser and off home to relive the match on LFC TV. Heaven.

So it's into the semi-final we go, against Chelsea. First leg at Anfield. As always The Kop was magnificent. In a very, very tight game, more like a chess game, both teams cancelled each other out. Chances were very few and far between. But just before half time we got the breakthrough. Dirk Kuyt puts the reds 1-0 up. The second half was much of the same. It was nerve racking. The ninety minutes are up and into injury time. Fuck me, four minutes of injury time. Chelsea were throwing everything at us, then it came. What a horrible feeling. No way back. Chelsea score with literally seconds to go. The very unlucky John Arne Riise scores an own goal. What a sickener. I felt so sorry for Riise. It turned out to be the beginning of the end for him. But all in all Riise was a really good player for our beloved redmen. So it's back down to that London for the second leg to that bastard of a place, Stamford Bridge. It turned out to be a bridge too far. We finally got beat 3-2 on the night, 4-3 on aggregate. It was a very, very tight game. The midfield of both sides were giving nothing away. Then the first goal came from Didier Drogba. 1-0 Chelsea. The second half starts and it's so tight again. The travelling redmen were doing their best to drive the team forward, then it came. The brilliant Fernando Torres makes it 1-1. The travelling redmen were bouncing and I mean bouncing. About four thousand redmen were bouncing to the sound of "his armband proved he was red, Torres, Torres, You'll never walk alone it says Torres, Torres, We bought the boy from sunny Spain, he gets the ball and scores again. Fernando Torres, Liverpool's number nine". After that the game was as tight as a drum. No one wanted to take a chance. So ninety minutes are up and it's into extra time. Nerve racking. Then eight minutes into the first period of extra time Chelsea get a penalty. Lampard makes no mistake, 2-1 Chelsea. Then right on half time of extra time Drogba makes it 3-1 on the night, 4-1 on aggregate. Babbel pulls one back with about four minutes left but it was too little too late. Final whistles goes. I'm absolutely gutted. What a horrible journey home. I don't think I spoke another word all the way home. So near to yet another European Cup Final. We would've played them pricks Man United in the final but it just wasn't to be.

We get off to a fabulous start in 2008/09, winning eight and drawing two of the first ten games. The first game of the season was away to Sunderland. We got all three points thanks to an 82nd minute goal from Fernando Torres but as always, them horrible Sunderland Police made sure our journey home would not be a nice one. They kept all the coaches back for about forty-five minutes, then when we finally got moving it was the usual Police escort to the motorway, then an escort onto the motorway keeping all the coaches on the inside lane, with motorbikes and unmarked cars stopping any lane changing. We were doing about forty miles an hour! They wouldn't let us pull into any of the service stations or even turn off the motorway onto an A road. They had a Police vehicle at every junction and service station stopping us from coming off. It was unbelievable. They had no right whatsoever to do this but it is the Police. It got even worse the following season. The whole coach was going fucking nuts. No drink on board at all. No booze, coke, lemo, no water, nothing. Unbelievable the way they treated us. Fuck them, we are not English, we are Scouse! After two wins and a draw it was Manure next up at Anfield. It's always nice to beat them bastards. Nice? That is the biggest under-statement ever. It was glorious. A beautiful own goal from Wes Brown, a man who loved lap dancers that much, he married one. The other goal was from Ryan Babel (the blurt). Anyway, every time Wes Brown was anywhere near The Kop end, I was giving him loads of verbals from where I sit in the Upper Centenary. I've got a very loud voice, some people say I've got a big gob. But I let it go on him. I shouted "Hey Wes, your wife gives a lovely dance. And it was only a fiver". All the people who have been sitting around me for the past however many years were loving it. Some of them were pissing themselves laughing. I didn't stop the whole game. You could see it was affecting him. He was glaring up towards me. It was boss. Big Frank, who sits next to me on one side, and Big Steve, who sits the other side, and a kid named Spam who was sitting directly in front of me. I think we must've missed fifteen minutes or so of the game through hilarious laughter. It just put the icing on the cake after a 2-1 win. And it was great to give them Mancs a taste of our Scouse humour. Laugh out fucking loud. Then came our first defeat of the season, away at Tottenham. We scored with our first attack through Dirk Kuyt in the first few minutes. Then it all went pear shaped, they hit back and finally beat us 2-1. That was a fucking horrible journey home, I slept most of the way. But we then go on another great run, fifteen games without defeat. But sadly eight of those fifteen were draws. The run came to an end at Middlesbrough, that's one twat of a place. We lost 2-0.

With only eleven games left it was a three horse race for the title: Us, Manure, and Chelsea. Only a handful of points in it but those Mancs kept winning when we were drawing. As it happened, Middlesbrough was the last time we lost that season, meaning we only lost two games in the whole league season. We gave it one hell of a go and went on one almighty run, winning ten of the last eleven games, drawing the other. After beating Sunderland at Anfield, next up it was down to Old Trafford. We totally destroyed them 4-1 and had all of us redmen dreaming of winning the title. Then after destroying Aston Villa 5-0 at Anfield it was off to that London yet again. It was Fulham this time. As always the coach bounced down the motorways, all the lads having a ball. It was a very tight game. 0-0 at Half Time. About twenty minutes to go and it was still 0-0. We were pressing but with no joy. Then I turned to three of four of the lads off the coach, I think it was John, Neil, Lee, and Zack, I said to them "Don't worry lads, we're going to win this. We're going to bring on little Yossi Benayoun and he'll grab the winner in the last few minutes". Time was running out, it was coming to the last minutes and fuck me it happened. Little Yossi Benayoun. Get in. 1-0. The travelling redmen went mental. An absolutely brilliant finish to the game and a brilliant journey home. A swift stop at the Off License and it was party time all the way home. The music was blaring, everyone dancing in the aisles of the coach. No one wanted the journey to end. What a trip that was. Next up we destroy Blackburn 4-0 at Anfield. Then came an incredible game at Anfield against Arsenal. After going behind a couple of times the score ended in an incredible 4-4 draw, with Benayoun grabbing the equaliser in the ninetieth minute yet again. The atmosphere was absolutely brilliant, but a draw meant we had it all to do. With only five games left and only three or four points separating Manure and us, it was points dropped. I was gutted driving home after the game.

And I was even more gutted at about half six the next morning when my wife Anmmarie got up to open the shop for work. As she got out of bed she looked out of the window to see what the weather was like. Then she turned to me and said "Gerry, did you leave the car at the match or what?" I said "No, I drove home." She said "Well it's not up the path". I jumped up and looked out of the window, fuck me it was gone. Been robbed, but that wasn't the end of it. We came downstairs to find out the house had been burgled. Then it hit me. "Oh no" I shouted. I ran past my bird and straight upstairs to see if my Liverpool shrine was still intact. I was dreading opening the door. Wow what a relief when I did open it. Thank fuck them robbing bastards didn't have the bottle to come upstairs. They missed out on a nice few bob, as I have numerous signed shirts, balls, programmes as well as other memorabilia in there. It would've destroyed me but thank God it never happened. I went round to see Jamie Carragher a couple of days later to get a few shirts signed for this charity event I was helping with. I told him what had happened and he just looked at me and said "Fuck me lad, not only are them burglars targeting us players, they are also starting to target the top fans as well". We had a laugh about it. Anyway back to the games. We did all we possibly could by winning the last five games but sadly it wasn't enough. We lost the league by four points to Manure. In the FA Cup, it was out in the fourth round by, of all people, that shite from across the park. After a 1-1 draw at Anfield, they beat us 1-0 at Goodison. Same again in the league cup, out in the fourth round to Tottenham, 4-2 at White Hart Lane. We get to the quarter final in the European Cup, yet again against Chelsea. That was after destroying Real Madrid in the last sixteen. We won 1-0 in Madrid thanks to little Yossi Benayoun yet again. I was absolutely gutted I couldn't go but what can I do? But I really enjoyed the return game at Anfield. We totally destroyed the mighty Real Madrid 4-0. Yes, 4-0. Thanks to goals from the brilliant Stevie Gerrard (2), Fernando Torres and a very, very rare goal from Dossena. Not that rare really as he also scored in the 4-1 win at Old Trafford the week before. So it's the first leg of the quarter final at Anfield against Chelsea. As always the crowd was really pumped up for this one. They gave their all, but sadly on the night Chelsea played really well and deservedly beat our beloved redmen 3-1. It started so well. Torres scoring after five minutes, 1-0, but after that it all went horribly wrong. So we have left ourselves a mountain and a half to climb. The coach journey down was the same as always. Everyone confident we could pull it back. In an incredible game we needed to score at least three. We went one better than that and scored four, but so did Chelsea. It finished 4-4 on the night so that was the end for us. All in all it has been a really good season, only losing two games in the league all season, but sadly all those draws cost us in the end. So it's yet another season over. No silverware in the cabinet.

By now most of our beloved red fans are not happy at all. That pair of cowboys, Hicks and Gillette were full of broken promises. Full of shit. The Spirit of Shankly Group was formed and they let that pair of cowboys know, in no uncertain terms, that we wouldn't put up with listening to all these lies anymore. These next two seasons are without a doubt the worst two seasons I have ever witnessed at Anfield. There were all sorts of demonstrations going on outside Anfield. At one time there was even a chance that out beloved Liverpool Football Club would go into administration. Fuck me, people were talking about us doing a Leeds – they were once a massive club but look at them now. It was horrible going to the games. You could just feel it. It was like a nightmare where you just can't wake up and find out it was only a dream. But it wasn't a dream. We were in big, big trouble. Rafa Benitez was not a happy man. It was also affecting the players on the pitch. We lost two of the first three league games, 2-1 at White Hart lane with Gerrard scoring from the spot, and 3-1 at Villa Park with Torres scoring a consolation goal. We never recovered from that really bad start. I think all redmen knew we faced a major battle for qualification to the Champions League, and so it proved. We ended up finishing in a miserable 7th place. Fernando Torres had done his knee in after setting up a Europa League semi-final showdown with his old club, Atletico Madrid. Also there were stories floating round about Benitez's agent holding talks with the Juventus board. Plus Xabi Alonso moved on to Real Madrid. I love Rafa but that was the worst decision he made for Liverpool Football Club. No doubt about it, this has to be the worst season I have ever witnessed over the past fifty five years or so.

Some nights I couldn't sleep, dreading getting up in the morning to read the papers and watch Sky Sports. I just couldn't believe this nightmare was happening to our beloved Liverpool Football Club. The only chink of light to brighten these darkest days was the last game of the season. It was at Anfield against

Chelsea. I tell you what lads, it will have to go down as one of the weirdest games I have ever seen because believe me, most redmen wanted us to lose this game, and we did. We were well and truly beaten, 2-0, but it meant that Chelsea were crowned champions ahead of that Manure from down the East Lancs. At the end of the game the Chelsea fans were buzzing at winning the league. They were chanting "You're ancient history, you're ancient history". The Kop was silent, lacking either the will or the evidence to disagree with the Chelsea fans. What a devastating season that turned out to be. Like every Liverpool fan I was battered and drained. All my energy had been sucked away from me. All I want to do know is forget all about it, and try and relax for a few months before we start it all over again. Me and the other bird in my life, Annmarie (what a woman) had a really relaxing holiday in Egypt. Just lazed on the sun-loungers by the pool and read a few Liverpool books to cheer me up. I read Michael Shield's book. It was so sad. I wrote him a long letter a couple of months after he was initially arrested in 2005, Istanbul, telling him of my experience of being locked up abroad in 1980. I just told him 'Don't worry son, the power of all us scousers, all our beloved redmen will help you through this storm. You'll never walk alone lad'. He came on our coach for one of the games after he got out. I can't really remember which game it was. He sat next to me all the way there and back. We had a really good chat. He was such a nice kid. He'd lost about five or six stone, but looked good because he was a bit of a fat kid. He won't mind me saying that because I had a boss laugh with him when the conversation came to birds. (No, not the Liver bird). I said "Come on lad, you have had a touch. Now you're nice and slim, quite good looking. You should have no problems pulling the ladies". Good luck in the future son and I'll see you soon. Back to Egypt. I met this boss family from Stamford in Lincolnshire. It was our first day there so all I wanted to do was lay there by the pool. So I get down the pool nice and early with the Liver bird tattooed on my chest and one of my numerous Liverpool shirts on my back. I notice this big guy, about forty eight years of age with a beautiful big tattoo on his leg of our beloved Liverpool Football Club. We immediately bonded as one member to another of the greatest football club in the world (arguably). But there is no argument about who are the greatest fans on the earth, and our beloved redmen hold that title in most quarters. Anyway we had a great time talking about LFC. His name was Paul Webb and his lovely wife Jane. He thinks he's fucking Tarzan. Such a nice guy and Jane a lovely lady. Only messing Jane, she doesn't like getting called a lady. Anyway I invited them down to come and watch a game at Anfield. I sorted out his tickets and as a really nice surprise I sorted out some tickets to meet the players after the game in the players' lounge. The game was against West Ham which we won 3-0. They stayed in my house for the weekend with one of their sons, Jamie. It was his birthday on the day of the match so it was such a pleasure for me to be able to make it one of the best birthdays he's ever had. Anyway we had a great holiday and now it's time to go home for the new season.

The media were giving us loads, Liverpool this, Liverpool that. The nightmare was getting worse. Then it happened. On the 3rd June, about twelve hours before my fifty-ninth birthday, the headlines in the paper read 'Benitez leaves Liverpool'. Rafa said "It is a sad day for me to announce that I will no longer be the manager of Liverpool Football Club. I would like to thank all the staff and the players for their efforts. Also I would like to thank the magnificent fans for all your support over the years. I am very, very proud to say I was your manager. Thank you so much once more and always remember you'll never walk alone". I was absolutely gutted. Those fucking god damn Yanks. Full of promises, full of bullshit. I felt so sorry, not only for Rafa but for his lovely wife and children. They remind me of Jan Molby's family. Such nice people. They are without a doubt adopted scousers, forever in the history of our beloved redmen. So Rafa, me and my massive, massive red family wish you are your family the best of luck in the future. You and your family will never ever walk alone. And thank you so so, so much for your very generous £96,000 donation to the Hillsborough fund. You are just simply class Rafa. Wow, Istanbul. I will take them memories to my grave. Even to this day, seven years later, I still have to pinch myself and ask 'Did that really happen

Gerry?' Fuck me it did. I've never in my life been through so many different emotions in any game I have seen. And that's a lot of games well over two thousand. So I can't pay you any higher compliment than that Rafa. I think in a way it was a relief for Rafa and his family. The stories were flying all round Liverpool that Benitez wasn't looking good. He was white and gaunt, all through too much worry and too little sleep. He picked up infections and coughs and kept coming out in cold sweats. When some of his friends told him how he looked he said "No I'm alright" and invented stories about his daughter waking him up all through the night. The truth was Liverpool's decline was affecting him badly. And as a result he would stay up all night watching videos of football, devising ways of getting Liverpool out of trouble. Rafa's wife Montse said she loved living in their Caldy home on the Wirral and had no desire to move back to Spain, or anywhere else for that matter. Apparently she was just breaking down in tears all the while. So I think Rafa made the right decision for himself and his family. Thank you once again Rafa. I wish you and your family a happy and healthy life. YNWA.

THE MANAGERIAL MERRY-GO-ROUND

A S ALWAYS ALL SORTS OF NAMES cropped up for the new Liverpool managers job. There was Harry Redknapp but he said he didn't fancy it, Gus Hiddink swiftly let it be known that he wasn't interested, in fact the only man to openly tout for the job was Sven Goran Eriksson, who came out with the biggest load of bullshit I have ever heard. He quoted that he has been a Liverpool fan all his life. But in the end the new manager would be Roy Hodgson from Fulham. So it's off to the Jewellers for me to buy another silver salver. As well as myself, many, many Liverpool supporters were disappointed that King Kenny didn't get the job. And in hindsight we were correct. Anyway after seven months, one miserable defeat after another, the fans were chanting Hodgson for England, followed by the chants of Dalglish. In the end the club were forced to send an embarrassing distress call to a cruise ship in the Persian Gulf, begging the prodigal son to return and save the season. Me and millions of Liverpool fans were delighted. I did feel a little bit sorry for Hodgson. It was such a massive job to fill. Just a little too big for him. He seemed a nice guy. I went up to Melwood as I usually do to welcome him with his silver salver wishing him all the best at his appointment as Liverpool manager. So it's back to the jewellers yet again to get another silver salver for King Kenny. That's another £120. I inscribed on the salver 'Welcome back King Kenny. Let's have the same again, from Gerry Blayney and Billy Swann (deceased)'. Kenny just looked at me and laughed as if to say 'You're not asking much are you Gerry'. Well he soon had our beloved redmen moving swiftly up the table, from third from bottom to end up finishing in seventh place, just missing out on qualification to the Europa League on the last game of the season at Anfield against Tottenham. We lost 2-0. Myself and many, many others were not upset with that defeat costing us a place in Europe.

In fact I was happy. As far as I'm concerned and many, many more redmen, it was a blessing in disguise because to reach the final of the Europa League you have to play a minimum of twenty-two games. Fuck me that's a third of a league season. Far too many games, far too much travel. It would definitely hinder our chances of qualifying for the Champions League the following season.

Then the news every Liverpool fan in the world had been waiting for finally came. After forty-four months of, I don't know what, it was over. A relief. Them bastard Yanks had finally gone. Things could only get better without them cowboys. So after the usual media hype, our new owners were yet another company from America, but I assure you these Yanks are not just in it for the money. They had pedigree. They like winning. They made the Boston Red Sox famous and my gut feeling is that they will restore our fame. The Yanks are dead. Long live the Yanks. It's just a breath of fresh air to me. I just knew this was the start of a new beginning for our beloved redmen, but let's not get carried away. Rome wasn't built in a day. So redmen, we need to be patient, it might take a good few seasons.

The Yanks didn't wait long to show the cash to Dalglish, who went out and bought Luis Suarez for £22million. I'd only seen clips of him but he looked brilliant and the thought of him teaming up with Torres was mouth-watering. But it all turned sour when Fernando Torres left for Chelsea with only about two hours left of the transfer deadline. We got £50million for him so it wasn't that bad. Then about one hour later we signed Andy Carroll from Newcastle United for £35million. A lot of money for a young lad but we did well out of the Torres deal so fuck the ladyboy. I've lost all my respect for that man, especially as I went out of my way for him. In his first season at Anfield his wife gave birth to a little girl. Eva her name if my memory serves me right. Anyway I got Torres a beautiful present for his daughter. I got him something that you can't buy in the shops. My Auntie is really good with a needle. She makes these beautiful tapestries, about the size of a birthday card and all hand stitched. It takes her about two or three days to do. She puts the date of birth, and then the weight of the baby. His wife must've been delighted. I told Jamie Carragher that I was getting it made for him so Jamie told him I was getting it done. He asked Jamie could I possibly get the weight put in Kilos, not pounds and ounces. Anyway I was very busy at the time so I gave it to Jamie to give to him at Melwood. I also wrote him a letter telling him how much our beloved redmen loved him and I asked him would he give me a telephone call, or even better to write me a small letter in reply so I could put it alongside my collection of shirts, letters, balls, all my memorabilia. But nothing. Not a dickie bird. Fuck him. The ungrateful bastard. Anyway the new owners wasted no time giving Kenny more money for new players as well as Luis Suarez. Kenny brought in Stewart Downing from Villa, Charlie Adam from Blackpool, Jordan Henderson from Sunderland and Jose Enrique from Newcastle, spending at total of about £80million. He also brought in a young unknown, Uruguayan centre half Sebastian Coates, plus a great free transfer, Craig Bellamy from Man City. The feeling among all of our massive family is so different than that of the last two seasons. At least now we have a bit of hope. But as I've said before we must be patient. So here we go, into the 2011–12 season.

★

It's Friday night, around 10.15. I'm just watching Sky Sports. Everyone is dead excited with the new season starting tomorrow. So it's off to bed. I can't sleep. I feel like a junkie waiting for my next fix. I finally drift off to dream about our beloved redmen. Then before I knew it, it was morning. So I'm up and ready and it's off to Anfield. I usually leave my home in Crosby at about quarter to two. By the time I get parked up it's about quarter past two. So it's a quick pint or two in The Twelfth Man pub. A good friend of mine Robbie Rogers, also a great red, runs the pub. It's fucking rammed every game. But Robbie always makes sure I don't have to queue up. He always sorts me out. No charge as well. A good mate Robbie. Thanks a lot lad. I leave the pub around 2.40pm. It's only a five minute walk to the game. That's for most people. But for me it takes about twelve minutes as me old legs are struggling these days so I have to take it nice and easy. First of all, I salute the Shankly statue, then I make my way round to the Anfield Rd end to the Hillsborough Memorial. I kiss the first two fingers of my right hand and spread them right across my son's name, Peter Andrew Harrison. I've kissed that stone at every home game since the tragedy. Then it's into the game. I sit in the Upper Centenary towards The Kop end, literally ten yards or so from the scoreboard where all the police observation goes on. Just as the players are entering the pitch towards The Kop end, Jamie Carragher runs towards where I sit, or should I say stand. I always stand on my seat and thump my heart with my right hand and Carra responds with a fisted salute. It was really funny a couple of seasons ago. This new steward started on our entrance. He was a fucking man mountain, bigger than big Ron Yeats. Anyway as I stand on my seat to greet Carra and the boys I hear this big shout from less than ten yards away. He shouts to me "Hey soft lad, sit down now." I just looked at him, gave him a quick "No" and then it was so funny. Loads of people around me started to shout at him. "Shut it lad. Don't you know who he is?" one fella shouted. Wow, what a compliment.

Anyway back to the first game. Everyone was made up with the return of King Kenny. First up was Sunderland at Anfield. The crowd were buzzing and it didn't take long to erupt. After only four minutes the magnificent Suarez is clean through on the goalkeeper. He calmly goes around the goalkeeper only for the last man to bring him down. No doubt about it's a penalty and a sending off. But no! That stupid ref Dowd gave the penalty but didn't send the defender off. He totally bottled it. It was only four minutes into the opening game of the season. If that would've been four or five games into the season he would have definitely sent the player off. But no. We missed the penalty and to make it worse they still had the full eleven players on the pitch. Suarez then did score and we went 1-0 up. We were playing well then all of a sudden, right out of the blue, it's 1-1. Then after that we missed chance after chance after chance. To Sunderland's credit they defended brilliantly. It finishes 1-1. So next up it's Arsenal away at The Emirates. What a boss stadium. It's class. As usual we get picked up at the Village Inn in Aintree, a nice big brekkie before we get on the coach. So it's off to that London yet again. As always it was a boss trip on the way down the motorways. Nice music and loads of banter between one another. The booze was flowing plus whatever else. All the usual suspects on board. That lunatic, my mate James Miller, I love him to death but I am afraid he is a lunatic. Funny as fuck though. Then there's Fletch who runs the coach. Me and Fletch have become really good friends over the years. He runs the coach and doesn't make a penny. Sometimes he's putting money in to make it up. Then there's Graham, Fletch's sidekick. Then Lee Brennan, nice lad, wouldn't like to fight him though. There's allsorts on our coach. Bricklayers, sparks, roofers, builders, shopfitters, and also shoplifters… only messin'. As always the music was boss thanks to Lee O'Conner the music man. Then there's Neil, the stats man and me mate Zack. Then at the back of the bus where I sit with all the lunatics there's Mogga, Scott Jones and Macca who are two of my favourite people on the coach, Kinney, Tommo, Brad, Callum, John Stewart, Joanna. Then there's Micah, wow what a tattoo he's got on his back. More or less the whole of his back. There's loads of other lads who go on the coach but it's so hard remembering all their names. Don't go mad if I've missed you out lads, I can't remember everyone's name. So we arrive at the Emirates, everyone bouncing. We start the game really well. Then Arsenal have a player sent off and we end up winning the game 2-0, an own goal and in the ninetieth minute the little genius pops up to make it 2-0. Happy days. I had a tenner on Liverpool 2-0, Suarez last goal. A nice few hundred quid in me bin. So it's a lovely journey home, fifty odd redmen going off their heads on the coach. Beautiful. As always when we win the journey home was so fast.

Next up was the Carling Cup away to Exeter City. We couldn't get enough people for the coach, it's just not feasible. A midweek game which a lot of people cannot afford. So it's a drive job. And boy is it some drive. Approximately a five hundred mile round trip.

I went with me mate Chappy, Billy the farmer, a kid named Jay and Rickie the fat cunt! Haha only messin' lad, I'm a skinny cunt so what? I'd arranged to meet them at the Jolly Miller boozer at 12 o'clock. They came in a Ford Focus, definitely too small for five people, nearly six with Ricky. Also it stunk of cow shit. So I says "Come on, we'll go in my sixteen year old Galaxy, plenty of room in that". And 'Betsy' the Galaxy flew there and back, no problem. We get in the game pretty early to watch the reds warming up. Then I saw one of me mates Paul Edwards and his son Jake (great young redman in the making). Jake wanted me to get a programme and a shirt signed by Carra for him. He's only about fifteen yards away warming up so I shouts "Jamie, here lad". Jamie came over and obliged as always. Boy was little Jake buzzing. The game itself was a nice comfortable 3-1 win but we didn't get home until about three in the morning. Slept like a baby. Then after a 3-1 win at Anfield against Bolton in the league it was Stoke City away. It turned out to be our first defeat of the season. How the fuck we lost that game I'll never know. I'd have been gutted with a draw as we absolutely destroyed them. We should've won by at least three clear goals but it just wasn't our day. So next up it was Tottenham away, boy was that a day to forget. We couldn't get enough people for the coach again. We could fill it easily every game but its hard work for some of the lads to get tickets, plus the fucking price of them.

Anyway, I go on the train with about ten or twelve lads off the coach. Dead quick the trains nowadays. Just over two hours to get to London, but I don't like them. You can't have a smoke, there's no loud music and usually a booze ban. Anyway the game was sickening. We got tonked 4-0. Mind you we had two players sent off which made it more or less impossible. It was a dry train on the way home and it was just full of bizzies so near impossible to sneak anything on. We managed to get a few beers on but that was that. Anyway as we are pulling up into Lime St we noticed this kid getting dragged off the train by four bizzies. They just lashed him to the ground literally punching and kicking him. You could hear the screams all over Lime St. They went far too far. There was no need for that at all. So I decided to shout over "Alright lads I think he's had enough, don't you?" This big mountain of a copper just glared as me as he came walking towards me. I thought "Oh fuck here we go." He just pushed his face right into me and said "Fuck off unless you want some". So I just butted him about four times and knocked him out. Only messin' lads. I just had to swallow it and fuck off. I can't wait to get to bed.

Three days later it's yet another twat of a journey away to Brighton & Hove Albion in the Carling Cup. With the coach struggling for numbers again I felt so, so sorry for loads of young redmen. Fuck me this is three away games in eleven days. How the fuck these young redmen can afford to go to every game I don't know. I'm afraid that football these days is all about money. It's more or less a week's wages going to a London away game. £35 a coach, between £50-65 for a match ticket, a pie, pint and programme with your ale money and a taxi home after the game it's near enough £150. A fucking joke. But if you love the mighty reds what can you do? You'll find the money some way. Anyway the travelling redmen made it to the game in their droves, by hook or by crook. Lovely new little ground. I drove down again with the same lads but this time we went in Chappy's car, a beautiful motor. A long, long drive, just over a five hundred and fifty mile round trip. We get to the ground where loads of young redmen were looking for tickets but me old mate Stevie G had sent quite a few tickets down with a kid named Joe the red to give them to any of the lads who hadn't got a ticket. It's about time Stevie had some good press. I'm telling you redmen, the next day I told the local shopkeepers; newsagents, butchers, fruit and veg shops, as they're all Liverpool fans - I told them all to spread it about. Nice one Stevie lad, a Liverpool legend. The game itself was a comfortable 2-1 win. It could've been so many more but a win's a win. We'll take it. It was a long drive home. I hate driving home from the games. On a coach it's different. You can enjoy the victory much, much more with fifty or so travelling redmen. Next up it's Wolverhampton at Anfield. 2-1 win but again it could've been so many more. Then we play the blue shite from across the park. As I've said before, I hate going there. It's fucking horrible. Before the Heysel disaster it was world renowned the friendliness between the fans. No other city in world football came anywhere near it. But nowadays it's just pure hatred. The chants of 'Murderers, Murderers' hurts me so much. It's just so hard to take from fellow scousers who should know better. But as normal we punch them little blue bastards with a 2-0 victory. Little Luis Suarez bags the last goal getting my little bet up again, Liverpool 2-0, Suarez last goal. 25-1, 33-1, I can't really remember but something like that. That'll pay for my next away game with a bit of change over.

Then we have that horrible purple nosed bastard and his cronies from down the East Lancs at Anfield. The game was at Anfield. Stevie G returned from injury after missing the opening nine games. It didn't take him long. Get in. Stevie G, 1-0. We were much the better side but somehow they managed to score and held on for a draw. We well deserved the victory. The same thing the next game. Home to newly promoted Norwich City. 1-1 again when we should've won by three or four. Next up was Stoke City away in the fourth round of the League Cup. A nice little hour and a half journey and a 2-1 victory. Suarez bagged both goals. What a player we have got here. Wow! I just love watching him. I've never seen a player like him. West Brom are next up away at The Hawthorns. I've got great memories of going there as you have read earlier on in the book. We played really well and finally won the game 2-0 thanks to goals from Andy Carroll and Charlie Adam. Then it's another of the promoted clubs Swansea City at Anfield. This is just getting ridiculous. Yet another draw - 0-0.

Then we play at horrible Chelsea. I've already told you how much I hate going there. Without a doubt it's my most hated away journey. I just can't believe how horrible the fans are. Absolute scum (the bizzies aren't much better) and there's always some kind of trouble. It's never changed in my forty-six years of going down there. As normal the travelling redmen are well and truly up for this one. With that rat Torres plus those ridiculous plastic flags trying to create an atmosphere. The travelling redmen taunted them for the entire game. Totally outclassed them on the field and also on

the terraces. Our scouse humour was at its best. We finally win
the game with goals from Maxi and a cracker from Glen Johnson
in the 87th minute giving us a 2-1 win. I forgot to mention last
season at Chelsea. Me and a few mates, Chappy and Billy the
farmer, we were heading back towards the coaches after the game
and as always there was loads of little groups of them bastard rent
boys looking for trouble. Just as we were crossing the road I notice
this little group, about six or seven of the bastards. They weren't
kids, they were in their mid-thirties to early forties.

As we walked past them they started giving it loads, the usual
'scouse cunts' and so on. We just carried on walking and then they
shouted something about Hillsborough. I went off me cake and
shouted back "Fuck you rent boys come and have a go if you think
you can" the next thing we know they just ran at us. We were
having a go back then a bizzie comes from nowhere and slams me
against the police van and has my arms up me back. I was gutted,
thinking we're going to be locked in the cells all night. I had only
a couple of quid in me pocket. What a nightmare! Then all of a
sudden this other bizzie came rushing over and said to the other
one "You've got it wrong, let him go. I seen it all, the Chelsea fans
attacked him and his mates". Fuck me lucky or what? Two other
bizzies had me mate Chappy with his arms up his back so I rushes
over and says "Come on mate it's nothing to do with us" but at
first he didn't want to know. But the bizzie was right behind me.
He put them in the picture and told them what happened. They
finally let us go with the usual "Fuck off back to Liverpool you
scouse bastards" or something like that. We had a laugh about it on
the coach and it was a lovely drive back. Anyway we played Man
City next. Yet another draw. 1-1, followed by a 1-0 away to Fulham.

Most of the new signings were finding it really hard to settle
in but Dalglish's best buy by a country mile was the incomparable
Luis Suarez. In my fifty five years watching the redmen I have
never seen a player do the things he does with that football. He is
world class and is going to be a Liverpool legend. (If we can keep
hold of him). He ended up scoring 17 goals in his first season. He
missed loads of chances and a few people were having a little go

at him. Those people haven't got a fucking clue. 17 goals? Not bad considering he got an eight game ban as well for racial abuse against Patrice Evra of Man United. Mark my words he will score at least 25 goals next season, maybe more. Anyway back to the games, after a win against QPR at Anfield and a 2-0 away win at Aston Villa, we win only one of the next six league games, losing three and drawing two. Stevie G had been out injured but he decided to come to the Villa game on the coach with his mates. So we are inside Villa Park and one of the lads turned to me and said "There's Stevie G over there. He's shouting you to go over to him." So I just looked at the lad and all his mates and said "Sorry about this lads, he's a fucking nuisance". Only joking of course Steven. So I was right over to him, hugging him and having a good chat. It was great. Anyway after the game its back to the car park to get on the coach. Two young boys I know, about fifteen years of age, Ben and John Paul, sons of my very good friend John Calvert, said to me "Stevie Gerrard is on a coach over there. Any chance of getting his autograph for us?" I said "I'll do better than that, I'll take you on the coach to see him". So we walked over to the coach, went to get on and this fella, the coach driver, says "No one can get on here mate". The two kids just looked at me dead sad. I just winked at them and said "Watch this". I said to the driver "Just go and tell him Gerry Blayney is here". "I've been told that no one is allowed on the coach" he said. I just looked at him and said "Do yourself a favour mate, just go and do it now". He reluctantly turned to walk down the coach and within a minute and said "Sorry about that mate just go on". The two kids were buzzing. He signed shirts and programmes for them, anything they had really. Happy days, they were made up.

It didn't look good at all in the league but at least we are still in the two cup competitions, the League Cup and the FA Cup. But it got even worse in the last sixteen games. We won only five, losing a massive nine games, and drawing two. But two of them games were probably the highlights of the league season. The first one was at Anfield against the blue shite. I just love it when we tear into them and boy did Stevie G give it to them. He tore them apart scoring a magnificent hat-trick in a 3-0 win. As always the stupid blue bastards where chanting "The baby's not yours" referring to one of his kids, but Stevie, with his typical scouse humour, put the match ball up the front of his shirt as the game finished and taunted them blue bastards to death, pointing towards the ball under his shirt as though he was pregnant. Pure scouse class. Smoke it blue boys. Then there was the 3-0 away win at Norwich City with another hat-trick from the incomparable Luis Suarez. Wow! I've seen some fabulous hat-tricks watching our beloved redmen in the last fifty five years but this one from Luis Suarez was the best I've ever seen. Three absolutely stunning goals. One from well wide from outside the box with a stunning drive, another from outside the box, more central this time, and then an absolute gem when he lobbed the keeper from the half way line. I can't remember who played the ball to him but as it came to him he just took one touch to control it and then in an instant he just let fly. What a magnificent goal. What a magnificent hat-trick. So it's back to the cups. We are looking really good in the League Cup, Carling Cup or whatever you want to call it. After knocking Stoke out we got drawn against them horrible bastards Chelsea at Stamford Bridge. As always it was a boss journey down there on the coach with the usual suspects. The game itself was glorious. As always, we taunted them cockney rent boys to death and destroyed their team on the field. A nice comfortable 2-0 win thanks to goal from Maxi Rodriguez and a rare goal from Martin Kelly. A boss journey home as it always is when we turn them rentboys over. Next up it's the Semi Final against money bags Manchester City, a two legged affair. The first leg was away in Manchester and thanks to a 13th minute penalty from the irresistible Stevie G we win 1-0. So it's back to Anfield for the second leg. In a really exciting game it ends up 2-2 with goals from Stevie G yet again from the penalty spot, and the goal that finally put us through from Craig Bellamy with fifteen minutes to go. So it's off to Wembley.

This was my thirty-third visit to Wembley, two or three behind probably Liverpool's greatest ever supporter Lenny Woods. We were playing the mighty Cardiff City ha-ha. But I tell you what lads, they gave us one hell of a game. And to be honest we were so, so lucky to win it in the end. After drawing 1-1 with a goal from Martin Skrtl it went to extra time, with Dirk Kuyt scoring, but it ended 2-2. Penalties. Cardiff should've won the game when they missed a sitter in the last couple of minutes of extra time. I was really confident now of winning on penalties as we have won twelve of the last thirteen penalty shootouts. First up it was Stevie G who missed his pen. Oh no. But then they miss, then Charlie Adam steps up and blasts one about ten yards over the bar. What a miss. Not going well. Then they scored, wow it's getting very nervy now. Up steps Kuyt, get in, back in it again. Then they hit the post, then Downing scores. Then they score to make it 2-2 with one penalty each to go. Glen Johnson steps up, keeps his cool and scores, advantage Liverpool. Their final penalty taker was Anthony Gerrard, Stevie G's cousin. Thank God he missed. Game over and another trophy in the cabinet.

In the FA Cup we drew Oldham Athletic at Anfield in the third round. No problem, we won 5-1 thanks to goals from Bellamy, Gerrard, Shelvey, Carroll and a very rare goal from the underachieving Stewart Downing. Next up, wow what a draw. We get Man United at Anfield. It is so, so sweet when we beat them and we did it thanks to goals from Daniel Agger and the winner from Dirk Kuyt in the 88th minute. I really, really enjoyed that win. Fuck you, you Manc bastards. Next up we get Brighton & Hove Albion at Anfield. We absolutely destroyed them 6-1 with goals from Skrtl, Carroll, Suarez, and a very rare goal from me old mate Jamie Carragher. Plus two own goals. Then we get paired with Stoke City in the quarter final at Anfield. We win 2-1, Suarez at it yet again with the first goal after 23 minutes. Then another rare goal from Downing. So it's into the semi-final. We get paired with the blue shite to be played at Wembley. It was just a mass of scousers mingling with each other so it was a bit of a refreshing change. I didn't see any trouble at all amongst the fans and our beloved redmen didn't let us down. They broke all the Evertonians hearts beating them 2-1. Everton took a 1-0 lead but then a disastrous mistake by Distin let Luis Suarez in to level it up. Then in the

87th minute a glorious header from Andy Carroll. What a glorious feeling beating Everton at Wembley. So we are in the final to play that fucking Chelsea but it just wasn't our day. We finally lose the game 2-1. What a horrible journey home. I don't think I spoke a word for about an hour and a half. But what can we do. A horrible ending to a horrible season. And there was worse to come.

The new owners decided that it was time for Dalglish to be replaced. It was such a sad day for our beloved redmen to let Dalglish go, but in all fairness I think it was the right decision. It was a horrible pre-season, not knowing what was going to happen. All sorts of names came up and eventually we signed Brendan Rodgers, the Swansea manager. He was only young but he had done a marvellous job at Swansea. His style of football suits our beloved Liverpool FC down to the ground so we will just have to wait and see what the future holds. As always it's another trip to the jewellers to get my silver salver to give to the new manager. So it's off to Melwood to meet him. He was a really humble and nice man who I took to straight away. He read the inscription on the salver which read 'All the best Brendan on your first year managing the mighty reds from Gerry Blayney & Billy Swann (deceased)'. After reading the inscription he just looked at me and said "Us paddies get everywhere". Then we got talking about me dad. I told Brendan that me dad was born in Belfast and as a kid his dad took him to watch Glentoran in the Irish League. We had a lovely chat for about fifteen minutes then as I was about to leave Brendan said to me "Is that right Gerry? Do you get all the new managers a silver salver?" I turned to him and said "That's right Brendan". Then he said to me "You must've spent a nice few bob over the last few seasons. Let's hope you don't have to buy another one for many, many, many years". That was so nice to hear. Brendan didn't take long to sign some desperately needed new players. He brought in Joe Allan from his former club Swansea and Fabio Borini from Roma.

Well this is it, another season in my amazing journey supporting our beloved redmen all over England and Europe. I am so privileged and proud to be a member of the greatest family of football fans on the planet. I would also like to say a massive thank you to all the redmen and women who helped me get through the tragedy of Hillsborough. My plan was to finish this book last season but with all that has happened over the Hillsborough inquiry and the fantastic news that followed, I just had to put this season in. After twenty-three years the truth has finally started to come out. Now the whole world knows what every Liverpool fan has known for the past twenty-three years or so. The full story hasn't come out yet, but it will and until that day I will not rest. I want those responsible for the disaster to be punished and disgraced. And also jailed. I can't really believe that after a quarter of a century, and setback after setback, that the truth has finally come out. Now all we need is justice. But what is justice? There is no justice for the ninety-six families, but this will help.

So the season starts, first up West Brom away. We got well beat, 3-0. Then after a 2-2 draw at home with Manchester City, Skrtl and Suarez scoring, it was down to the Emirates to play Arsenal. As normal the coach was bouncing all the way down there, with some new faces on board as well. About six or seven lads from Huyton started coming on our coach. They were boss. They loved the coach, they ended up coming on it for most of the season with us. There was one kid I really hit it off with. A kid named Dunny, who loved the reds just like I do. I can't really remember all the other names but they are all good lads. It wasn't a very nice journey home though as we got beat 2-0. While I'm name dropping I would never forgive myself if I never put in, without a doubt, one of the best reds on the planet. It's Phil McKewon (probably spelt it wrong, sorry mate!) who has taken over Wilcox Travels after Bobby died. Anyway back to the games. After drawing with Sunderland and getting beat by Man United it was off down to Norwich. Boy does Luis Suarez love playing them, scoring yet another glorious hat-trick in a 5-2 win. Suarez has been outstanding in every game so far. He is just a joy to watch. But apart from Suarez, things weren't really looking very good. The next five games was one win and four draws. Suarez scored four times in those five games. Then he hit another two in the 3-0 win at home to Wigan. There just seemed to be no consistency in the team, apart from Suarez of course. Winning one week, losing the next, and too many draws. We badly needed another striker to take the burden off Suarez. Then finally, in the January sales, Brendan signs Daniel Sturridge for £12m from Chelsea. He fitted in straightaway. He made his debut at Old Trafford, scoring in a 2-1 defeat. He ended up with 11 goals in 16 appearances. He slotted in with Suarez beautifully. In the January window we also signed Phillipe Coutinho for £8.5m from Inter Milan. Wow, what a player. He just slotted in perfectly, supplying Sturridge and Suarez with the ammunition they need. After such a disappointing two thirds of the season, we win eight and draw four in the last twelve games of the season. But it was far too late, finishing a disappointing seventh in the table. With only five games left we are at home to Chelsea. The game itself finished 2-2 but the happenings in the game totally destroyed the whole season. Suarez, who had basically carried us for two thirds of the season scoring goals, let himself and Liverpool Football Club down. He tried to bite Ivanovic of Chelsea. Where was his fucking head? That was it. The press had a field day. He eventually got banned for ten games meaning he would miss the last four games of the season and the first six of next. But then it got much worse than that, if it could get any worse. Suarez decided he has had enough of the media so it looks like we might have lost him. I was absolutely gutted. As I have said before I have never seen a player like this kid. And I just know that wherever he goes he is going to be a sensation. But no player is bigger than the club. Funnily enough in the last four games Suarez wasn't missed at all. We thumped Newcastle 6-0 away, a 0-0 draw a home to Everton, a 3-1 away win at Fulham (Sturridge hat-trick), and then in the last game of the season QPR we won 1-0 thanks to the new kid on the block Coutinho. Wow, wow. He is going to be some player.

That game was also Jamie Carragher's last for the club after 737 games. Wow! What a career. What a player! And what a person! I can't thank you enough Jamie for everything you have done for Liverpool Football Club and for everything you have done for me personally, giving me your shirt from the Inter Milan game, for signing hundreds of programmes for me and shirts for charities. Thanks a billion Jay. Well redmen, I hope you have enjoyed reading this book as much as I have writing it. I would also like to thank two fanatical girls who follow our beloved redmen. The first girl, without a doubt, the best female Liverpool supporter in the world, is Sharon Long. She is from somewhere in Wales. She has been following Liverpool all over England and Europe. I see her at every Liverpool away game. Sadly the girl is wheelchair bound. Boy that is what you call support. She is in a wheelchair and she follows them everywhere. I give her a little kiss every away game, and she gives me a big smile. You'll never walk alone girl. The other girl is the daughter of a good friend of mine, Nicky Galvin from the north end. She goes everywhere with her dad, Europe, the lot. She is only eighteen but I think she has been going abroad for about ten years. You'll never walk alone girl. I'd also like to thank the three girls who sit by me in the Upper Centenary, sorry girls I just can't remember your names as I'm writing this. Oh, I nearly forgot, along with the fantastic Hillsborough news, "THE WITCH IS DEAD". That rat Thatcher has finally died. The news came out just before the away game at Reading. We were struggling to get a coach together but within hours of her dying the coach was booked up solid. Wow, what a day out that was. The drive down on the coach was brilliant. All the chants were about Thatcher. Inside the ground it was absolutely mental. People drinking and throwing lagers over each other celebrating. The bizzies didn't know what was going on. They just looked at everyone in amazement. Even the Reading fans were taking pictures on their phones and joining in with the celebrations.

I would just like to say sorry to any great redmen I haven't mentioned in the book. I'm terrible with names and there are that many people you bump into at the match. It's impossible for me to remember you all, but I've just remembered two. The two Vinny's – the Vinny who runs the coach with Chappy, top redman, and my new mate Vinny. Vinny Brady. Loves the reds like me. Then there's me new mate, Sean. He works in my local newsagents.

★

I intended to finish this book at the end of 2013 but with the good news about Hillsborough and with the remarkable season we've just had I thought I'd finish on a high. Like Brendan Rodgers I was really pleased that we didn't qualify for that stupid Europa League. I know at the end of the day a trophy is a trophy, but having to play a minimum of 22 games to get to the final is over half a league season. The travel all over Europe would definitely hinder our chances of pushing for the Champions League, which was our aim at the start of the season. As it was Suarez was going to miss the first 5 games due to suspension, and he would be dearly missed. First up its Stoke City at Anfield. In a very tight game we win 1-0 thanks to a goal from Daniel Sturridge. The next two gamnes finish the same, 1-0 away at Aston Villa with Sturridge scoring the only goal, and a glorious win against the Mancs at Anfield, Sturridge bagging the only goal yet again. Next a 2-2 draw away at Swansea, Sturridge again and one from Victor Moses, a loan player from Chelsea. Boy is he shit, no way in a million years will our beloved redmen sign him on a permanent deal. Next up is Southampton at Anfield. Fuck me they destroyed us. It was only 1-0 but it could have been 2 or 3. They played really well and deserved a victory. Next its away to Sunderland and the return of the magnificent Louis Suarez. Wow! In my fifty-seven years watching our beloved redmen, I have never seen anything like him. He is just unique. And it didn't take him long to make his mark. He scored twice in a 3-1 away win. One of them was an absolute stunner. Sturridge got the other. Boy is Danny boy on fire. Next a comfortable 3-1 home win against Crystal Palace. Sturridge, Suarez and Gerrard scored the goals and then a 2-2 draw at Newcastle. Gerrard from the spot and another from the incomparable Suarez. Simply a joy to watch.

It got even better for little Louis in the next game at home to West Brom. He bagged a glorious hat-trick and Sturridge once again got the other. Wow. Without a doubt they are the best front two in the Premier League and so exciting to watch. Next up we are away at Arsenal. We get well and truly beaten 2-0. Arsenal deserved the victory. It was certainly a wake up call for our beloved redmen but we bounce back against Fulham at Anfield, destroying them 4-0. An own goal, one from Skrtel and another two for the little genius Louis Suarez. Next up it's the blue shite at Goodison. Wow. What a game. It finished in a 3-3 draw. Coutinho scored after five minutes and then Suarez made it two. But in an unbelievable finish Everton went 3-2 up before Daniel Sturridge netted in the 89th minute to make it 3-3. We were really confident going into the next game at Hull City but it all turned sour. We got thumped 3-1, Gerrard scoring a consolation goal. Yet once more we bounce back straight away by hammering Norwich City at Anfield. Wow they must hate Suarez. He absolutely destroyed them, scoring four times with Raheem Sterling getting the fifth. Then another great win at Anfield against West Ham, 4-1, with goals from Sakho, Suarez and two own goals.

The Tottenham game took on a bit of significance. Our away form was up and down but, what a night! The coach I had travelled with last season was having problems. There were a few knobheads causing trouble so I decided to go on another coach run by two great redmen, Chappy and Vinny. It's a boss coach, run really, really well. A few of my mates off Fletch's coach decided to come with me. There's John Chidlow (love him, top red) his brother Ian, and a kid call Tommo. What a night it turned out to be. We destroyed Tottenham 5-0 with two from Suarez, one from Henderson, and an absolute cracker from young Jon Flannagan. Boy did the kid enjoy that moment. I know his dad and his uncle Paul well. It's so nice when one of our own make the grade with our beloved redmen. Sterling scored the last goal in the last minutes. All the reds were bouncing everywhere. It was an unbelievable atmosphere. As we got on the coach to travel home there was a few Tottenham fans, all in there fifties probably. They just looked at the coach and started clapping. What a glorious journey home, everybody dancing and singing all the way, it set the tone for the rest of the season. Next up was Cardiff City at Anfield, again we enjoyed a nice comfortable 3-1 win with two more from the little genius Suarez and one from the ever improving Sterling. Next it's moneybags City. They had been steamrollering opponents at home, scoring a record amount of goals so most assumed we'd go the same way. But though we lost the game 2-1, believe me if we had got a draw I'd have been disappointed. We dominated the game, but that's football. Next it's away to those horrible horrible bastards Chelsea. We go 1-0 up with a goal from Skrtel but we lose the game 2-1. I really believe we deserved a draw, we are going to have to bounce back now. Two big defeats in a row. We bounce back in a big big way going unbeaten in the next thirteen games, yes thirteen, winning eleven and drawing two. First up of the streak was Hull City at Anfield. We owed them one and the reds duly obliged with a comfortable 2-0 win. A rare goal from Daniel Agger and the other from Suarez. The next game was crazy at Stoke. It finished 5-3. An own, goal, a Gerrard pen, Sterling and two more from the irresistible Suarez. Then Aston Villa away. The dirty horrible scumbags. A few dirty bastards tried to give me a bit of aggro after the game but they soon got on their toes after a few redmen seen what was going on. The game finished in a 2-2 draw with goals from Sturridge and Stevie G from the spot. Next up it's the blue shite from across the park. They are playing brilliantly, right up there in the mix. But they copped it at Anfield. We totally destroyed them on the pitch, and in the terraces. Wow, 4-0. It could have been 10! Stevie G scored first, then Sturridge bagged two more. Then King Luis made it four, with forty minutes left to go. Were so good to watch. I enjoyed that game immensely, like forty odd thousand other Liverpool fans. It was just poetry in motion, watching the blue shite just blown out of sight. We stumble at West Brom throwing away a 1-0 lead thanks to the on fire Stuuridge. It was looking like an easy win until Kolo Toure somehow lost his concentration and passed the ball straight to ex-blue nose Victor Anichebe who scored. What a bad bad mistake. Toure was holding his head in dis belief. Horrible result. It felt like a defeat. But we are still well in the hunt for the Champions League. Brendan Rodgers is getting the best out of all the players and getting the fans dreaming of getting back. Next came Arsenal at Anfield. They were flying at the time - top of the league but we brought them down to earth with ease in one of the best displays I have seen in many a season. We destroyed them 5-1. We were awesome to a man. What a team performance! The goals came from Skrtel (2), Sterling (2) and yet another from Daniel Sturridge. Next was a very very nervy game away at Fulham. It was 2-2 going into the last minute and then we got a penalty. I just couldn't watch it. I turned my back and looked at the travelling redmen. They went wild. Get in. 3-2, Stevie G. The other goals came from Sturridge and the brilliant Brazilian Phillipe Coutinho. What a brilliant journey down the motorway. The redmen are starting to believe now.

I've been so wrapped up with the league that I have forgotten about the cup competitions. In the league cup we scraped through the first round against Notts County after extra time 4-2, goals from Sterling, Henderson, and yet another two from the goal machine Sturridge but we got knocked out by them shites from down the M62 Man Utd, 1-0. Then in the FA Cup we beat Oldham at Anfield 2-0 with an own goal and one from Aspas. In the next round we beat Bournemouth 2-0 with goals from Moses and Sturridge before facing Arsenal at the Emirates. They were well up for revenge after that 5-1 spanking at Anfield eight days earlier and we lost the game 2-1, Gerrard getting our goal from the spot. It was a horrible journey home. So that's it. Full concentration on the league. Next up was Swansea at Anfield in a crazy crazy game. We just scraped home, winning 4-3 with goals from Henderson (2) and Sturridge (2). Next up it's back down the motorway to play Southampton. They are playing really well at the moment, especially at home, but the nerves are blown away with a really good 3-0 win. But believe me Southampton played their part in the game. Suarez, Sterling and Gerrard got the goals. What a boss journey home on the coach. It was literally bouncing. Everybody was really starting to believe now. But before we got out of Southampton there was about twenty, maybe thirty Southampton skinheads waiting by a roundabout ready to attack the coaches. It was mayhem.

Next it's them horrible bastards Man Utd at Old Trafford. We totally ripped them to bits. 3-0. Could have been a lot more. Stevie G scored two penalties and also hit the post with another pen, and of course, little Luis Suarez grabbed the other. Next up its Cardiff City away. As always the coach is buzzing, everybody dreaming, not of qualifying for the Champions League by now but of winning the Premier League. As we got outside the ground the coaches were pulling in and the front coach got attacked by a mob of Cardiff hooligans. They were throwing bricks, bottles, all sorts of things at the coach. All the lads on the coach got off to defend themselves. It was like a throwback to the seventies. I thought all this had gone, but it sadly hasn't. The Cardiff hooligans were ripping drainpipes off houses and attacking the travelling redmen – there were running battles everywhere. Me and me mate Lee were caught right in the middle of it all. I nearly got involved as a drainpipe was lashed towards me. I was going nuts and wanting to fight back. But luckily for me Lee, Lee Rogers, dragged me away. Thanks Lee. The bizzies shit themselves and just let it all go off. This big cunt was trying to drag the door off the front of the coach. Big mistake. The driver jumped off and knocked the big cunt spark out. He got what he deserved. He must have been in his late forties. The bizzies finally got involved. Loads of people got nicked and that was that. The game itself was crazy. We soon found ourselves 1-0 down but the amazing Luis Suarez equalised. Cardiff came right back and took the lead again before Martin Skrtel made it 2-2. It just got better and better in the second half. We took all the points in a 6-3 win with the other goals coming from Skrtel again, Sturridge, and another two for the greatest player on the planet Luis Suarez, netting his hat-trick in the ninetieth minute. He is just a joy to watch. What a beautiful journey home, everyone dancing and singing. I was drunk on emotion. Charlie was on form, turning everyone on as he always does.

Next up it's bottom of the league Sunderland at home. We cruise into a 2-0 lead, Stevie G and Sturridge scoring. It was looking so easy. We were playing well. But Sunderland pulled one back in around the seventy fifth minute and the game totally changed. They threw everything at us. My nerves were gone, and so were some of the players. We were making mistake after mistake. But we hung on to earn a hard three points. Next it's Tottenham at Anfield. We done more or less the same to them as we did at White Heart Lane, beating them 4-0 with goals from Suarez, Henderson,

Coutinho and an own goal. Believe me redmen, this Brazilian wizard Coutinho is gonna be some player. Just six more games to go and we are right up there, there's nothing in it between us, Chelsea and Man City. Next it's back down to that London to play West Ham. In a very tricky game we get the three points thanks to two penalties from Stevie G, winning 2-1. The coach journeys home are getting more and more exciting. Everyone singing 'we're gonna win the league, we're gonna win the league'.

Then comes the big test against title rivals Man City at Anfield. Normally I get to Anfield about half an hour before kick off but this time I got there at about half eleven. Everywhere was chocka, Anfield Road was just a mass of red and white, flares going off everywhere. Everyone was waiting for the team coach to arrive. I hadn't seen scenes like that for many a year. I think It terrified someof the Man City players as they arrived on the coach. The game started and our beloved redmen took the game right to City. After only six minutes Raheem Sterling had the Kop going mental. Then Martin Skrtel made it 2-0 after 25 minutes. We were rampant and should have scored more. 2-0 at half time. But a different City turned up for the second half. Silva was running the show finding gaps everywhere. His first goal took a deflection off Glen Johnson, then Silva made it 2-2. They were taking control. I was so nervous. But we found another gear and finally won it 3-2 thanks to the brilliant Coutinho following a mis-kick from City captain Vincent Kompany. Wow! What a game! We were top of the league with four games to go and the title was in our own hands.

Next it's Norwich away. What a long journey, which wasn't helped by Sky Sports having it live at midday which meant we had to leave Liverpool at four in the morning. Quite a few of the lads decided to stay out all night in town, then just get a taxi to the Oak Tree pub in Huyton to be picked up by the coach. That Sky do my fuckin head in, what a ridiculous time. But it was worth it to see our beloved redmen take another step towards the title, winning 3-2. Goals came from Sterling (2) and yet another from the genius Suarez. Them Norwich fans must hate him. He just loves scoring against them. Four earlier on in the season, plus a couple of hat-tricks in previous seasons, can't blame them can we. Just three games left and we only need seven points to win the title, so we can afford to draw one.

The next and biggest hurdle came next at with that horrible, horrible club Chelsea and mouth almighty Mourinho. I arrived at Anfield around the same time as the previous week to wait for the team coach to arrive. As against Man City, it was just a mass of red and white. Everybody believed that we could win our first title in 24 years. But heartbreakingly we lose the game. Chelsea came for a point. They actually started wasting time as early as the second minute. They slowed the game down and put ten men behind the ball. We tried everything to break through, the Kop willing them on, but just before half time a crucial slip by the magnificent Stevie G let in Demba Ba to stride away and make it 1-0. Gerrard looked devastated. The second half was more of the same. It was horrible to watch. I've seen some teams defend but this was the worst I've ever seen. It was a joke. Chelsea players were going down at every opportunity and wasting time. I don't think the referee gave a warning until about the eightieth minute. We threw everything at them to no avail, then in the last minute Chelsea broke away with Torres of all people who squared the ball to Willian. Game over. It was a horrible drive back to my home in Crosby. I don't think I spoke a word in two days. It was just so hard to take. Now it was out of our hands as Man City won again meaning if they won their last three games the title was theirs.

With heavy hearts we headed down to Crystal Palace. It was a very weird journey going down there. Everyone was still gutted at losing to Chelsea. I didn't have a ticket. I got let down. I was going fucking nuts. I was hoping to get one down there but no such luck. The touts were selling them for as much as £400 a ticket. There was no way I could afford that and there was no way of bunking in. I couldn't get near the turnstiles, stewards and bizzies everywhere. So I had to watch it in a pub on the big screen with about three hundred other Liverpool fans who couldn't get tickets. It was bouncing the pub. The reds went into a 3-0 lead after fifty five minutes. Goals came from Jo Allen, Sturridge and another for the greatest player on the planet, taking his tally to 31 league goals for the season. Obviously I'm talking about Suarez. We started to chase the goal difference that City had on us. Big mistake. Palace brought on a very young striker who caused mayhem and before we knew it, Palace had pulled the three goals back to make it 3-3. What a horrible end to the game. The coach journey home was one of the worst I've ever endured. I didn't speak a word for two hours. Everyone knew that was the end of our dream. We beat Newcastle 2-1 in the last game of the season with Agger and Sturridge scoring to go out on a bit of a high while City won their games in hand and beat West Ham on the last day of the season to win the league.

Nevertheless, what a magnificent season. We were just so good to watch. I think every neutral wanted Liverpool to win the league. It was our aim at the beginning of the season was to get into the Champions League. We achieved that and much, much more, finishing runners up by two points to Man City. It was so cruel. Our beloved redmen gave everything and more, but it just wasn't to be. But Brendan Rodgers has brought the best out of Liverpool. I am so looking forward to next season. The sleeping giants have been awoken. Beware. Everyone. We will go again next season.

Luis Suarez won the player of the year award and it was always unlikely that we'd keep hold of him after a season like that, the season of his life. I think he can still get better at Barcelona, unbelievable, he's an absolute joy to watch. I wish him nothing but the best. He gave everything to Liverpool in the past three seasons. I am convicted he will be voted best player in the world next season. Mark my words.

I would just like to mention all the people on the new coach who I have been going the match with all season. First there's Bernie. Top redman. Then Billy the farmer, John and Ian, Katie, Yozza, Lee and Steve, and two Brazillian identical twin sisters, Selena and Shara, fit as fuck, lol. Then there's Motty, Willo, Ryan, Big Jimbo, Ben (really good lad) and all the others who travelled with me to the game from the Oak Tree pub from Huyton. Also, the name of this book is 'In My Blood' well we have Shankly blood on the coach in the shape of his grandson Chris.

Before I go I must mention Hillsborough. Massive steps have finally been taken and it's only a matter of time now before we get full closure and hopefully plenty of prison sentences too. It really hurts me to talk about Hillsborough so I will finish this book off now.

YNWA